HOW TO USE

Adobe®

Photoshop® CS2

Daniel Giordan
with revisions by Doug Nelson

SAMS

Sams Publishing
800 East 96th Street
Indianapolis, Indiana 46240

How To Use Adobe® Photoshop® CS2

International Standard Book Number: 0-672-32751-1

Library of Congress Catalog Card Number: 2004097761

Printed in the United States of America

First Printing: August 2005

08 07 06 05   4 3 2 1

Trademarks

All terms mentioned in this book that are known to be trademarks or service marks have been appropriately capitalized. Sams Publishing cannot attest to the accuracy of this information. Use of a term in this book should not be regarded as affecting the validity of any trademark or service mark.

Adobe and Photoshop are registered trademarks of Adobe Systems, Incorporated.

Warning and Disclaimer

Every effort has been made to make this book as complete and as accurate as possible, but no warranty or fitness is implied. The information provided is on an "as is" basis. The author and the publisher shall have neither liability nor responsibility to any person or entity with respect to any loss or damages arising from the information contained in this book.

Bulk Sales

Sams Publishing offers excellent discounts on this book when ordered in quantity for bulk purchases or special sales. For more information, please contact

U.S. Corporate and Government Sales
1-800-382-3419
corpsales@pearsontechgroup.com

For sales outside the United States, please contact
International Sales
international@pearsoned.com

Acquisitions Editor
Betsy Brown

Development Editor
Alice Martina Smith

Managing Editor
Charlotte Clapp

Project Editor
Mandie Frank

Production Editor
Megan Wade

Indexer
Ken Johnson

Technical Editor
Mara Zebest

Publishing Coordinator
Vanessa Evans

Designer
Anne Jones

Page Layout
TnT Design, Inc.

Contents at a Glance

Contents

About the Authors

Daniel Giordan is an artist and designer who works as the design director for AOL Web Properties, coordinating the publishing designs for online properties such as Netscape, CompuServe, MapQuest, AIM, ICQ, and others. In addition to this book, he has authored four other books on Photoshop, including *The Art of Photoshop*, *Using Photoshop*, and *Dynamic Photoshop*. He has written other books addressing subjects such as Dreamweaver, Kai's PowerTools, and general design subjects. Dan also writes a monthly column for *Photoshop User* magazine.

With a master's degree in fine arts, Dan also paints and works with photography while indulging an excessive interest in capturing every moment of his son's life on film.

Doug Nelson is the man Photoshop book publishers and authors call on to vet their books. He is a Photoshop alpha- and beta-tester and has written a monthly techniques column for *Photoshop Fix* magazine. His website, RetouchPRO.com, is responsible for introducing thousands to a new hobby, hundreds to a new career, and at least two to a new spouse.

Acknowledgments

Where do I start here? So many thanks, so little time....

Let me start by thanking everyone at Adobe for building the software application most responsible for the ongoing evolution and refinement in computer graphics. Photoshop is the world's most popular design program; nothing else even comes close.

I also want to thank Alice Martina Smith, Betsy Brown, Mandie Frank, and the whole team of editors and designers at Sams Publishing. When I start feeling like my part of the project is overwhelming, I think about these people who are juggling details and deadlines for up to 12 different titles at a time—and all I have to worry about is what's on page 56.

Finally (primarily), I must thank God and my family for all their support. Writing this book was a huge task that consumed the overwhelming majority of my time and attention. Even when I wasn't writing, I was thinking about content, solutions, and upcoming deadlines. Although I've made every effort to keep Barb and Josh in my sights, I'm sure that my attention has slipped over the past few weeks. Thank you, Barb, for putting up with the schedule, my moods, and my absence. I thank God every day for you and Josh, and I thank Him for what He's done for all of us.

Dedication

This book is for Barb and Josh.

We Want to Hear from You!

As the reader of this book, *you* are our most important critic and commentator. We value your opinion and want to know what we're doing right, what we could do better, what areas you'd like to see us publish in, and any other words of wisdom you're willing to pass our way.

You can email or write me directly to let me know what you did or didn't like about this book—as well as what we can do to make our books stronger.

Please note that I cannot help you with technical problems related to the topic of this book, and that due to the high volume of mail I receive, I might not be able to reply to every message.

When you write, please be sure to include this book's title and author as well as your name and phone or email address. I will carefully review your comments and share them with the author and editors who worked on the book.

Email: graphics@samspublishing.com

Mail: Mark Taber
            Associate Publisher
            Sams Publishing
            800 East 96th Street
            Indianapolis, IN 46240 USA

Reader Services

For more information about this book or others from Sams Publishing, visit our website at www.samspublishing.com. Type the ISBN (excluding hyphens) or the title of the book in the Search box to find the book you're looking for.

How to Use This Book

The Complete Visual Reference

Each part of this book consists of a series of short instructional tasks designed to help you understand the information you need to get the most out of Photoshop.

Each task includes a series of easy-to-understand steps designed to guide you through the procedure.

 Click: Click the left mouse button once.

 Double-click: Click the left mouse button twice in rapid succession.

 Right-click: Click the right mouse button once.

 Selection: This circle highlights the area that is discussed in the step.

 Keyboard: Type information or data into the indicated location.

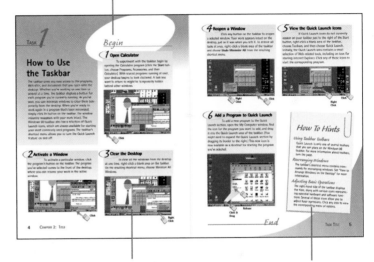

Each step is fully illustrated to show you how it looks onscreen.

Extra hints that tell you how to accomplish a goal are provided in most tasks.

Drag & Drop: Position the mouse pointer over the object, click and hold the left mouse button, drag the object to its new location, and release the mouse button.

Screen elements (such as menus, icons, windows, and so on), as well as things you enter or select, appear in **boldface** type.

Continues

If you see this symbol, it means that the task you're in continues on the next page.

Introduction

*T*he history of image-editing applications should be divided into two categories: BP and AP (Before Photoshop and After Photoshop). Before Photoshop, various bitmap applications were available, some of which were very good. There was Pixel Paint Pro, Studio 8, Digital Darkroom, and of course MacPaint. Like dinosaurs facing extinction, all these applications faded away after the comet called Photoshop fell to earth in the late 1980s.

I am told that Photoshop got its start in 1987 as a personal project of Thomas Knoll (a doctoral candidate in computer science at the University of Michigan). Thomas Knoll wrote a programming routine to display grayscale images on a black-and-white monitor. Thomas showed the program to his brother, John Knoll, who at the time worked at Industrial Light and Magic (the special-effects studio started by George Lucas). Intrigued by the possibilities of this program, John asked Thomas to help him write a program for processing digital image files. The brothers expanded the program to include color capabilities, soft-edge masks, plug-in filter support, and many of the features that became the foundation for Photoshop's success. This was at a time when graphic file formats were all over the map and PostScript had already begun to take shape in the marketplace to help standardize a solution to many of the problems facing the computer graphics world. Photoshop was unique in its mathematical approach to images—rather than a program that simply pushed pixels around, everyone saw Photoshop as another means to promote PostScript and printing. Little did they realize the influence it would later have, especially because more people take photographs than use line illustrations.

One could argue that Photoshop is the most influential facilitator for the growth of digital graphics since the Macintosh. And although the Mac got us started in the mid-1980s, Adobe has kept things moving forward with interface standards and cross-platform compatibility that make graphics accessible to just about every computer in the world. This universality has made Photoshop the core application driving new advances in the computer graphics world. Photoshop combines with After Effects for professional video editing, with Quark and InDesign for industry-standard page layout, and with Illustrator and FreeHand for desktop illustration. In all these instances, Photoshop sits right in the middle. Photoshop also drives the advancement of digital photography and professional web design.

It was the boom in web design books in the early 1990s that prompted Adobe to launch a complementary application to Photoshop called ImageReady. Although Photoshop was the creative powerhouse, ImageReady excelled in prepping images for the Web: compressing file sizes; converting colors; and building clean, concise animations. ImageReady also featured a bare-bones set of image-editing tools for basic image editing.

Because this book covers Photoshop CS2, it also addresses how ImageReady supports graphic design workflow and integration with Photoshop, especially where web design is concerned. Therefore, you will see ImageReady written into some of the task instructions—and even featured in a few standalone tasks. Because of the redundant feature set created when they were separate programs, some of the tasks described for Photoshop can be executed in virtually the same way in ImageReady.

And another thing: Because Adobe does such an excellent job of building cross-platform applications, you should not be concerned that most of the screen shots in the book are Windows based. Everything works the same on the Mac (except for the keystrokes, which I've identified for both systems).

Whether you're working with ImageReady or Photoshop, this book is designed to get you up and running quickly, with straightforward solutions to your questions. The challenge comes from the fact that Photoshop's complexity cannot always be clearly addressed in seven steps or less. I've tried to address the details as much as I can, expounding in the How-To Hints sections and task and part openers. Although the format of this book resists long narratives and detailed explanations, a ton of solid information is still packed into the tasks that follow. I was very pleased that we were able to drill a bit deeper into some of the advanced features in this book, and I hope it helps you push things further and get the most out of Photoshop.

Task

Getting Started with Photoshop

Most people look at Photoshop as a program that has many levels of complexity. They say things such as, "I probably don't use 10% of the program," or "I just use it to open my digital camera images." Although it's true that Photoshop has a deep level of complexity, it's also true that the program is easy for the beginner to use. This is one of the features that has made Photoshop so popular: It's easy to jump in and get started and, as your needs grow, the program grows right along with you.

The first step in getting started is to set up Photoshop to work the way you want it to work. How do you set the preferences? What about customizing the desktop or setting ruler increments? You should consider a few customizable features, as well as specific tools built in to the program that can come in handy with almost any file on which you might be working.

Because Adobe includes ImageReady as part of Photoshop CS2, you also should consider how to optimize ImageReady for the way you work and familiarize yourself with how ImageReady integrates with Photoshop. Because ImageReady is focused more on web design, consider whether ImageReady's slicing, scripting, and optimization controls offer advantages over those provided by Photoshop. Specifically, check out the control ImageReady provides over HTML protocols, naming conventions, and other control sets in the ImageReady **Preferences** box.

Adobe now ships Bridge, which is a standalone file-access application you can use to locate and then open a file in any of the Creative Suite 2 applications—Photoshop, Illustrator, GoLive, InDesign, and Camera Raw (a plug-in that lets you access and use Raw files as they come off your digital camera). With Bridge, you have opportunities to optimize how these two applications work as well, so you should become familiar with the **Preferences** windows for these applications. ●

Welcome to Photoshop, Bridge, Camera Raw, and ImageReady

This task is a basic introduction to Photoshop, ImageReady, Camera Raw, and Bridge. In this task, you launch each program and evaluate the general workspace.

Begin

1 Launch Photoshop

In Windows, click the **Start** button and select **All Programs, Adobe Photoshop CS2**. On a Mac, open the folder labeled **Adobe Photoshop CS2** and double-click the **Adobe Photoshop CS2** icon. Click items on the **Welcome Screen** to gain easy access to tutorials and documentation of new features; click the **Close** button to launch Photoshop's main screen areas.

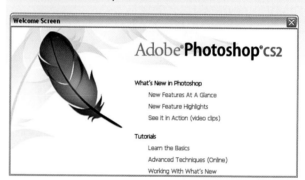

2 The Basic Photoshop Screen Areas

After closing the **Welcome Screen**, you'll see the full range of Photoshop controls. The toolbox is on the left side of the screen and contains all the Photoshop tools. The most commonly used Photoshop palettes appear on the right, and the menu bar appears across the top of the screen. The **Options** bar runs under the menu bar and contains the modifiers for each tool you select, the **Go to Bridge** button, and the **Palette Well**.

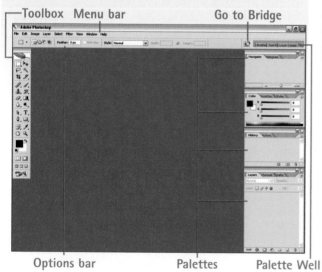

Toolbox Menu bar   Go to Bridge

Options bar   Palettes   Palette Well

3 Launch ImageReady

In Windows, click the **Start** button and select **Programs, Adobe ImageReady CS2**. On a Mac, open the folder labeled **Adobe Photoshop CS2** and double-click the **Adobe ImageReady CS2** icon. The ImageReady desktop looks very similar to the Photoshop desktop. Closer examination, however, reveals that some of the tool icons and palettes are different and that the **Slice**, **Table**, and **Image Map** palettes appear in the lower-right corner of the screen.

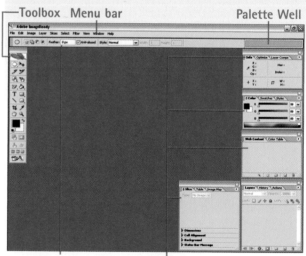

Toolbox Menu bar   Palette Well

Options bar   Palettes

4 The Basic Bridge Screen Areas

In Windows, click the **Start** button and select **Programs, Adobe Bridge**. On a Mac, open the **Adobe Bridge** folder and double-click the **Bridge** icon. If Photoshop is already open, click the **Go to Bridge** button located on the **Options** bar. Along the top are the menu commands. The large content area contains thumbnails of the images in the current folder; at the very bottom are the status information and display buttons.

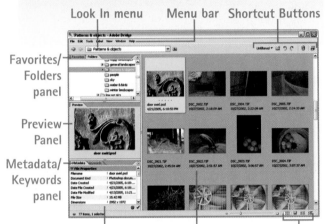

Look In menu   Menu bar   Shortcut Buttons

Favorites/ Folders panel

Preview Panel

Metadata/ Keywords panel

Status information   Content area   Display buttons

5 The Basic Camera Raw Screen Areas

Camera Raw isn't a standalone application, but whenever you open a Raw file in Photoshop or Bridge, you are presented with the Camera Raw interface. The title shows some basic file information. Below that are the tools, view options, and RGB values display. To the right of the image area are the **Histogram** display and adjustment sliders. Under the image area are the **Zoom** controls and **Workflow** options. At the bottom right are buttons for **Save** (saves the adjusted image as a file), **Open** (opens the adjusted image in Photoshop), **Done** (saves just the adjustments), and **Cancel** (discards any changes and closes Camera Raw).

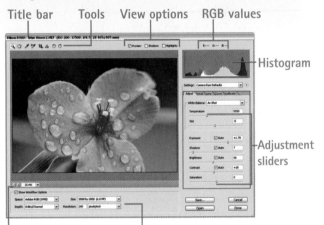

Title bar   Tools   View options   RGB values

Histogram

Adjustment sliders

Zoom controls   Workflow options

6 Adobe Help Center Screen Areas

The **Help** command in all CS2 applications now launches the Adobe Help Center. Beneath the top row of buttons are the **Navigation** and **Commands** buttons, along with the **Search** box. On the left side are the **Help Topics** titles, and along the bottom are the **Previous Topic** and **Next Topic** buttons.

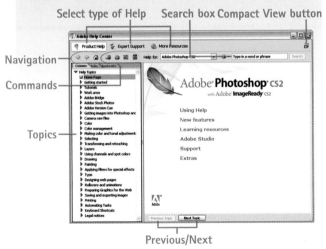

Select type of Help   Search box Compact View button

Navigation

Commands

Topics

Previous/Next

How-To Hints

Jumping from Photoshop to ImageReady

Switching from Photoshop to ImageReady is as easy as clicking the **Edit in** button at the bottom of the toolbox. If you are in Photoshop when you click this button, ImageReady opens. If you're in ImageReady when you click it, Photoshop opens. In Windows, press **Ctrl+Shift+M**; on the Mac, press ⌘**-Shift-M** to jump from one application to the other. Your active image automatically transfers to the application you move to.

End

How to Use the Toolbox

Each time you launch Photoshop or ImageReady, the toolbox appears on the screen, usually in the upper-left corner. In the process of editing an image, you will go to the toolbox frequently to select various selection, painting, and specialty tools. This task outlines what you'll find in the toolbox and how to access it.

Begin

1 Open the Photoshop Toolbox

The toolbox should appear automatically on the desktop, but it can be closed, which means you have to reopen it. To open the toolbox, select **Window**, **Tools**.

2 Select a Photoshop Tool

Click a tool to select it. If the tool button contains a small triangle in the lower-right corner, that tool offers additional tool options in a pop-out menu. Click and hold the tool button to view the pop-out menu; drag through the pop-out menu to select one of the additional tools.

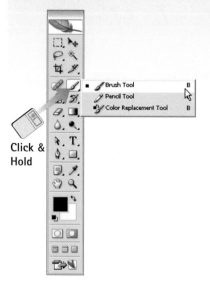

Click & Hold

3 Open the ImageReady Toolbox

The ImageReady toolbox should appear on the desktop as soon as ImageReady opens. Like its Photoshop counterpart, the ImageReady toolbox also can be closed, requiring you to reopen it. To open the toolbox in ImageReady, select **Window**, **Tools**.

4 Select an ImageReady Tool

Click a tool to select it. If the tool button contains a small triangle in the lower-right corner, that tool offers additional tool options in a pop-out menu. Click and hold the tool button to view the pop-out menu; drag through the pop-out menu to select one of the additional tools.

Click & Hold

5 Jump Between ImageReady and Photoshop

Click the **Edit in** button at the bottom of either the Photoshop or the ImageReady toolbox to move between Photoshop and ImageReady. This technique is especially useful when you have a file open and want to use features from both applications. You can also perform this command from a menu by selecting **File, Edit in Photoshop/ImageReady** or by pressing **Ctrl+Shift+M** (Windows) or **⌘-Shift-M** (Mac).

Click

End

How-To Hints

Path to Adobe Online

Click the **Adobe Online** button at the top of the toolbox (the feather icon) to access the **Adobe.com** website. Alternatively, select **Help, Photoshop Online** from the menu bar.

Configuring the Jump to Menu

By default, you can jump to Photoshop or ImageReady by clicking the **Edit in** button. You can access alternative graphics editors as well as HTML editors by creating a shortcut or alias to a desired application and dragging it to the following location on the Mac: **Adobe\Photoshop CS2\Helpers\Jump To Graphics Editor** (or **Jump To HTML Editor**). In Windows, create the shortcut to the desired application by opening Windows Explorer, right-clicking the application's filename, and selecting **Create Shortcut** from the context menu. Then drag the shortcut to the following location: **Program Files\Adobe\Photoshop CS2\Helpers\Jump To Graphics Editor** (or **Jump To HTML Editor**).

How to Use the Menu Bars

The menu bars in Photoshop and ImageReady operate like the menu bars in any other application. Click the menu name so that the menu drops down; then click any option to select it. Select an option that has a solid right-facing arrowhead, and a submenu pops out. Select an option that has a three-dot ellipsis (...) following it, and a dialog box opens. This task looks at the grouping of the various menus to help you understand the functionality associated with each one.

Begin

1 The Photoshop File Menu

You use the Photoshop **File** menu to address the basic opening, closing, and saving of files. This menu covers the import/export of files, workflow management and automated tasks, as well as page setup and print options. It also contains the **Exit** command (**Quit** on the Mac) for closing the application. *Note:* Photoshop for Mac OS X features a **Photoshop** menu that includes the **Preferences**, **Hide**, and **Quit** commands.

2 The Photoshop Edit and Image Menus

You use the Photoshop **Edit** and **Image** menus to specify most of the standard global changes to an open image. You'll find controls for cut and paste, transformations, fill, stroke, pattern, preferences (Windows users only; Mac users find preferences in the **Photoshop** menu), and color settings on the **Edit** menu. On the **Image** menu, you'll find options for color mode, adjustment options, crop, canvas size, and image size.

3 The Photoshop Layer Menu

The Photoshop **Layer** menu covers all the layer options—creating and deleting layers, merging layers, applying layer effects, and clipping masks. You can find most of these same controls on the **Layers** *palette menu*.

4 The Photoshop Select Menu

You use the Photoshop **Select** menu to control selection options within the program. These options include inverting selections, feathering, selection modifiers, and saving and loading selections.

5 The Photoshop Filter Menu

Simply put, the Photoshop **Filter** menu contains all the native Photoshop filters, divided into four filter interface groups and 14 subheadings. The **Filter** menu also can include any third-party filters you might have loaded in the Photoshop plug-ins folder.

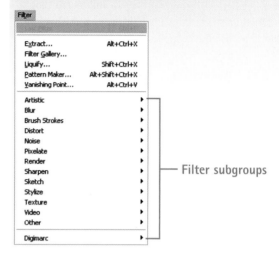

Filter subgroups

6 The Photoshop View and Window Menus

You use the **View** menu to control zooming and previews, as well as the visibility of rulers and guides. The **Window** menu lets you launch and close any of the 19 palettes. In addition, the **Window** menu lists all open file windows so you can move a file to the front of the screen simply by choosing it from this menu.

7 The Photoshop and ImageReady Help Menus

The ImageReady and Photoshop **Help** menus let you launch Adobe's **Help Center**. The Photoshop version provides access to the two file wizards as well as the **Adobe Online** and **Adobe Updates** services. Both versions also have several **How-to** tips.

ImageReady Help menu

Photoshop Help menu

Continues

8 The ImageReady File Menu

You use the ImageReady **File** menu to open, close, and save files, as well as to save files optimized as GIFs or JPEGs. This menu also covers the import and export of files, HTML browser previews, and recent files. The **File** menu also contains the **Exit** command (**Quit** on the Mac) for closing the application.

9 The ImageReady Edit and Image Menus

You use the ImageReady **Edit** and **Image** menus to control most of the standard global changes to an open image. Controls for cutting and pasting image data and HTML, as well as options for transformations, fill, stroke, pattern, and setting preferences are located on the **Edit** menu. The **Image** menu is more limited than its Photoshop counterpart; it offers canvas and image size controls, as well as a few adjustment options.

10 The ImageReady Layer Menu

The ImageReady **Layer** menu covers all the layer options—creating and deleting layers, merging, applying layer styles, and grouping. It also offers control over layer-to-imagemap conversion, slice and imagemap layer creation, and precise layer placement and locking. You can find many of these same controls in the **Layers** palette menu.

11 The ImageReady Slices Menu

The **Slices** menu specifies the handling of image slices. A *slice* is the portion of the image when ImageReady divides an image into smaller pieces for optimization and display in an HTML table. This menu specifies how image slices are created, modified, linked, and deleted. You can also preview JavaScript rollovers and link slices and slice selections. If it has to do with slices, you'll find that option on this menu.

12 The ImageReady Select Menu

You use the ImageReady **Select** menu to control selection options within the program. These options include inverting selections, feathering, selection modifiers, and saving and loading selections.

13 The ImageReady Filter Menu

The ImageReady **Filter** menu contains 101 filters divided into 14 subheadings. This menu also includes **Liquify**, the **Filter Gallery**, and any third-party filters you might have loaded into the plug-ins folder.

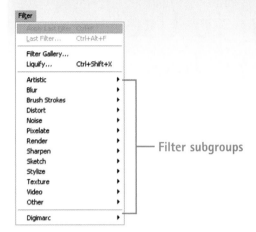

Filter subgroups

14 The ImageReady View and Window Menus

You use the **View** menu to control zooming and previews as well as the visibility of rulers and guides. The **Window** menu lets you launch and close any of the 19 ImageReady palettes. In addition, it also lists all open file windows and all the window arrangement commands.

End

How-To Hints

Why Menus Are Grayed Out

Menu commands are *context sensitive*, meaning they are accessible only if they can actually be used. For this reason, if a command is grayed out and unresponsive, you cannot use it in the given situation.

Keeping Up with Photoshop Updates and Information

Adobe has made it easy to stay abreast of news, trends, and technical issues with links available from within Photoshop itself. To view the Photoshop product page, which includes current listings of Photoshop tech notes, news, and events, select **Help, Photoshop Online**. To launch Adobe Updater and check for product updates, select **Help, Updates**. These both access the Adobe website using your Internet connection.

How to Use Photoshop and ImageReady Palettes

Photoshop and ImageReady use a system of 25 floating palettes to group items and controls such as brushes and tool options. You can open and close palettes on demand and easily compress or expand them to optimize your workspace.

Begin

1 Examine a Group of Palettes

To open a palette in ImageReady or Photoshop, open the **Window** menu and then select the palette you want to launch. To optimize your workspace, the application groups multiple palettes in a single window and separates them with tabs. If the palette you want is hidden, click its tab to bring it to the front of the window.

Multiple palettes in a single window

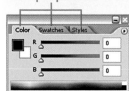

2 Collapse and Expand a Palette

To collapse or expand a palette in Windows, click the **Minimize/Maximize** button. On a Mac, click the green **Resize** button. To collapse a palette all the way down to only the tab names, double-click the tab. Double-click again to fully expand the palette.

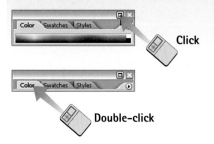

Click

Double-click

3 Resize a Palette

To resize most palettes (some cannot be resized), click and drag the lower-right corner of the window. To return a palette to its default size, click the **Minimize/Maximize** button (Windows) or the green **Resize** button (Mac).

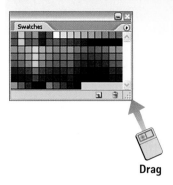

Drag

4 Tools and the Options Bar

The **Options** bars in ImageReady and Photoshop vary depending on the tool selected in the toolbox. By default, the **Options** bar runs across the top of the screen, docked just below the menu bar. Should you close it, you can reopen it by selecting **Window**, **Options** or by double-clicking a tool in the toolbox.

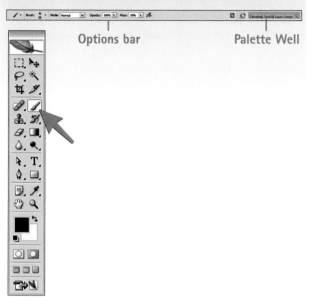

Options bar   Palette Well

5 The Palette Menu

A *palette menu* lists options related to the functionality of the associated palette. To open any palette menu, click the black triangle in the upper-right corner of the palette; click again to make a selection from the list of options.

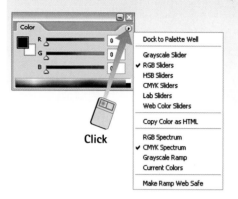

Click

6 Use the Palette Shortcut Buttons

At the bottom of some palettes are shortcut buttons for easy access to common tasks. To find out what each button does, first make sure that the **Show Tool Tips** option is selected in the **Options** section of the **General Preferences** box (select **Edit**, **Preferences**, **General**). With this option turned on, you can then simply position your mouse pointer over a button to read the description. See Task 10, "How to Set Photoshop Preferences," for more information.

Create a new layer

How-To Hints

Grouping and Placing Palettes

To move a palette into another palette group, click and hold the palette's tab and drag it to the target palette window. To separate a palette as a standalone window, click the tab and drag it to an empty area on the desktop. Note that the **Options** bar includes a *palette well* (the gray rectangle to the right of the bar; it is not shown in many figures in this book) that holds palettes and keeps their title tabs visible for easy access. Drag a palette to the well to add it; click once on its tab to expand or collapse it.

As you open and reposition palettes, Photoshop remembers their sizes and where you used them last. To reset the palettes to their defaults each time you open them, select **Edit**, **Preferences**, **General**; the **General Preferences** box opens. Disable the **Save Palette Locations** option—you must restart Photoshop before the changes take effect.

End

How to Use the Color Picker

The **Color Picker** is the standard interface for selecting a color in Photoshop or ImageReady. It allows fast and intuitive color selection from millions of colors. The **Color Picker** also offers PANTONE color matching and web-safe color choices.

Begin

1 Set Color Picker Preferences

Select **File**, **Preferences**, **General** to open the **Preferences** window to the **General** page (in OS X, select **Photoshop/ImageReady**, **Preferences**, **General**). Select **Adobe** from the **Color Picker** drop-down list. Although you could select the **Windows** or **Apple** color picker from this list, the **Adobe** version is the recommended choice. Click **OK** to close the dialog box.

Click

2 Launch the Color Picker

In the toolbox, click the **Foreground** color swatch to launch the **Color Picker** dialog box.

Click

3 Set the Hue

Click and drag the white triangles on the **Hue** slider to select the desired hue. As you drag, notice that the range of colors displayed in the large **Select Foreground Color** window changes.

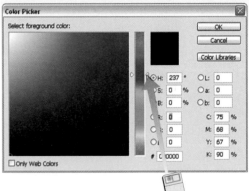

Drag

4 Select a Value

Move the mouse pointer into the **Select Foreground Color** window. Notice that the pointer changes into a sample dot as you do so. Click in the color window to select a color; that color selection is reflected in the color swatch in the upper right of the dialog box.

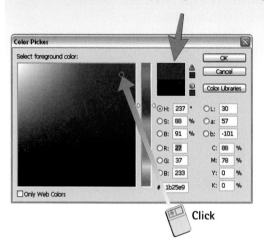

 Click

5 Check the Gamut Warnings

If the color you selected falls outside the printable CMYK color gamut, a triangle with an exclamation point appears next to the selected color. The color box that appears below the triangle is the nearest in-gamut color based on the current conversion settings. If the color you selected does not fall within the web browser-safe color palette, a cube appears just below the triangle, with another color box that indicates the nearest web-safe color. Click in either box to select that color.

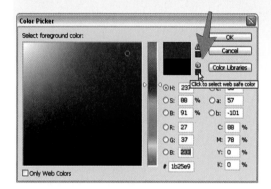

6 Select PANTONE-Type Colors

In the **Color Picker**, click the **Color Libraries** button to open the **Color Libraries** dialog box. Select a color-matching system from the **Book** drop-down list and type the color number (if you know it). Otherwise, drag the white triangles into the approximate area, and then click a swatch to select a color. Click the **Picker** button to go back to the Photoshop **Color Picker**, or click **OK** to select the color and close the color-selection dialog boxes.

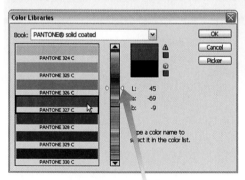

Click

End

 Click

How-To Hints

Comparing Relative Values

By default, the **Select Color** window in the **Color Picker** is based on a color's hue. In other words, the **H:** is the default active selection. Click in any of the other boxes—which represent Brightness (**B:**), Saturation (**S:**), RGB, CMYK, and Lab—to change the way color is displayed in the window. You also can enter a numerical value in any of these fields to change the current color value numerically.

Entering a Hexadecimal Color or Checking Only Web Colors

Type a hexadecimal value in the **#** box at the bottom of the **Color Picker** to select web colors (colors that will display in most web browsers). You can also enable the **Only Web Colors** check box, which forces the **Select Color** window to display only a web-safe color range.

TASK **6**

How to Select a Color

Task 5 explained how to use the **Color Picker** to select a color. This task looks at the ways you can specify a color in Photoshop. The methods described in this task use a combination of working with the **Color Picker**, sampling colors from images, and using preset swatches. Use the method that best suits the task at hand.

1 Select a Foreground Color

Click the **Foreground** color swatch in the tool-box to launch the **Color Picker**. Follow the steps in Task 5, "How to Use the Color Picker," to select a color.

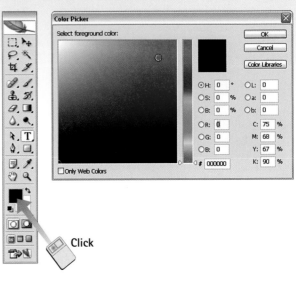

Click

2 Select a Background Color

Click the **Background** color swatch in the toolbox to launch the **Color Picker**. Follow the steps in Task 5 to select a color.

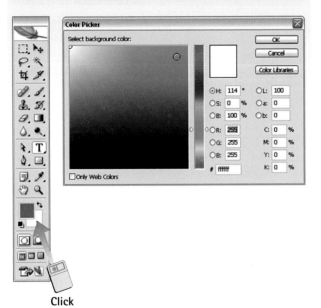

Click

3 Sample a Color

Click the **Eyedropper** tool in the toolbox. Move the tool in the image over the color you want to sample and click to select the desired color. The color you select becomes the foreground color (check the color swatch in the toolbox). **Alt**+click the color (Windows) or **Option**+click the color (Mac) to sample a background color.

Click

4 Use the Color Palette

Select **Window, Color** to open the **Color** palette. Click either its foreground or background swatch. Move the RGB sliders as necessary to mix the desired color; watch the color you are creating in the swatch on the left side of the palette or in the toolbox. You can select additional color models and options from the **Color** palette menu.

Drag

5 Use the Color Swatches

Select **Window, Swatches** to open the **Swatches** palette, which contains an array of preset color swatches. Click the desired color to select it (it becomes the foreground color in the toolbox; **Alt/Option**+click for the background color). To add the current foreground color as a swatch on this palette, move the pointer to an empty space on the palette until the pointer changes to the **Paint Bucket**; click to add the color as a swatch on the palette.

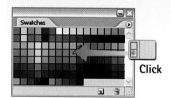

Click

End

How-To Hints

Color Switcher

To switch the foreground and background colors in the toolbox, click the **Switch Colors** button (the double-headed, curved arrow to the right of the **Foreground** color swatch in the toolbox). Alternatively, press the **X** key to switch the foreground and background colors.

Reverting to Black and White

Click the **Default Colors** button in the toolbox (the small, black square on top of the white square to the left of the **Background** color swatch) to reset the foreground and background colors to black and white. Alternatively, press the **D** key to set the foreground and background colors to black and white.

How to Browse Files in Bridge

Adobe Bridge is the new replacement for the file browser. Because it is a separate application from Photoshop, it offers many advantages over the file browser, including the capability to be run on its own. It also offers many advantages over the system file browser (Explorer or Selectr) including the capability to preview Raw files and file data. If you have other Adobe Creative Suite applications, they can also use Bridge, and they will add their own set of features.

Begin

1 Launch Bridge

Bridge can be launched in several ways. It has its own entry under in the Windows **Programs** menu (double-click the **Bridge** icon in the **Adobe Bridge** folder on the Mac), or you can launch it by selecting **File, Browse** in Photoshop. The easiest way is to click the **Go to Bridge** button located on the Photoshop **Options** bar next to the **Palette Well**.

Click

2 Resize the Panels

The default Bridge layout has four panels you can resize by dragging the divider bars. When you have a layout you prefer, Bridge uses that layout each time it is launched until you drag the divider bars into new positions.

Drag

3 Navigate to the Folder

Click the **Folders** tab and navigate the directory tree until you can highlight your desired folder. A plus sign next to a folder name indicates that it has subfolders. Click the plus sign to expand a folder, or click the minus sign to collapse it.

 Click

4 Locate Your File

Using the scrollbar along the right edge of the content area, scroll through the thumbnails until you find the image you're looking for. The default view in the content area shows the filename and creation date. Click an image thumbnail once to load the image in the **Preview** panel on the left side of the Bridge window.

Click

5 Manage Your File

If your image needs to be rotated, click either the clockwise or counterclockwise rotation button located on the toolbar above the thumbnails. You can also delete the file from the hard disk (click to select it and then click the trash can icon) or drag the thumbnail to a different folder.

Rotate image Trash can

6 Open Your File

If the file you're looking at is the one you want to load, double-click its thumbnail to open it. If it is a Raw file, it opens in Camera Raw—most image file formats open in Photoshop. Nonimage files open in their associated applications. You can change which applications to use when opening specific file types in the **Preferences** window (select **Edit, Preferences** in Windows or **Bridge, Preferences** on the Mac).

End

How-To Hints

Multiple Selection

To select more than one thumbnail in a single folder (you can't select images from multiple folders), click the first thumbnail, press and hold the **Ctrl** key (Windows) or the ⌘ key (Mac), and click each additional thumbnail you want to select. If you want to select a range, click the first thumbnail, press and hold the **Shift** key, and click the last thumbnail in the range. Any command you use in Bridge applies to all the selected thumbnails (select **File, Open** instead of double-clicking to open multiple files).

Advanced Bridge

Bridge looks deceptively simple. Take the time to explore all the menus and submenus, and you'll find a surprising array of commands that go far beyond the simple viewing of files. You can order prints online, rename files in batches, and even select files for use with Photoshop's automated features (such as **Picture Package** and **Contact Sheet II**).

How to Use Rulers, Grids, and Guides

The importance of rulers and guides has grown considerably in the last few revisions of Photoshop. *Guides* are user-defined alignment lines. New for CS2 are Smart Guides that appear automatically anytime two objects are aligned. The *grid* is an underlying matrix of lines you can use for the general alignment of all the items on a page. The enhanced text (type) features have made text-alignment issues much easier to address. In addition, designers are creating complete web pages in Photoshop and ImageReady, which necessitates using guides and grids to maintain spacing and alignment.

Begin

1 Set Ruler Preferences

Select **Edit**, **Preferences**, **Units & Rulers** to open the **Preferences** window to the **Units & Rulers** page. From the **Rulers** drop-down list in the **Units** section, select the desired unit of measurement (select from **Pixels**, **Inches**, **Centimeters**, **Millimeters**, **Points**, **Picas**, and **Percent**) and then click **OK**. In this instance, you do not have to restart Photoshop for the preference change to take effect.

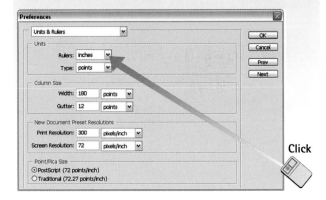

Click

2 Activate Rulers

Select **View**, **Rulers** to make the rulers visible around the top and left edges of the image area.

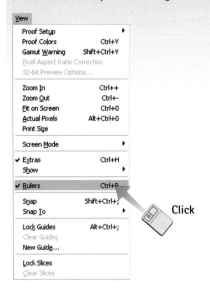

Click

3 Set Guides Preferences

Select **Edit**, **Preferences**, **Guides**, **Grid & Slices** to open the **Preferences** window to the **Guides**, **Grid & Slices** page. Here you can specify the color and format of the guide and gridlines, as well as the spacing for the grid. Click the color swatches to select a custom color, or use the **Color** drop-down lists to select from preset colors. You can also select slice colors and toggle slice numbers on and off.

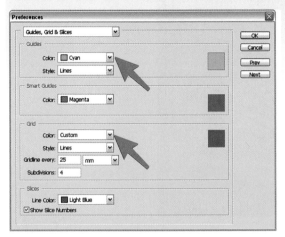

4 Create and Activate Guides

To create a guide, click in the ruler area and drag into the image area. A vertical or horizontal guide follows the tool, depending on which ruler you started with. You can drag out as many guides as you need. You can also place a guide in a specific place by selecting **View, New Guide** and entering the orientation and pixel position in the dialog box that appears. To move a guide, use the **Move** tool to drag the guide into a new position.

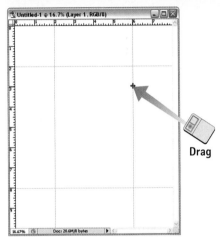

Drag

5 Set Snap-to Parameters

To precisely align elements to guides and grids as you drag the elements, select **View, Snap to, Guides** or **View, Snap to, Grid**. Select these commands again to turn them off.

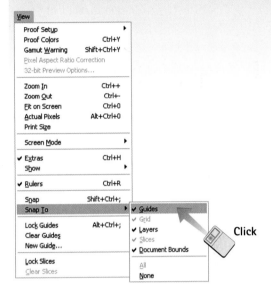

Click

6 Lock Guides As Needed

To lock the guides in place, select **View, Lock Guides**. When you lock the guide lines, you prevent them from moving accidentally, especially when you are using numerous guides.

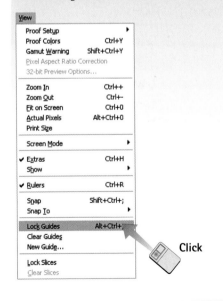

Click

End

How-To Hints

Web Measurements

When working with a web design, set the ruler increments to **Pixels** on the **Units & Rulers** page of the **Preferences** window. Then scroll the image against the rulers to take rough measurements of page elements. An alternative way to make quick measurements is to use the **Measure** tool to measure areas within your images.

Using Smart Guides

Select **View, Show, Smart Guides** to enable a new feature for Photoshop CS2: Smart Guides. As you're dragging an object on a layer, **Smart Guides** looks at the layers below it and flashes a temporary guideline when it thinks you've aligned with the top, bottom, or middle of another object.

How to Use Color Management

It is important to specify how Photoshop will display the color characteristics for each image file you open. These characteristics are divided among the RGB color model (for screen viewing and inkjet printing) and CMYK or grayscale color models (for offset printing). Each model allows for a different range of color, which can dramatically impact the final design.

Select **Edit, Color Settings** to open the **Color Settings** dialog box. You use this dialog box to set the default color spaces and color management options for all the files you open in Photoshop.

It is impossible to accurately display the entirety of any color model (such as RGB or CMYK) on a monitor. A *color space profile* determines how color values appear on your monitor when viewed in Photoshop. The profile includes a *gamut* (the range of colors the profile can represent) and mapping details that tell the monitor which color to display for a particular pixel's color value. A *working space* is the default color space profile assigned to new documents.

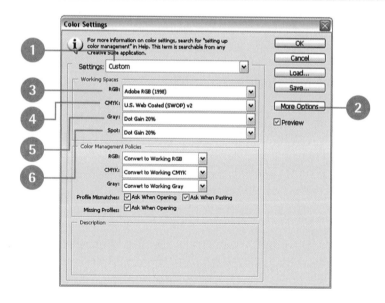

1. **Settings pop-up menu:** Click the arrow to display a list of color management presets designed for specific tasks. Use the **Settings** presets if you are unsure how to proceed, provided that your objective fits with the predefined settings. Options are **Monitor Color** (essentially turns off color management), **Colorsync Workflow** (Mac only), **North America General Purpose 2**, **North America Prepress 2**, and **North America Web/Internet**. Changing any of the menu listings that follow converts this setting to **Custom**.

2. **More/Fewer Options button:** Expands or contracts the window to show or hide advanced controls.

Working Spaces Section

3 RGB pop-up menu: Click the arrow to display a list of RGB working space profiles:

Adobe RGB (1998): Presents a wide range of colors and is therefore a good choice for general work in RGB. All RGB profiles include a large range in colors that will cause many colors to fall outside the CMYK color range (something to consider for RGB-to-CMYK color conversions).

Apple RGB: Based on the original Apple RGB monitor (gamma 1.8, Trinitron primaries, 6500K white point). It works well for legacy graphic files because this was the standard for older versions of Adobe Photoshop and Illustrator.

ColorMatch RGB: Matches the color space of Radius Pressview monitors. This option should be used when working within that workflow environment.

sRGB IEC61966-2.1: Matches the native color range for most PC monitors and is becoming standard for many cameras, scanners, printers, and software applications. This option is ideal for web work, but its smaller color range can cause problems for print production.

Monitor Profiles: If you have loaded a monitor profile for your current monitor, you might see a profile option for it in the **RGB** list. If you select your monitor's profile, Photoshop acts as though all color management were turned off. This option is the same as selecting **Monitor Color** from the **Settings** pop-up menu.

Color Management Profiles: If other color management options are loaded on your system (such as **ColorSync RGB**), you might see profiles for them listed in the **RGB** list. The profiles you see listed usually reflect the current settings for each option.

Device Profiles: Color space profiles are different from device profiles. However, because of the way operating systems store profiles, you might find profiles listed here for cameras, scanners, printers, and other devices. *This is not the correct place to select one of these device profiles.*

4 CMYK pop-up menu: Click the arrow to display a list of CMYK color space profiles—from generic to industry-standard and custom settings. Select from the **Custom, Load,** or **Save CMYK, Euroscale, Japan,** and **U.S.** prepress options. Check with your printing specialist, but if you're unsure which setting to use, the default option **U.S. Web Coated (SWOP)v2** is the recommended setting and is standard for most CMYK work.

5 Gray pop-up menu: This option specifies how grayscale images are displayed. Options simulate **Dot Gain** percentages (10%–30%), **1.8 Gamma** (Mac), and **2.2 Gamma** (PC). Use **Dot Gain** percentages if you're going to send the image to offset printing, as dictated by your printing specialist. If unknown, leave the default setting of **Dot Gain 20%**.

6 Spot pop-up menu: This option specifies how spot color channels and duotones are displayed. Options simulate **Dot Gain** percentages (10%–30%). If unknown, leave the default setting of **Dot Gain 20%**.

Continues

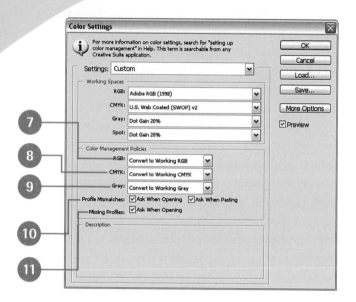

Color Management Policies Section

7 **RGB pop-up menu:** Specifies mapping between different RGB color space profiles, as can occur with embedded profile conflicts and the moving of profiles between multiple documents. Options include the following:

> **Off:** Ignores and discards profiles when you are opening files and doesn't assign a color space profile when creating new files.
>
> **Preserve Embedded Profiles:** Preserves embedded profiles when you are opening files. In the case of mismatches between the working space and the embedded profile, the embedded profile is used.
>
> **Convert to Working RGB:** Converts to the current RGB working space when you are opening files with no embedded profile. In the case of mismatches between the working space and embedded profile, the working space color model is used.

8 **CMYK pop-up menu:** Specifies mapping between different CMYK color space profiles, as can occur with embedded profile conflicts and when moving profiles between multiple documents. Options include the following:

> **Off:** Ignores and discards profiles when you are opening files and doesn't assign a color space profile when creating new files.
>
> **Preserve Embedded Profiles:** Preserves embedded profiles when you are opening files. In the case of mismatches between the working space and the embedded profile, the embedded profile is used.
>
> **Convert to Working CMYK:** Converts to the current CMYK working space when you are opening files with no embedded profile. In the case of mismatches between the working space and the embedded profile, the working space color model is used.

9 **Gray pop-up menu:** Specifies mapping between different grayscale image profiles, as can occur with embedded profile conflicts and the moving of profiles between multiple documents. Options include the following:

> **Off:** Ignores and discards profiles when you are opening files and doesn't assign a color space profile when creating new files.
>
> **Preserve Embedded Profiles:** Preserves embedded profiles when you are opening files. In the case of mismatches between the working space and the embedded profile, the embedded profile is used.
>
> **Convert to Working Gray:** Converts to the current grayscale working space when you are opening files with no embedded profile. In the case of mismatches between the working space and the embedded profile, the working space color model is used.

10 **Profile Mismatches check boxes:** Specify when you should be notified about profile conflicts. The **Ask when Opening** check box notifies you of mismatches as a file is opened and offers the option of overriding the embedded profile in favor of the current working space. The **Ask when Pasting** check box notifies you of mismatches when image data is brought into an existing file, as would occur through pasting, drag-and-drop, or importing.

11 **Missing Profiles Ask when Opening check box:** When you are opening a file, this option notifies you that there are no associated profiles and allows you to select one. This requires the related profile option to be turned on.

Continues

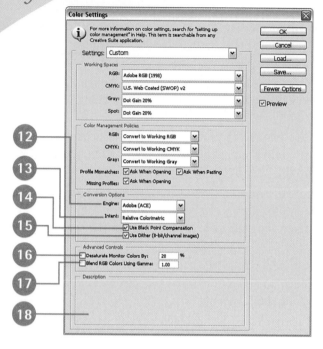

Conversion Options Section

If you click the **More Options** button at the upper-right side of the dialog box, the following additional options become available:

12 **Engine pop-up menu:** Specifies the color management system or method to be used when converting between color spaces. Options include the following:

> **Adobe (ACE):** The Adobe Color Management System and Color Engine. Adobe recommends this option for most users.

> **Apple ColorSync (Mac only):** Uses the Apple ColorSync color management and matching system, including associated hardware or software profiles.

> **Apple CMM (Mac only):** Uses the Apple ColorSync color management system and the CMM color matching system.

> **Microsoft ICM (Windows only):** Uses the Microsoft Windows color matching system.

13 **Intent pop-up menu:** Controls the method for mapping one color space into another. Options include the following:

> **Perceptual:** Attempts to preserve the relative visual relationships between colors. This option works well with wide gamut images in which exact color matching is not critical but a natural color space is desired.

> **Saturation:** Requests high color saturation and bright colors. This option is good for business graphics and dynamic color effects.

Relative Colorimetric: Attempts to replicate the white point of the source file to the white point of the destination image. This option works well when the color ranges of both images are within the working color space. Adobe recommends this for most conversions.

Absolute Colorimetric: Does a direct match of source and destination images, without adjusting the white point. This option should be used when the exact match of a specific color is required (as with a logo). Colors outside the working color space are flattened, and all contrast within these areas are lost.

(14) **Use Black Point Compensation check box:** Adjusts the black point when converting colors between color spaces. Enabling this check box ensures that the full color range of the working space is optimized.

(15) **Use Dither (8-Bit/Channel Images) check box:** Uses a color dithering method to specify colors when converting between color spaces. This option reduces banding but increases file size.

Advanced Controls Section

(16) **Desaturate Monitor Colors by check box and field:** Allows you to desaturate colors by a prescribed percentage. This is a good option to use if you're trying to view an image with a color range that's larger than that of the current monitor. Because this is a rare occurrence, Adobe recommends this option for expert users only.

(17) **Blend RGB Colors Using Gamma check box and field:** Provides control over how painted colors or layers blend in **Normal** blending mode. Enables image colors to be combined using a specified gamma value. **Gamma 1.0** is considered to be the most accurate with the fewest artifacts. This option overrides any existing color spaces for the combined colors. The only reason I can think of for using this option is to match Photoshop to another application's color-conversion process.

(18) **Description field:** When you drag the mouse pointer over any of the sections and menus in the **Color Settings** dialog box, a short description of the item appears in this field.

End

How-To Hints

Opening Files and Dialog Boxes

If you have enabled the **Ask when Opening** check box in the **Profile Mismatches** section, you see a dialog box each time a file is opened with a profile that does not match the current working space profile (as specified in the **Working Spaces** section). If **Ask when Opening** is selected in the **Missing Profiles** section, the dialog box appears each time a file is opened that has a mismatched profile or no profile at all. Although you can avoid these dialog boxes by disabling the **Ask when Opening** check box, you run the risk of unwanted color shifts as you open images (if you do not understand the options offered in this dialog box). You're better off taking some time to understand which space works best for your workflow and image types and managing the profiles through the controls described here.

TASK

How to Set Photoshop Preferences

General Controls

Select **Edit**, **Preferences**, **General** to open the **Preferences** box to the **General** page (in Mac OS X, select **Photoshop**, **Preferences**, **General**). You use this page of the **Preferences** box to control interpolation, the **Color Picker** option, and a number of other general application parameters.

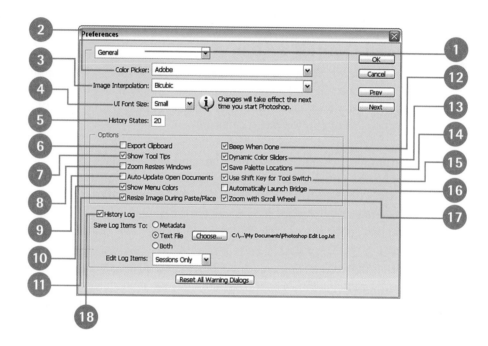

① **Preferences Title pop-up menu:** Click the arrow to display a list of other pages in the **Preferences** box; select an option to open that page. Also, the **Next** and **Prev** buttons jump forward or backward to the choices in this list.

② **Color Picker pop-up menu:** Click the arrow to display a list of Color Picker options; select the **Adobe** or **Apple/Windows Color Picker**.

③ **Image Interpolation pop-up menu:** Click the arrow to display a list of interpolation options. Select **Nearest Neighbor**, **Bilinear**, **Bicubic**, **Bicubic Smoother**, or **Bicubic Sharper**. In most cases, use **Bicubic Smoother** when enlarging an image and use **Bicubic Sharper** when reducing or downsampling. Each image is different, however, so experiment for best results.

4   **UI Font Size:** This option allows control over the size of text for user interface items such as the text that appears on the tabs of palettes. By default it is set to **Small**.

5   **History States:** By default this number is set to **20**, which means Photoshop stores (via the **History** palette) the last 20 steps performed on an image. A larger number gives you greater control in how many steps you can go back (if needed), but the tradeoff is that it also requires more memory to store that information in the **History** palette.

6   **Export Clipboard check box:** This option attempts to export the current **Clipboard** contents when Photoshop is closed. Leave this option disabled because it slows the shutdown process and because the exported format is almost always incompatible.

7   **Show Tool Tips check box:** Activatesthe pop-up tool descriptions when you hover the cursor over the interface elements.

8   **Zoom Resizes Windows check box:** Resizes image windows when zooming in and out of the image from the keyboard.

9   **Auto-Update Open Documents check box:** Updates open documents automatically.

10   **Show Menu Colors check box:** Enables the color display for custom menus.

11   **Resize Image During Paste/Place check box:** Determines whether to resize pasted or placed images that are larger than the Photoshop document.

12   **Beep when Done check box:** Emits an audible beep when a task is complete.

13   **Dynamic Color Sliders check box:** Updates the current color selections in the **Color** palette in real time as the sliders are adjusted. Disable this check box for a slight performance increase.

14   **Save Palette Locations check box:** Reopens palettes in the same place and at the same size as they were when they were closed, or when Photoshop is closed.

15   **Use Shift Key for Tool Switch check box:** Enables the use of the **Shift** key along with the letter key assigned to the tool to toggle tool selections within a group of tools. When unchecked, simply repeatedly press the letter key assigned to the tool to toggle between the grouped tool selections.

16   **Automatically Launch Bridge check box:** Automatically launches Bridge in the background whenever Photoshop is opened.

17   **Zoom with Scroll Wheel check box:** This determines whether scrolling or zooming is the default action for a mouse with a scroll wheel option.

18   **History Log check box:** Enable this check box to generate an ongoing log of activities executed within each session of Photoshop.

Continues

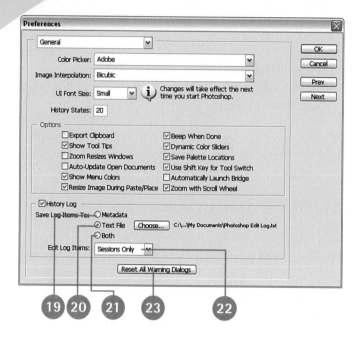

19 **Save Log Items to Metadata:** Saves the history log in XML-base metadata format within the file.

20 **Save Log Items to Text File:** Saves the history log as a generic text file. Click the **Choose** button to designate the save location for the history log text file. Click and navigate to the desired destination folder.

21 **Save Log Items to Both:** Creates a history log record in both metadata and generic text formats.

22 **Edit Log Items pop-up menu:** Select from **Concise**, **Detailed**, and **Sessions Only** history log formats. **Concise** shows the opening and closing of files and of the application itself, plus the edits recorded in the **History** palette. **Detailed** shows everything **Concise** does, plus every edit used and the file paths. **Sessions Only** records only the start date and time, with no editing data stored.

23 **Reset All Warning Dialogs button:** Resets all warning messages to their defaults.

File Handling

Click the **Next** button to go to the **File Handling** preferences dialog box or select **Edit, Preferences, File Handling** to launch the **File Handling Preferences** box (in Mac OS X, select **Photoshop, Preferences, File Handling**). You use this page to specify how a file is saved (including previews and thumbnails) and for compatibility issues for files that might need to be opened or viewed in older versions of Photoshop.

Mac only

Preferences Title pop-up menu: Click the arrow to display a list of other pages in the **Preferences** window; select an option to open that page. Currently it should be set to **File Handling** to view the options discussed here.

Image Previews pop-up menu: Click the arrow to display a list of save options and then select one of these options: **Always Save**, **Never Save**, or **Ask when Saving**.

Icon check box (Mac only): Saves an icon preview for viewing within windows on the desktop.

Full Size check box (Mac only): Saves a 72dpi file version for applications that can open only low-resolution Photoshop files.

Macintosh Thumbnail check box (Mac only): Creates a thumbnail that is displayed in Macintosh systems in the **Open** dialog box.

Windows Thumbnail check box (Mac only): Creates a thumbnail that is displayed in Windows systems.

Continues

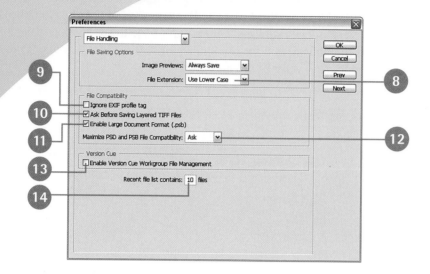

7 **Append File Extension pop-up menu (Mac only):** Adds file extensions as a file is saved, based on the file format. Click the arrow to display a list including **Always**, **Never**, and **Ask when Saving**.

8 **Use Lower Case check box:** Adds the file extension using lowercase letters. In Windows, the **File Extension** pop-up menu offers the choice between automatically adding extensions to file-names in **Use Upper Case** or **Use Lower Case** letters.

9 **Ignore EXIF Profile Tag check box:** Does not apply the color tag when contained within Exchangeable Image File information. EXIF information is typically saved from digital camera settings, and some photographers prefer to disable the wide-gamut tags.

10 **Ask Before Saving Layered TIFF Files check box:** Prompts to include additional save options when saving TIFF files after adding layers.

11 **Enable Large Document Format (.psb) check box:** Enables Photoshop to recognize Large Document Format files, extending the maximum file dimensions to 300,000 × 300,000 pixels. If this check box is disabled, Photoshop defaults to a limit of 30,000 × 30,000 pixels.

12 **Maximize PSD and PSB File Compatibility pop-up menu:** Determines when and how Photoshop embeds a flattened version of the image within the file for compatibility with other software. Options in the pop-up menu are **Ask**, **Always**, and **Never**.

13 **Enable Version Cue Workgroup File Management check box:** Turns on version-control capabilities for workgroup-based development.

14 **Recent File List Contains field:** Type a number in the box to set the number of recent files to be displayed in the **Recent Files** pop-up menu that appears when you select **File**, **Open Recent**.

Display & Cursors

Click the **Next** button to go to the **Display & Cursors Preferences** window or select **Edit**, **Preferences**, **Display & Cursors** to open the **Preferences** window to the **Display & Cursors** page (in Mac OS X, select **Photoshop**, **Preferences**, **Display & Cursors**). You use this page to specify brush and cursor shapes and sizes.

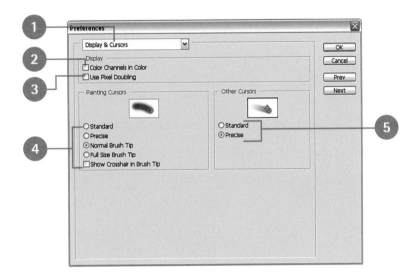

1 **Preferences Title pop-up menu:** Click the arrow to display a list of other pages in the **Preferences** box; select an option to open that page. Currently it should be set to **Display & Cursors** to view the options discussed below.

2 **Color Channels in Color check box:** Displays the color channels in color rather than in grayscale.

3 **Use Pixel Doubling check box:** Enables faster previews by temporarily reducing the resolution of the preview (it does not affect the actual file, only the preview).

4 **Painting Cursors radio buttons:** You can select **Standard** (icon), **Precise** (cross hairs), **Normal Brush Tip** (actual shape and size of the brush tip), or **Full Size Brush Tip** (actual shape with visual indications of a soft or hard edge) for the painting cursor. In addition, a **Show Crosshair in Brush Tip** check box can be enabled along with either the **Normal Brush Tip** or **Full Size Brush Tip** options to see a crosshair inside the brush tip.

5 **Other Cursors radio buttons:** Enable you to select between a **Standard** (icon) and **Precise** (cross hairs) cursor for the nonpainting tools.

Continues

Transparency & Gamut

Click the **Next** button to go to the **Transparency & Gamut Preferences** window or select **Edit**, **Preferences**, **Transparency & Gamut** to open the **Preferences** window to the **Transparency & Gamut** page (in Mac OS X, select **Photoshop**, **Preferences**, **Transparency & Gamut**). You use this page to specify how transparency is shown in a file, as well as to select the gamut warning color format.

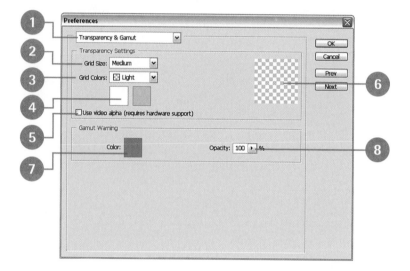

1 **Preferences Title pop-up menu:** Click the arrow to display a list of other pages in the **Preferences** window; select an option to open that page. Currently it should be set to **Transparency & Gamut** to view the options discussed here.

2 **Grid Size pop-up menu:** Controls the size of the checkerboard used to indicate transparency. Options are **None**, **Small**, **Medium**, and **Large**.

3 **Grid Colors pop-up menu:** Controls the color of the checkerboard used to indicate transparency. Options are **Light**, **Medium**, **Dark**, **Red**, **Orange**, **Green**, **Blue**, **Purple**, and **Custom**.

4 **Custom color swatches:** Click one or both of the swatches to select custom colors for the transparency checkerboard.

5 **Use Video Alpha check box:** Enables video alpha capability (a special effect transparency technique available with certain video boards).

6 **Transparency preview window:** Shows the current checkerboard pattern.

7 **Gamut Warning Color swatch:** Click to display the **Color Picker** so you can select the color that will show in place of the out-of-gamut color.

8 **Gamut Warning Opacity slider:** Click and drag the slider to control the transparency of the color you've chosen to replace the out-of-gamut color.

Units & Rulers

Select **Edit**, **Preferences**, **Units & Rulers** to open the **Preferences** window to the **Units & Rulers** page (in Mac OS X, select **Photoshop**, **Preferences**, **Units & Rulers**). You use this page to specify the format and measurements for rulers and columns.

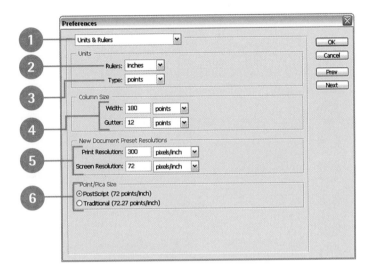

1 **Preferences Title pop-up menu:** Click the arrow to display a list of other pages in the **Preferences** window; select an option to open that page. Currently it should be set to **Units & Rulers** to view the options discussed here.

2 **Rulers Units pop-up menu:** Click the arrow to display a list of the units of measurement for Photoshop rulers. Options include **Pixels**, **Inches**, **Centimeters**, **Millimeters**, **Points**, **Picas**, and **Percent**.

3 **Type Units pop-up menu:** Click the arrow to display a list of the units of measurement for type (text) specifications. Options include **Pixels**, **Points**, and **Millimeters.**

4 **Column Size Width and Gutter pop-up menus:** Enter the width of a target column and the width of the *gutter* (the space between columns) for layout purposes. When resizing an image or a canvas, the units you specify here are the ones you see when you select **Columns** in the **New, Image Size, or Canvas Size** dialog box.

5 **New Document Preset Resolutions fields:** Pop-up menus control pixels per inch or centimeters. Enter default new document resolutions for print or screen in the fields.

6 **Point/Pica Size radio buttons:** Select either the **PostScript** or the **Traditional** measurement system.

Continues

Guides, Grid & Slices

Click the **Next** button to go to the **Guides, Grid & Slices Preferences** window or select **Edit, Preferences, Guides, Grid & Slices** to open the **Preferences** window to the **Guides, Grid & Slices** page (in Mac OS X, select **Photoshop, Preferences, Guides, Grids & Slices**). You use this page to control interpolation and a number of other general application parameters.

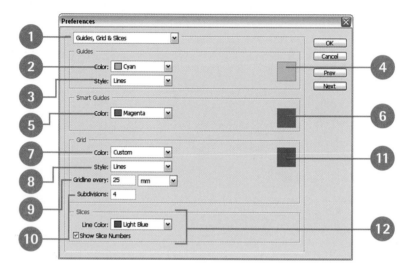

(1) **Preferences Title pop-up menu:** Click the arrow to display a list of other pages in the **Preferences** window; select an option to open that page. Currently it should be set to **Guides, Grid & Slices** to view the options discussed here.

(2) **Guides Color pop-up menu:** Select the color of the guide lines. Choices are **Light Blue, Light Red, Green, Medium Blue, Yellow, Magenta, Cyan, Light Gray, Black,** and **Custom**.

(3) **Guides Style pop-up menu:** Determines the format of the guides. Options are solid **Lines** and **Dashed Lines**.

(4) **Guides color swatch:** Click to open the **Color Picker** so you can select a custom guide color.

(5) **Smart Guides Color pop-menu:** Select the color of the smart guide lines. Choices are **Light Blue, Light Red, Green, Medium Blue, Yellow, Magenta, Cyan, Light Gray, Black,** and **Custom**.

(6) **Smart Guides color swatch:** Click to open the **Color Picker** so you can select a custom smart guide color.

(7) **Grid Color pop-up menu:** Select the color of the grid. Choices are **Light Blue, Light Red, Green, Medium Blue, Yellow, Magenta, Cyan, Light Gray, Black,** and **Custom**.

(8) **Grid Style pop-up menu:** Determines the format of the grid. Options are solid **Lines, Dots,** and **Dashed Lines**.

(9) **Gridline controls:** Select the unit of measurement from the pop-up menu for the main grid divisions. Choices are **Pixels, Inches, Centimeters, Points, Picas,** and **Percent**. After you select a unit, type the number of units between gridlines.

(10) **Subdivisions:** Determines how many subdivisions fall between each main gridline. Enter the desired value in the field.

(11) **Grid color swatch:** Click to open the **Color Picker** so you can select a custom grid color.

(12) **Slices options:** Select slices line color from the **Line Color** pop-up menu. Choices are **Light Blue, Light Red, Green, Medium Blue, Yellow, Magenta, Cyan, Light Gray,** and **Black**. To show slice numbers, enable the **Show Slice Numbers** check box.

Plug-ins & Scratch Disks

Click the **Next** button to go to the **Plug-ins & Scratch Disks Preferences** window box or select **Edit, Preferences, Plug-Ins & Scratch Disks** to open the **Preferences** window to the **Plug-Ins & Scratch Disks** page (in Mac OS X, select **Photoshop, Preferences, Plug-ins & Scratch Disks**). You use this page to tell Photoshop where to look for plug-ins and scratch disks.

Plug-ins are utilities and filters that extend Photoshop's core functionality. The default Photoshop plug-ins folder is located under the main Photoshop directory; install any plug-ins there. However, for sharing with other applications or housekeeping purposes, you might want to use a separate folder for any third-party plug-ins. This page of the **Preferences** window enables you to specify an additional folder for Photoshop to access.

As Photoshop manipulates files, it temporarily appropriates hard disk space to free up RAM memory. When you work with larger files, it's even more important to have free disk space for the scratch disk. This page of the **Preferences** box is also the place for you to tell Photoshop which drives to use for the scratch disk.

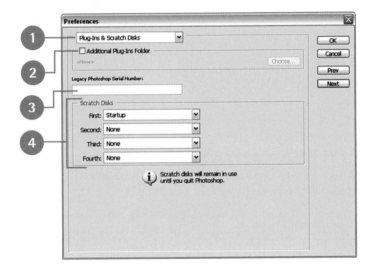

1. **Preferences Title pop-up menu:** Click the arrow to display a list of other pages in the Preferences window; select an option to open that page. Currently it should be set to **Plug-Ins & Scratch Disks** to view the options discussed here.

2. **Additional Plug-ins Folder check box and Choose button:** Enable the check box and click **Choose** to navigate to an additional plug-ins folder.

3. **Legacy Photoshop Serial Number field:** Enter the old-style Photoshop serial number in the field as required by certain plug-ins.

4. **Scratch Disks pop-up menus:** Click to select up to four disks that will serve as scratch disks. All mounted disks are listed as scratch disk options. You might need more than one scratch disk if you work with particularly large image files.

Continues

Memory & Image Cache

Click the Next button to go to the **Memory & Image Cache Preferences** window or select **Edit, Preferences, Memory & Image Cache** to open the **Preferences** window to the **Memory & Image Cache** page (in Mac OS X, select **Photoshop, Preferences, Memory & Image Cache**). You use this page to allocate RAM to the application and to set the number of caching levels—a Photoshop method for speeding screen redraw.

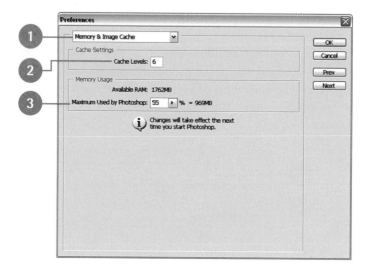

1. **Preferences Title pop-up menu:** Click the arrow to display a list of other pages in the **Preferences** window; select an option to open that page. Currently it should be set to **Memory & Image Cache** to view the options discussed here.

2. **Cache Levels field:** Enter the number of cache levels you want to use. A higher number speeds redraws but requires more RAM and can increase the time it takes to open an image.

3. **Memory Usage/Maximum Used by Photoshop:** Allocates the percentage of available memory (shown as available RAM) to be used by Photoshop. The slider control allocates from 36MB to 100% of available memory.

Type

Click the **Next** button to go to the **Type Preferences** window or select **Edit**, **Preferences**, **Type** to open the **Preferences** window to the **Type** page (in Mac OS X, select **Photoshop**, **Preferences**, **Type**). You use this page to turn on smart quotes and customize how the type options look.

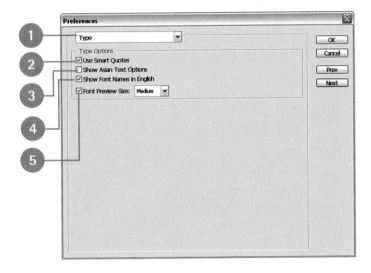

1 **Preferences Title pop-up menu:** Click the arrow to display a list of other pages in the **Preferences** window; select an option to open that page. Currently it should be set to **Type** to view the options discussed here.

2 **Use Smart Quotes check box:** Uses curly quotes (quotation marks that curl in on both ends of a sentence) instead of straight quotes.

3 **Show Asian Text Options check box:** Displays text options for installed Asian character sets in the character and paragraph text palettes.

4 **Show Font Names in English check box:** Displays Asian font names in English.

5 **Font Preview Size check box and pop-up menu:** Determine the size of the font preview on the **Type** tool **Options** bar and the **Character** palette. Select from **Small**, **Medium** (the default), or **Large**.

End

How to Set ImageReady Preferences

General Controls

Select Edit, Preferences, General to open the Preferences window to the General page (in Mac OS X, select ImageReady, Preferences, General). You use this page to control interpolation, the Color Picker option, and a number of other general application parameters.

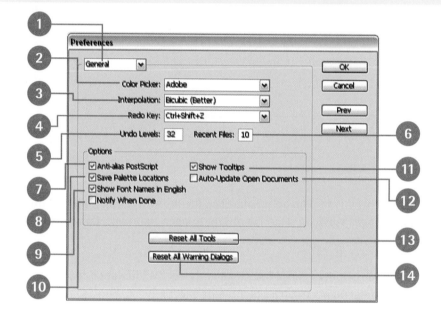

1. **Preferences Title pop-up menu:** Click the arrow to display a list of other pages in the Preferences window; select an option to open that page. Currently it should be set to **General** to view the options discussed here.

2. **Color Picker pop-up menu:** Click the arrow to display the list of options; then select the **Adobe** or **System** option.

3. **Interpolation pop-up menu:** Click the arrow to display a list of interpolation options. Select **Nearest Neighbor (Faster), Bilinear, Bicubic (Better), Bicubic Smoother,** or **Bicubic Sharper.** In most cases, use **Bicubic Smoother** when enlarging an image and use **Bicubic Sharper** when reducing or downsampling. Each image is different, however, so experiment for best results.

4 **Redo Key pop-up menu:** Click the arrow to select the key combination that redoes an undone command.

5 **Undo Levels field:** Determines the number of undo states supported by the **History** palette. Type a value in the field to change the setting. The higher you set this number, the more memory ImageReady uses to store the changes.

6 **Recent Files field:** Type the number of recent files you want to appear in the **Recent Files** submenu.

7 **Anti-alias PostScript check box:** Select this option to achieve smooth results when placing or importing PDF or EPS images.

8 **Save Palette Locations check box:** Reopens palettes in the same place and at the same size as when they were closed or when ImageReady was closed.

9 **Show Font Names in English check box:** Displays all font names in English.

10 **Notify when Done check box:** Enable this check box to produce a notification when tasks are completed.

11 **Show Tooltips check box:** Activates the pop-up tool descriptions when you hover the mouse pointer over the interface elements.

12 **Auto-Update Open Documents check box:** Updates open files automatically.

13 **Use System Shortcuts check box (Mac only):** Enable this check box if you want to use shortcut commands that are Mac OS X specific.

14 **Reset All Tools button:** Resets all tools to their default configurations specified at the initial installation.

15 **Reset All Warning Dialogs button:** Resets all warning dialog boxes to their default configurations specified at the initial installation.

Continues

Slices

Click the **Next** button to go to the **Slices Preferences** window or select **Edit, Preferences, Slices** to open the **Preferences** window to the **Slices** page (in Mac OS X, select **ImageReady, Preferences, Slices**). You use this page to specify how ImageReady generates slices, including naming conventions, colors, and slice lines. A *slice* is the portion of the image when ImageReady divides an image into smaller pieces for optimization and display in an HTML table.

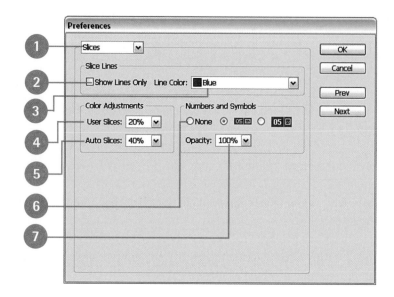

1. **Preferences Title pop-up menu:** Click the arrow to display a list of other pages in the **Preferences** window; select an option to open that page. Currently it should be set to **Slices** to view the options discussed here.

2. **Show Lines Only check box:** Shows only the slice lines when you view slices, omitting the transparent coloring.

3. **Line Color pop-up menu:** Specifies the color of the slice lines. Choices include 24 color options.

4. **Color Adjustments User Slices box and slider:** Determine the opacity for the color shading of the user slices (slices created manually by the user). Click the arrow and drag the slider or type a number value to change the setting.

5. **Color Adjustments Auto Slices box and slider:** Determine the opacity for the color shading of the auto slices (slices created automatically based on guide lines). Click the arrow and drag the slider or type a number value to change the setting.

6. **Numbers and Symbols radio buttons:** Control the size of slice numbers and icons. Select **None** or the small or large icon button.

7. **Numbers and Symbols Opacity box and slider:** Click the arrow and drag the slider or type a number value to control the opacity of the slice numbers and symbols.

Image Maps

Click the **Next** button to go to the **Image Maps Preferences** window or select **Edit, Preferences, Image Maps** to open the **Preferences** window to the **Image Maps** page (in Mac OS X, select **ImageReady, Preferences, Image Maps**). You use this page to specify how ImageReady displays image map information. An *image map* refers to the process of creating hot spots in web images that serve as links or triggers for other actions.

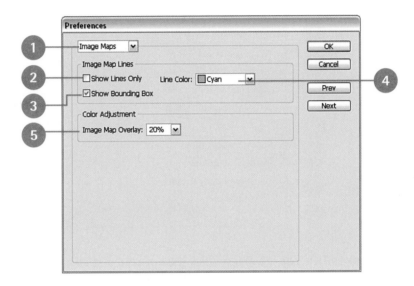

1. **Preferences Title pop-up menu:** Click the arrow to display a list of other pages in the **Preferences** window; select an option to open that page. Currently it should be set to **Image Maps** to view the options discussed here.

2. **Show Lines Only check box:** Uses an outline only with no overlay to designate an image map.

3. **Show Bounding Box check box:** Creates a rectangular bounding box around an image map.

4. **Line Color pop-up menu:** Allows you to select the line color for outlining image maps from a list of 24 line colors.

5. **Image Map Overlay box and slider:** Designate an image map with a white fill to separate it from the rest of the image. The slider value determines the fill opacity.

Continues

Guides and Grid

Click the **Next** button to go to the **Guides and Grid Preferences** window or select **Edit, Preferences, Guides and Grid** to open the **Preferences** window to the **Guides and Grid** page (in Mac OS X, select **ImageReady, Preferences, Guides and Grid**). You use this page to control guide and grid parameters.

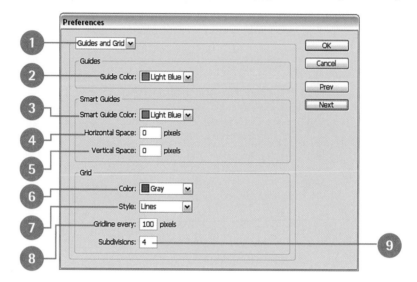

1. **Preferences Title pop-up menu:** Click the arrow to display a list of other pages in the **Preferences** window; select an option to open that page. Currently it should be set to **Guides and Grid** to view the options discussed here.

2. **Guide Color pop-up menu:** Select the color of the guide lines. Choices are **Gray, Light Blue, Red, Green, Blue, Yellow, Magenta, Cyan, Light Gray,** and **Black.**

3. **Smart Guide Color pop-up menu:** Smart guides automatically appear near the edges of objects as they're being dragged into alignment. This setting determines the color of the smart guides. Choices are **Gray, Light Blue, Red, Green, Blue, Yellow, Magenta, Cyan, Light Gray,** and **Black.**

4. **Horizontal Space field:** Enter a pixel value to determine horizontal padding around an object for the snap-to guides feature.

5. **Vertical Space field:** Enter a pixel value to determine vertical padding around an object for the snap-to guides feature.

6. **Grid Color pop-up menu:** Select the color of the grid. Choices are **Gray, Light Blue, Red, Green, Blue, Yellow, Magenta, Cyan, Light Gray,** and **Black.**

7. **Grid Style pop-up menu:** Determines the format of the grid. Options are solid **Lines, Dots,** and **Dashed Lines.**

8. **Gridline Every *X* Pixels field:** Enter a pixel value to determine the pixel spacing between gridlines.

9. **Subdivisions field:** Determines how many subdivisions fall between each main gridline. Enter the desired value in the field.

Optimization

Click the **Next** button to go to the **Optimization Preferences** window or select **Edit,**
Preferences, Optimization to open the **Preferences** window to the **Optimization** page (in Mac
OS X, select **ImageReady, Preferences, Optimization**). You use this page to specify how opti-
mization settings are calculated and displayed.

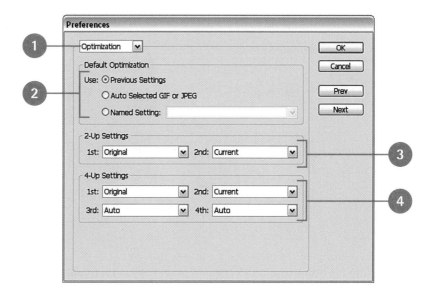

①　**Preferences Title pop-up menu:** Click the arrow to display a list of other pages in the
Preferences window; select an option to open that page. Currently it should be set to
Optimization to view the options discussed below.

②　**Default Optimization radio buttons:** Select how you want to generate optimization defaults
for an image. Choices are **Previous Settings, Auto Selected GIF or JPEG,** and **Named Setting.**
The **Named Setting** option allows you to select from a list of standard optimization defaults.

③　**2-Up Settings pop-up menus:** Determine which iterations of the image are displayed in the
2-Up window. Defaults for the first menu are **Original** and **Current,** but the second menu
allows you to select from a long list of optimized presets.

④　**4-Up Settings pop-up menus:** Determine which iterations of the image are displayed in the
4-Up window. Defaults are **Original** and **Current,** but you also can select from a long list of
optimized presets, including **Auto,** which uses the next logical level of compression.

Continues

Cursors

Click the **Next** button to go to the **Cursors Preferences** window or select **Edit, Preferences, Cursors** to open the **Preferences** window to the **Cursors** page (in Mac OS X, select **ImageReady, Preferences, Cursors**). You use this page to specify brush and cursor shapes and sizes.

Transparency

Click the **Next** button to go to the **Transparency Preferences** window or select **Edit, Preferences, Transparency** to open the **Preferences** window to the **Transparency** page (in Mac OS X, select **ImageReady, Preferences, Transparency**). You use this page to specify how transparency is depicted in a file.

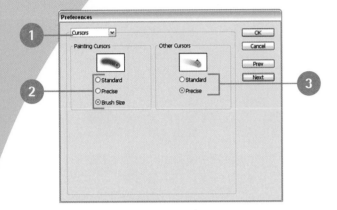

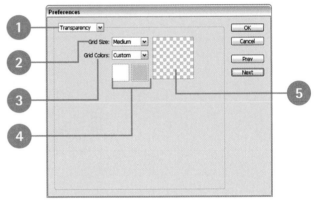

1 **Preferences Title pop-up menu:** Click the arrow to display a list of other pages in the **Preferences** window; select an option to open that page. Currently it should be set to Cursors to view the options discussed here.

2 **Painting Cursors radio buttons:** Select **Standard** (icon), **Precise** (cross hairs), or **Brush Size** (actual sized outline) as the shape of the painting cursor.

3 **Other Cursors radio buttons:** Select **Standard** (icon) or **Precise** (cross hairs) for the cursor shape.

1 **Preferences Title pop-up menu:** Click the arrow to display a list of other pages in the **Preferences** box; select an option to open that page. Currently it should be set to **Transparency** to view the options discussed here.

2 **Grid Size pop-up menu:** Controls the size of the checkerboard used to indicate transparency. Options are **None, Small, Medium,** and **Large**.

3 **Grid Colors pop-up menu:** Controls the color of the checkerboard used to indicate transparency. Options are **Light, Medium, Dark, Red, Orange, Green, Blue, Purple,** and **Custom**.

4 **Custom color swatches:** Click one or both of the swatches to select specific colors for the transparency checkerboard.

5 **Transparency preview window:** Shows the current transparency checkerboard pattern.

Plug-ins

Click the **Next** button to go to the **Plug-ins Preferences** window or select **Edit, Preferences, Plug-ins** to open the **Preferences** window to the **Plug-ins** page (in Mac OS X, select **ImageReady, Preferences, Plug-ins**). You use this page to tell ImageReady where to look for plug-ins. *Plug-ins* are utilities and filters that extend ImageReady's core functionality. The default plug-ins folder is located under the main Photoshop directory; install any plug-ins there. However, for sharing with other applications or housekeeping purposes, you might want to use a separate folder for any third-party plug-ins. This page of the **Preferences** window allows you to specify an additional folder for ImageReady to access.

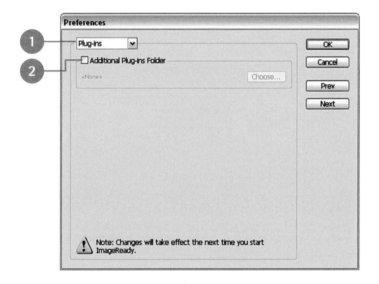

1 **Preferences Title pop-up menu:** Click the arrow to display a list of other pages in the **Preferences** window; select an option to open that page. Currently it should be set to **Plug-ins** to view the options discussed here.

2 **Additional Plug-ins Folder check box and Choose button:** Enable the check box and click **Choose** to navigate to an additional plug-ins folder.

End

12 How to Set Bridge Preferences

General Controls

Select **Edit, Preferences** to open the **Bridge Preferences** window (in Mac OS X, select **Bridge, Preferences**). Then select **General** from the list on the left. This page controls the appearance of Bridge and the basic information it displays.

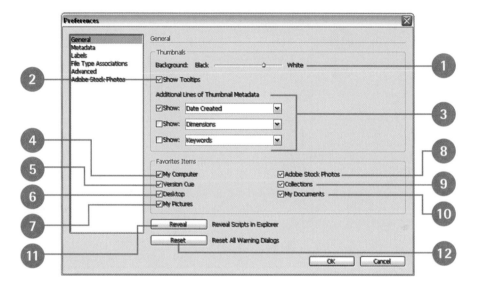

1 **Thumbnails Background slider:** A slider control ranging from black to white controls the darkness of the background behind the thumbnails.

2 **Show Tooltips check box:** If enabled, hovering the mouse pointer over a thumbnail or control pops up a brief description or help information.

3 **Additional Lines of Thumbnail Metadata check boxes and menus:** Select the file information to be displayed under each thumbnail. You can display up to three lines of information, and each line can display 1 of 17 types of metadata.

4 **My Computer check box:** When enabled, the **My Computer** folder appears on the **Favorites** tab in the Bridge window.

5 **Version Cue check box:** When enabled, a **Version Cue** icon appears on the **Favorites** tab in the Bridge window.

6 **Desktop check box:** When enabled, the **Desktop** folder appears on the **Favorites** tab in the Bridge window.

7 **My Pictures check box:** When enabled, the **My Pictures** folder appears on the **Favorites** tab in the Bridge window.

8 **Adobe Stock Photos check box:** When enabled, an icon for Adobe Stock Photos appears on the **Favorites** tab in the Bridge window.

9 **Collections check box:** When enabled, a **Collections** icon appears on the **Favorites** tab in the Bridge window.

10 **My Documents check box:** When enabled, the **My Documents** folder appears on the **Favorites** tab in the Bridge window.

11 **Reveal Scripts in Explorer/Finder:** Opens the folder that contains the scripts Bridge uses.

12 **Reset All Warning Dialogs:** Resets all warning dialog boxes back to their original installation defaults.

Continues

Metadata

Select **Edit**, **Preferences** to open the Bridge **Preferences** window (in Mac OS X, select **Bridge**, **Preferences**). Then select **Metadata** from the list on the left. This page controls which metadata sections and fields are displayed in the **Metadata** panel in the Bridge window. In the **Metadata** list in the **Preferences** window, you can expand or collapse the main categories by clicking the arrow to the left of the main category headings. If you enable the check box next to a main category heading, all the options in that category are automatically enabled, but you can enable and disable individual fields.

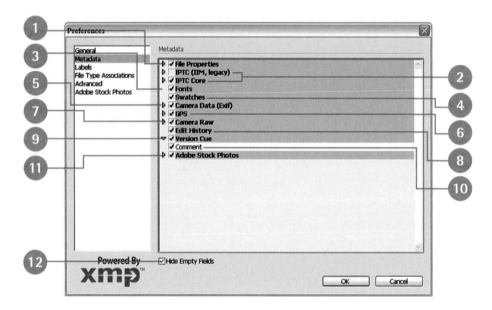

1   **File Properties check boxes:** These options describe the actual file, such as the date it was created, its size, and so on.

2   **IPTC check boxes:** These options provide editable text fields where information such as the photographer's name, the copyright date, where the image was taken, and any assigned keywords can be stored. **IPTC Core** is the current standard; **IPTC IIM** has been replaced by IPTC Core but is included for older files.

3   **Fonts check boxes:** Lists fonts used in InDesign files.

4   **Swatches check boxes:** Lists swatches used in InDesign files.

5   **Camera Data (Exif) check boxes:** These options show information recorded by the digital camera, including exposure information, camera model, lens used, and so on.

6 GPS check boxes: These options display navigational information recorded by cameras with global positioning systems.

7 Camera Raw check boxes: These options display the Camera Raw adjustment settings.

8 Edit History check boxes: This option displays the edit history if the **History Log** option is enabled in Photoshop preferences and set to **Metadata**.

9 Version Cue check boxes: These options lists information from Version Cue.

10 Comment check box: If enabled, this option allows you to enter a text comment about the image.

11 Adobe Stock Photos check boxes: These options list the data embedded in stock photos purchased from Adobe.

12 Hide Empty Fields check box: If enabled, fields with no data don't display in the **Metadata** panel.

Continues

Labels

Select **Edit, Preferences** to open the Bridge **Preferences** window (in Mac OS X, select **Bridge, Preferences**). Then select **Labels** from the list on the left. This page controls label naming and shortcuts.

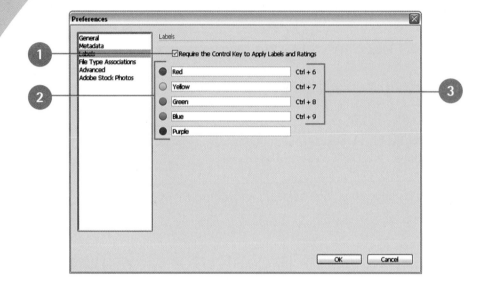

1 **Require the Control Key to Apply Labels and Ratings check box:** Adds the **Control** key to the shortcuts used to apply labels and ratings to files.

2 **Color Name:** Five label colors are available (**Red, Yellow, Green, Blue,** and **Purple**), but each label can have any name you like. Just click in the field next to the color dot and type your new label name.

3 **Shortcut combination:** Displays the keystroke combination used to assign the adjacent label. You cannot change the information here; your only option is whether to use the **Ctrl** key in combination with the assigned shortcut key by using the **Require the Control Key to Apply Labels and Ratings** check box. The purple label has no shortcut key available.

File Type Associations

Select **Edit**, **Preferences** to open the Bridge **Preferences** window (in Mac OS X, select **Bridge**, **Preferences**). Then select **File Type Associations** from the list on the left. This page controls which application Bridge will use to open different file types, overriding any operating system associations.

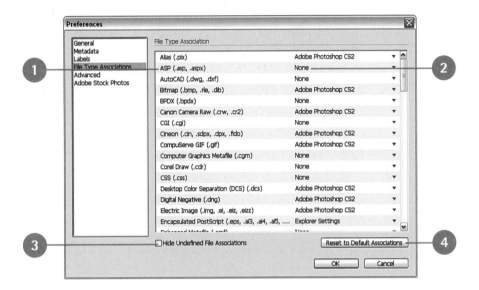

1 **File Type:** Displays the name of the file type, along with its associated two-, three-, or four-letter extension.

2 **Associated Program:** Displays the application Bridge will use to open a specific file type, or it displays **None** if no association is set. To add or change an association, click the program name (or the word None) to access the **Browse** tab, from which you can navigate to the desired application using your operating system's file browser.

3 **Hide Undefined File Associations check box:** Hides all file types with no associated application.

4 **Reset to Default Associations button:** Restores file type associations to their installation default settings.

Continues

Advanced Controls

Select **Edit, Preferences** to open the **Preferences** window (in Mac OS X, select **Bridge, Preferences**). Then select **Advanced** from the list on the left. This page controls Bridge performance.

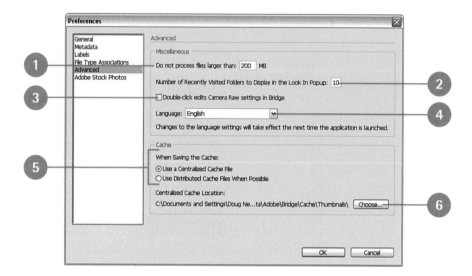

1 **Do Not Process Files Larger than X MB Field:** Creating thumbnails for large files can take some time, so you can set the maximum file size for which Bridge will display a thumbnail.

2 **Number of Recently Visited Folders to Display in the Look in Popup field:** The **Find** dialog box has a **Look in** pop-up menu that lists recently visited folders. This option sets the number of most recently visited folders to display in that pop-up menu.

3 **Double-click Edits Camera Raw Settings in Bridge check box:** If enabled, double-clicking a Raw file thumbnail opens the file directly in Camera Raw. If disabled, Photoshop launches and then the file opens in Camera Raw.

4 **Language menu:** Sets the language used for the Bridge interface. The options available here depend on the language of the Creative Suite applications installed.

5 **When Saving the Cache options:** Set to **Use a Centralized Cache File** to save thumbnails in a single large database. Set to **Use Distributed Cache Files when Possible** to store thumbnails in a small database in the same folder as the images.

6 **Centralized Cache Location and Choose button:** If a centralized cache is used, you can change the location for the cache by clicking the **Choose** button.

Adobe Stock Photos

Select **Edit**, **Preferences** to open the **Preferences** window (in Mac OS X, select **Bridge**, **Preferences**). Then select **Adobe Stock Photos** from the list on the left. This page controls all the options for Adobe Stock Photos.

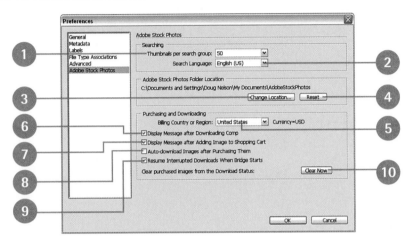

1   **Thumbnails per Search Group menu:** Searches can have thousands of matches. This option limits the number of thumbnails displayed per results page.

2   **Search Language menu:** This option sets the language to search in, without changing the Bridge interface language.

3   **Change Location button:** Click to select a new location for the Adobe Stock Photos folder.

4   **Reset button:** Click to restore the Adobe Stock Photos folder to its default location (the **My Documents** folder for Windows users, in the *<user login>*, **Documents** folder for Mac users).

5   **Billing Country or Region menu:** Select the default country or region from which you'll be paying for photos. The currency Adobe accepts from that country displays next to the country name.

6   **Display Message After Downloading Comp check box:** If enabled, it sends an alert message whenever your comp is finished downloading.

7   **Display Message After Adding Image to Shopping Cart check box:** If enabled, it sends an alert message whenever you add an image to your shopping cart.

8   **Auto-download Images After Purchasing Them check box:** If enabled, it automatically saves photos to the default folder after purchase.

9   **Resume Interrupted Downloads when Bridge Starts check box:** If enabled, it automatically resumes an interrupted download (for example, after a lost connection) the next time Bridge is launched.

10   **Clear Now button:** Clears purchased images from the **Download Status** display.

End

How to Set Camera Raw Preferences

In Bridge, select **Edit**, **Camera Raw Preferences** to open the **Preferences** window (in Mac OS X, select **Photoshop**, **Camera Raw Preferences**). You can also access the **Preferences** window from within the Camera Raw application by clicking the arrow at the upper right of the **Settings** area.

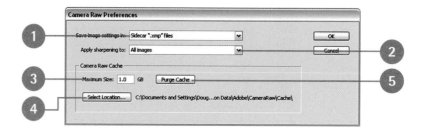

1 **Save Image Settings in drop-down menu:** Camera Raw never adjusts the actual Raw image file—adjustment settings are stored separately. Select whether to save adjustment settings in a central database or as individual Sidecar files in the same folder as the Raw image. Sidecar files have a .xmp extension.

2 **Apply Sharpening to drop-down menu:** If set to **Preview Images Only**, adjusting the sharpness from within Camera Raw doesn't actually sharpen the image—it sharpens just the preview of the image. Select **All Images** to actually apply sharpening to the image.

3 **Maximum Size field:** Camera Raw uses a cache to speed loading and recalculation of previews. Here you can change the maximum size of the Camera Raw cache.

4 **Select Location button:** Click to browse to a new location for the Camera Raw cache.

5 **Purge Cache button:** Should the cache get too large or corrupted, you can click this button to empty it.

End

Task

Optimizing Photoshop Projects

Although Photoshop often is thought of as a high-powered creative tool, it's also a nuts-and-bolts production tool. Most designers would rather spend their time building montages and creative designs, but too often they're saddled with less glamorous tasks such as cropping images and cataloging files.

The tasks in this part look at how to optimize your workflow, with tips and ideas on how to work faster and more efficiently. These tasks are valuable to master because you can apply them to other tasks, making everything you do a bit easier. In some situations, such as the tasks involving actions, these tips let you automate the entire process. Other tasks teach you to customize your workflow using keyboard shortcuts, file annotation, and batch processing. You'll also find tasks for sharing files and optimizing the features in the **History** palette. ●

How to Use Multiple Views

People are working with larger images than ever before. One challenge is being able to zoom in on work at a pixel level while still monitoring the overall look of the piece. The best way to address this issue is by using *multiple views*. Just open two separate windows of the same file, specify a high rate of magnification for editing in one window, and leave the other at full screen size to check your progress as you work.

Begin

1 Open the Main File

Select **File, Open** to display the **Open** dialog box. Select the file you want to work on and click **OK**.

Click

2 Set Desired Magnification

Click the **Zoom** tool in the toolbox and click the image. Watch the zoom percentage numbers in the lower-left corner of the screen. Continue clicking to zoom in to the magnification level that lets you see the area clearly. To zoom in on a particular area of the image, click the **Zoom** tool and drag to draw a marquee around the area you want to magnify.

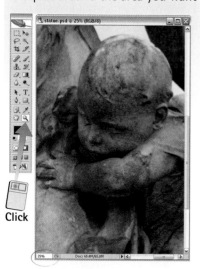

Click

3 Open a New View

To create a second window on this same image, select **Window, Arrange, New Window for <filename>**. You now have two windows with the same image on your desktop: One shows the full image, and the other shows a detailed zoom of a single area. You can create additional views for as many areas as necessary. (Don't worry about using up system resources when using multiple views. Your computer can handle it!)

4 Drag Windows into Position

Because the active window automatically appears on top of any other open windows, you should arrange the image windows so they're side by side. This arrangement allows you to see both the zoomed screen and the full screen at the same time. Drag the active window's title bar to arrange it where you want it.

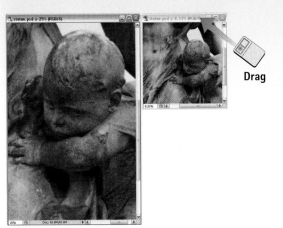

Drag

5 Edit the Image

Make any local edits to the image in either window. For example, you can paint, erase, or silhouette. (These and other tasks are explained later in this book.) As you work in one window, notice that the image is updated in real time in the other window.

6 Close Window to Reduce Number of Views

When you finish editing the image, close either of the view windows (click the **Close** box in the title bar) to revert to a single view and reduce onscreen clutter.

Click

How-To Hints

Synchronous Window Scrolling

You can scroll and pan the contents of multiple view windows by holding down the **Shift** key as you drag with the **Hand** tool. If you're using another tool, hold down the **spacebar** and the **Shift** key to temporarily change the cursor to the **Hand** tool.

Views and Proofing

Views can be useful when you're proofing an image in different color spaces. Open multiple views of the same image and select **View**, **Proof Setup**; then select the color model of your choice (such as **Macintosh RGB** or **Monitor RGB**). You can even select **Custom** and select the **Colorsync** profile of your choice. Multiple views are a great way to compare multiple color spaces side by side, using the same image.

End

How to Undo with the History Palette

The **History** palette is the control center for Photoshop's multiple undo capability. It allows you to revert an image back beyond what the simple **Edit, Undo** command can do. The **History** palette records each edit or command as a *layer tile*. Click a tile to revert the image to that earlier state. You can set features and options to optimize how the **History** palette works.

Begin

1 Open the History Palette

Select **Window, History** to open the **History** palette. The palette shows a snapshot at the top, representing the original state of the file as it was opened. As you make changes to the file, those changes are displayed as tiles running in descending order in the palette.

Snapshot

2 Set the Number of History States

Select **Edit, Preferences, General** to open the **General Preferences** dialog box. Set the number of states you want to record, with the understanding that any states that exceed this limit will be lost. If you set **History States** to **20**, for example, you cannot go back to what you did 21 steps ago. On the other hand, having more states is memory-intensive, so you must strike a happy medium between a **History** palette safety net and efficient allocation of memory and disk space. Click **OK** to save the history states and close the dialog box.

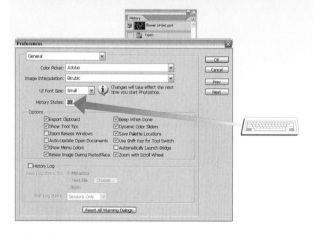

3 Take Snapshots

Another way to preserve a specific image state is to take a *snapshot*. Snapshots are independent of the standard image states mentioned in step 2 and remain available until you close or save the file. To take a snapshot, display the **History** palette menu and select **New Snapshot**. Give the snapshot a name in the dialog box that appears and click **OK**. A thumbnail of the snapshot appears in the upper part of the palette.

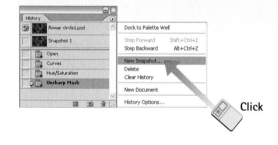
Click

4 Revert to a Previous State

To revert to a previous state or snapshot, select the corresponding tile in the **History** palette. The image in the active window reverts to the point in the editing process you selected. All tiles below the active tile are dimmed, but you can still revert to them by clicking them.

 Click

5 Create Duplicate Files

The **History** palette also lets you create a duplicate image file. After you create a duplicate, you can continue editing that duplicate, leaving the original in its previous state. To make a duplicate, select **New Document** from the **History** palette menu. Photoshop copies the image in a new window (without keeping track of any of the previous history states), which you can modify further or rename and save.

 Click

End

How-To Hints

Watching Those Brushstrokes

Remember that each time you click the mouse to apply a brushstroke, you consume a history state. Clicking away with multiple brushstrokes can consume all your history states in a hurry. Be sure to grab a snapshot before you start brushing, leaving you an escape route to a previous version.

Using the History Brush

You also can do great things with the Photoshop **History** brush, which allows you to brush in corrections using history states as a source. See Part 7, Task 4, "How to Use the History Brush," for details.

Snapshot Options

In the **Snapshot** dialog box that appears in step 3, you can control which portions of the image are archived. Select **Full Document**, **Merged Layers**, or **Current Layer** from the **From** menu as desired.

How to Create Custom Tool Presets

The custom tool preset options in Photoshop allow you to save all the variable settings associated with that tool. Specific brush sizes, feathering, blending modes, transparency, and other settings can be customized and loaded with a single click of the mouse. With custom tool presets, you can create customized brushes for specific tasks and store them in a floating palette or in toolsets for easy access.

Begin

1 Select the Tool

Tool presets can be created for any Photoshop tool. Select the desired tool from the toolbox. In this example, the **Brush** tool is selected.

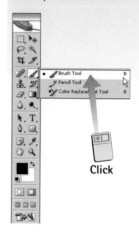

Click

2 Set the Tool Parameters

Modify the tool settings in the **Options** bar. You can save in the preset any settings you specify in the **Options** bar, along with the foreground color, if desired.

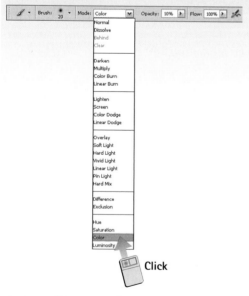

Click

3 Open the Tool Preset Palette

Select **Window, Tool Presets** to open the **Tool Presets** palette. The palette allows the option of showing all presets in the system or only the presets for the currently selected tool. Enable the **Current Tool Only** check box at the bottom of the palette to restrict the selection to only the presets for the current tool.

4 Save the Preset

Select **New Tool Preset** from the palette menu, or click the **New Tool Preset** icon at the bottom of the palette. Name the preset in the **New Tool Preset** window that appears. If desired, enable the **Include Color** check box to preserve the current foreground color selection as part of the preset.

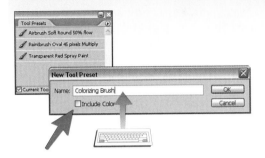

5 Load the Preset

Click the desired preset bar in the **Tool Presets** palette to load the preset options for the selected tool.

Click

End

How-To Hints

An Alternative Toolbox

If you leave the **Current Tool Only** check box disabled, all the presets for all the tools are visible in the **Tool Presets** palette. Now you can access specific presets as you need them, intuitively changing tools and parameters. It's like using the toolbox to select different tools, only now you can have a dozen variations on a tool instead of just one.

Using Scrubbing Slider Controls

Most numerical settings feature a scrubbing feature that allows a new way to modify the value. Position the mouse pointer over the setting label, such as the **Tolerance** label in the **Options** bar for the **Color Replacement** tool. The mouse pointer changes to a hand with arrows pointing left and right. Click and drag left or right to change the value.

Saving and Loading Sets

Sometimes specific projects require unique tool presets. You can create groups of presets and load them into the **Tool Presets** palette as needed. Use the **Save**, **Load**, or **Replace** tool preset commands in the palette menu. You can also select **Preset Manager** from the palette menu to launch the **Preset Manager** dialog box, where you can sort, load, save, rename, or delete your tool presets.

How to Create Custom Keyboard Shortcuts

Photoshop enables you to create and modify keyboard shortcuts for all application menus, palette menus, and tools. You can also remove any existing keyboard shortcuts and reassign them to another command or tool. Photoshop enables you to save multiple commands in shortcut sets that can correspond to workflow, tasks, or users. Thus, the same keystroke can generate different results, depending on which shortcut set you load.

Begin

1 Select or Create New Shortcut Set

Select **Edit, Keyboard Shortcuts** to launch the **Keyboard Shortcuts and Menus** dialog box. Select a target shortcut set from the **Set** pull-down menu at the top of the dialog box, or click the **New Set** button to the right of the menu to create a copy of the set that is currently loaded. The **Photoshop Defaults** keystroke set is automatically loaded if no other sets have been created.

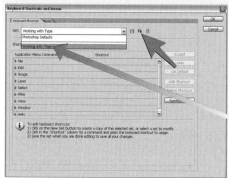

Click

2 Select Shortcut Type

Select a shortcut category from the **Shortcuts for** pull-down menu. The category options are **Application Menus**, **Palette Menus**, and **Tools**. When you select a shortcut category, the command list changes to reflect the options associated with that type.

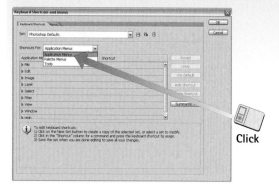

Click

3 Enter Keystroke

Select the tool or menu command you want to assign to a keyboard shortcut. Expand the list of menu commands by clicking the arrow to the left of each command, revealing subgroupings of individual commands. Enter the keystroke combination for the shortcut you want to assign to the tool or command, being sure to include the **Ctrl/⌘** key or a function key in addition to an alphanumeric key.

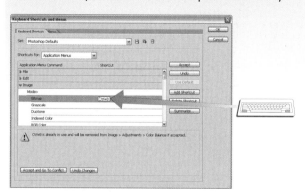

4 Resolve Any Conflicts

If the desired keystroke is already in use by another command, a prompt identifies the conflict and asks whether you want to remove the keyboard shortcut from the previous command. Click **Accept and Go to Conflict** or cancel the request by clicking **Undo Changes**. Clicking **Accept and Go to Conflict** opens the previous command and allows you to select an alternative keystroke for that command.

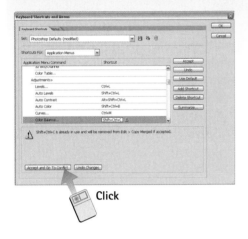

Click

5 Accept Changes

After you have entered all keyboard shortcuts, click **OK** to save changes to the set. Now whenever you press one of the assigned keyboard combinations, the associated command or tool is selected.

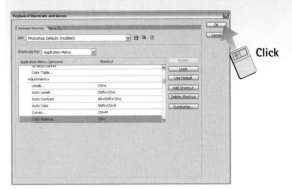

Click

6 About Menus

The **Menus** tab provides options for hiding seldom-used menu items or highlighting menu items with any color-coding system you might devise. Select **Application Menus** or **Palette Menus** from the **Menu for** drop-down list. Select the menu you want to affect and then select the specific menu command. Click the **Eye** icon to toggle visibility of that menu item, or select a highlight color from the drop-down list.

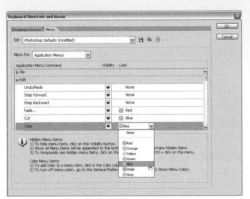

How-To Hints

Creating a Summary File

Remembering all the keystrokes you've assigned in a given set can be hard. To help you keep track, click the **Summarize** button in the **Keyboard Shortcuts** dialog box to create a complete list of shortcuts in a preformatted HTML document. The summary is handy for posting to an intranet or corporate website so everyone on the design team can reference and use the same set of shortcuts.

Deleting Sets and Shortcuts

In the **Keyboard Shortcuts** dialog box, highlight a command or tool name and click the **Delete Shortcut** button to delete the shortcut associated with that tool. To delete an entire shortcut set, click the **Delete Set** button to the left of the **OK** button.

End

How to Use the Preset Actions

Photoshop uses preset scripts called *actions* to automate repetitive tasks. For example, creating a drop shadow can involve inverting a selection, deleting a background, inverting the selection again, offsetting it, feathering it, and filling it with a transparent fill. Actions enable you to apply multiple steps such as these with a single mouse click. This can save you time—especially when you're processing multiple images in the same way. You can view actions in a simplified button mode (which allows for one-click application) and in a more detailed mode (in which you can examine each step in the action). In this task, you'll work in Button mode. You'll get more detailed information in the following tasks.

Begin

1 Open the Actions Palette

Select **Window, Actions** to open the **Actions** palette.

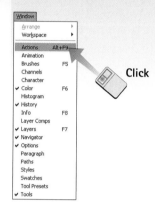

Click

2 Set Palette to Button Mode

Click and hold the arrow in the upper-right corner of the palette and drag to select **Button Mode**. The **Actions** palette changes to display all the actions as clickable buttons. Select this option again to disable **Button** mode and return the palette to the simple **List** mode.

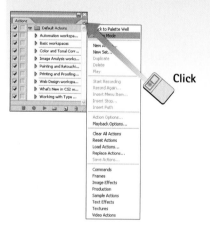

Click

3 Select an Area of the Image

Actions can be applied to a selected area of the image; in many cases, actions can be applied to the entire image. Click the **Marquee** tool and drag to select the area of the image you want to modify with an action.

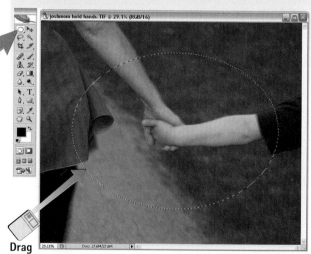

Drag

4 Click the Action Button

Click the desired action button in the Actions palette to execute the effect. You can apply multiple actions to the same selection—just click another action button.

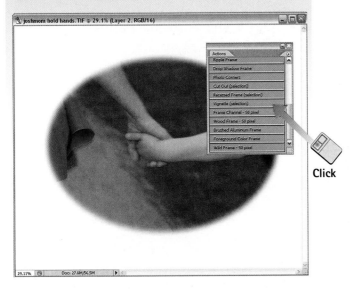

Click

End

How-To Hints

Keystroke Applications

If you deselect **Button Mode** from the **Actions** palette menu, you can set custom keystrokes for each action. For example, instead of going to the **Actions** palette to click the **Vignette** button, you could assign a keystroke such as **Shift+Ctrl+F2** that executes the **Vignette** action. In the **Actions** palette, select the action you want; then open the palette menu and drag down to select **Action Options**. In the dialog box that opens, specify a keystroke to launch the action.

More Photoshop Actions

Photoshop includes a host of action sets, accessible from the **Actions** palette menu. Select any of the sets listed at the bottom of the palette menu, or select **Load Actions** to load files with the **.atn** suffix. Each action set includes numerous actions that are useful in daily applications. The topics for the included action sets are **Commands, Frames, Image Effects, Production, Sample Actions, Text Effects, Textures,** and **Video Actions**.

How to Create Custom Actions

Although the preset actions that ship with Photoshop are useful, it won't be long before you'll feel the need to build your own. An action should be generic enough to work in a number of situations and on multiple images. Some editing tasks might not translate into actions. Keep trying, though, because building a clean action can give you a great deal of satisfaction, as well as save you a lot of time.

Begin

1 Open the Actions Palette

If the **Actions** palette is not currently displayed on your desktop, select **Window**, **Actions** to display the palette. If necessary, exit **Button** mode and return the palette to **List** mode (see step 2 in Task 5, "How to Use the Preset Actions").

2 Create a New Action

From the palette menu, select **New Action** to open the **New Action** dialog box. Type a name for the action you're going to record, and select the **Set** to which it will be added. You can create multiple sets of actions, which you can then select from the **Set** menu. If no other sets of actions are created, select from the **Default Actions** set that appears.

Click

3 Execute the Action

Click the **Record** button in the dialog box to begin recording the action. The **New Action** dialog box disappears to give you free access to the Photoshop application. In this example, I converted a file to grayscale, inverted it to create a negative image, and tweaked the tonal range with **Shadow/Highlight**.

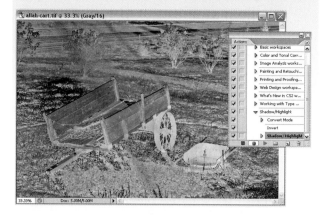

4 Select Stop Recording

After you perform all the steps of the action you want to record, select **Stop Recording** from the **Actions** palette menu to end the recording process.

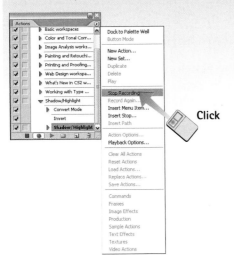

Click

5 Check the Action Sequence

Go to the **Actions** palette and find your newly created action in the list. Click the right-facing arrow to display the list of steps you recorded for that action.

6 Add Any Missing Steps

If necessary, you can add steps to the action sequence by selecting a step as an insertion point (here I selected **Shadow/Highlight**) and then selecting **Insert Menu Item** from the palette menu. Then type the name of the command as desired; Photoshop automatically records it and adds it to the action sequence *after* the selection. You also can select **Start Recording** and execute the commands to add steps after the selected command.

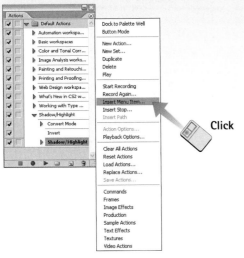

Click

How-To Hints

Cutting and Duplicating Actions

In the course of recording actions, certain tasks can become obsolete. To delete an action, select it in the **Actions** palette and select **Delete** from the **Actions** palette menu. In the dialog box that appears, click **OK** to delete the action.

It can also be helpful to duplicate an action and modify it to create a new result. Highlight the action to be copied and select **Duplicate** from the **Actions** palette menu. Click the triangle next to the action to expand it, showing the associated parameters. To change the settings, double-click the action, which launches an appropriate dialog box. Enter the new information and click **OK** to create the new action.

End

How to Set Up Batch Processing Options

As described in the preceding tasks, actions enable you to apply multiple commands to one image with a single mouse click. But what do you do if you have a folder of 200 image files that all need the same action? Although you could open each image file and apply the action, it would be much better to process all 200 images with just a single command. This is what the Photoshop **Batch** command does. The process involves specifying a target folder that contains all the images to be processed and then detailing how and where Photoshop saves the images created by the action.

Begin

1 Open the Actions Palette

If the **Actions** palette is not currently displayed on your desktop, select **Window, Actions** to display the palette. If necessary, exit **Button** mode and return the palette to **List** mode (see step 2 in Task 5, "How to Use the Preset Actions").

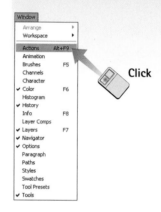
Click

2 Highlight the Action to Be Applied

In the **Actions** palette, click the action to be applied to all the images. The action is highlighted in the list. Ideally, you'll create the action first (refer to Task 6, "How to Create Custom Actions"); then select that action for the **Batch** command to use when it processes the files.

Click

3 Open the Batch Dialog Box

From the menu bar, select **File, Automate, Batch**. The **Batch** dialog box opens. The action you highlighted in step 2 appears in the **Play** section.

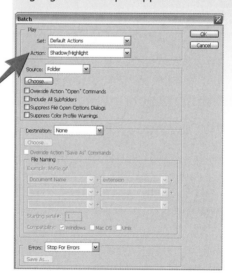

4 Select the Source Folder

From the **Source** drop-down list, select the **Folder** option and then click the **Select** button. In the **Browse for Folder** dialog box that appears, navigate to highlight the folder containing the images you want to process and click the **OK** button (the **Select** button for Macs). Back in the **Source** section, select options if you want to process images in subfolders. (For Macs, note that the file-selection dialog box is different from the Windows version shown here; use standard navigation techniques to select a source folder.)

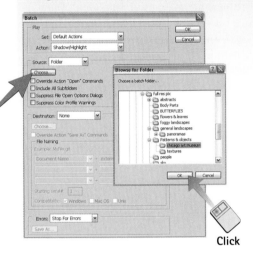

Click

5 Select the Destination Folder

Now specify where you want the changed images to be stored. From the **Destination** drop-down list, select **None** (the changed images remain open onscreen), **Save and Close** (the changed images are saved and stored in their original location), or **Folder** (you then click the **Select** button and navigate to the folder in which you want copies of the changed images to be stored). You can also specify a desired naming convention using the pop-up menus in the **File Naming** section of the **Batch** dialog box.

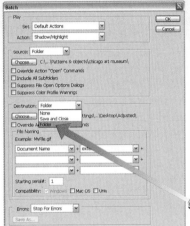

Click

6 Specify Error Handling

From the **Errors** drop-down list, select **Stop for Errors** (the process stops until errors are resolved) or **Log Errors to File** (the process continues and a list of errors is generated for later review). Click **OK** to begin running the selected action on the selected folders and subfolders.

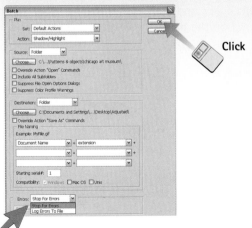

Click

How-To Hints

The Open and Save Commands

The **Batch** dialog box lets you designate special handling for opening and saving files. In many cases, individual actions include an **Open** command for a specific file or a **Save** or **Save As** command that stores files in a unique place.

Because these specific commands could conflict with processing a whole folder of different images, Photoshop lets you override a specific **Open** command in an action with a generic one that opens each image in the folder, regardless of how it is named. In a similar manner, the override **Save As** command stores each file in the folder specified, rather than in a unique place as specified in the action.

End

How to Optimize Color Files for Printing

Preparing a file for printing means a lot of different things. It could mean a complicated offset professional color project with film and plates, or it could refer to an inkjet proof or a laser print. For the sake of argument, this task refers to color printing on a press or proofing device. It is important that you check with your printer before prepping files and setting things up because all printers do things a bit differently. What follows are general guidelines for how to optimize a file for printing.

Begin

1 Determine Output Resolution

In most cases, you will print at 300ppi for high-quality images. You can reduce this number slightly for some offset presses (inkjet and color laser printers and copiers are even more forgiving). Open the **Image Size** dialog box by selecting **Image, Image Size**. If you know the resolution requirements of your printer, type them in the **Resolution** field; if you don't, type **300** as a baseline and select **pixels/inch**. Make sure the **Resample Image** check box is not selected to avoid degradation of image quality.

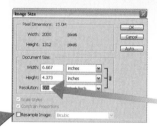

2 Set the Color Settings

Select **Edit, Color Settings** to open the **Color Settings** dialog box. Select **US Prepress Defaults** from the **Settings** menu (in OS X, select **Photoshop, Color Settings**). In the **Working Spaces** section, select the various profiles and parameters specified by your printer or leave the defaults. In the **Color Management Policies** section, select **Preserve Embedded Profiles** whenever a match or near match is available; otherwise, experiment with converting to the appropriate working spaces. See Part 1, Task 8, "How to Specify Photoshop Color Models."

3 Set Page Layout

Select **File, Print with Preview** to launch the **Print** dialog box. In the **Scaled Print Size** area, set the scale percentage as necessary to fit the image on the page size. Use the thumbnail image as a guide for entering the proper new value. If necessary, go to the **Position** area, deselect the **Center Image** check box, and drag the thumbnail image to reposition it on the page.

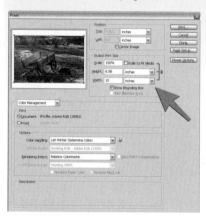

4 Check for Out-of-Gamut Colors

To print in color, you have to convert the color mode for your image to CMYK. Because the CMYK color format allows fewer colors than, say, the RGB format, you could lose some of the colors in your image during the color conversion. Select **View, Gamut Warning**. The gamut mask points out the areas where colors could be lost in the image so you can address the problems before the image goes to the printer.

Click

5 Correct Problem Colors

After you identify where the problem colors lie, select **View, Gamut Warning** again to turn off the gamut mask and then select **View, Proof Setup, Working CMYK**. Photoshop displays a preview of how the colors will look when they are converted. These color shifts are often subtle, and you might decide you can live with them. If not, edit the colors in your image using any of the color tools. (*Hint:* The **Sponge** tool can soften some saturated colors.)

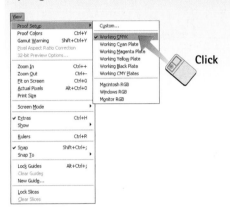

Click

6 Convert File to CMYK Color Mode

After you correct any color problems, convert the file to CMYK format. Select **Image, Mode, CMYK Color** to convert the file.

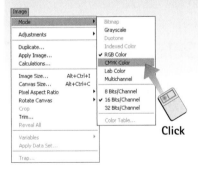

Click

7 Save File in Proper Format

Now save the file in the proper format as specified by your printer: Select **File, Save As** and then select the desired format from the **Format** menu. If in doubt, save the image as a **TIFF** file.

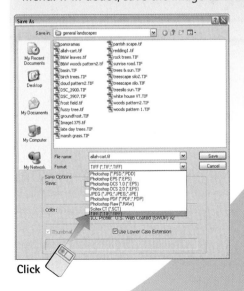

Click

End

Task

Selection Techniques

Sometimes you need to change just a portion of an image rather than make global changes. To do this effectively, you'll usually select just the portion of the image you want to change, isolating it from the rest of the image. Then you can use all of Photoshop's editing tools to change just the selected area, leaving the remaining image unchanged.

As you select objects or areas in an image, take the time to select those areas as accurately as possible. Selections that include fringe elements from the background or have poorly defined edges can destroy the realism and professional look of an image.

Photoshop goes to great lengths to provide a wide array of selection tools. The tasks in this part provide a solid overview of the various kinds of selections you can make in Photoshop, as well as how to modify, combine, and save selections after you've made them. The Photoshop selection tools let you isolate almost any kind of image area. It's well worth your time to learn as much as you can about image selections. ●

How to Select Geometric Areas

Selecting geometric areas such as circles, ovals, and rectangles is a common Photoshop task. Reasons for selecting geometric areas include lightening an area to place text on it, deleting a section of the image, and preparing to crop the image.

Begin

1 Open the File

Select **File, Open** to open the desired file.

Click

2 Select the Marquee Tool

Select the **Rectangular Marquee** tool to draw a rectangular selection; select the **Elliptical Marquee** tool to draw an oval selection. (Other tools offer the option of selecting a vertical or horizontal row of a single pixel.) To select any tool not currently visible in the toolbox, click and hold the current marquee tool; in the pop-out menu that appears, select the desired tool. The selected tool now appears on the toolbox button and in the **Options** bar at the top of the screen.

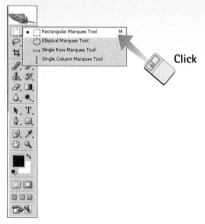

Click

3 Draw the Selection

Move the mouse pointer onto the image and click and drag to draw the selection. If the selection is not where you want it, click once outside the selection to deselect the area and drag to redraw the selection.

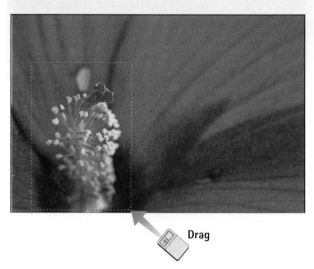

Drag

4 Move the Selection As Needed

After you create the selection, you can move the selection area (the ellipse or the rectangle, for example) to another area in the image. With the **Marquee** tool still selected, click *inside* the active selection and drag to move its location.

Drag

5 Deselect As Necessary

If you want to deselect the area and start over, choose **Select, Deselect** to deactivate the current selection. You also can deactivate a selection by clicking outside the selected area or by pressing **Ctrl+D** (Windows users) or **⌘+D** (Mac users) when using any of the marquee tools.

Click

End

How-To Hints

Selecting a Specific Size

To make a selection of a specific size, select **Fixed Size** from the **Style** menu in the **Options** bar and type the dimensions, in pixels, in the **Height** and **Width** fields. Click in the image to create a selection matching the dimensions you entered.

Selecting a Size Ratio

To select a perfect circle or square, press and hold the **Shift** key as you drag the selection. To constrain any other size ratio (that is, to drag a selection area that preserves a height/width ratio), select **Fixed Aspect Ratio** from the **Style** menu in the **Options** bar and type values for the desired width-to-height ratio.

Drawing from the Center Out

To draw a selection from the center out instead of drawing it from a corner down, hold the **Alt** key (Windows users) or the **Option** key (Mac users) as you drag.

How to Use the Polygonal Lasso Tool

The **Polygonal Lasso** tool lets you make selections with straight-line segments so you can create complex geometric areas such as star bursts and objects in perspective. It does not let you create curved segments, however, so be sure the area you want to select is suited for this tool.

Begin

1 Open the File

Select **File**, **Open** and select the desired file, or click the **Go to Bridge** icon in the **Options** bar to open **Bridge** and then double-click the desired image thumbnail to launch the image.

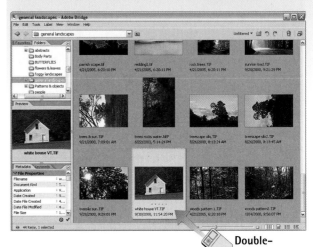

Double-click

2 Select the Polygonal Lasso Tool

Click and hold the **Lasso** tool in the toolbox and drag to select the **Polygonal Lasso** tool from the pop-out menu that appears. Note that the selected tool now appears on the toolbox button and in the **Options** bar at the top of the screen.

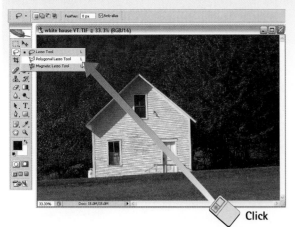

Click

3 Click the First Point

Move the pointer onto the image and click to place the first anchor point. After placing the first point, notice that a straight line extends between the anchor point and the mouse pointer. This line indicates the selection line that will be created when you click to place another anchor point.

Click

4 Add Other Points As Needed

Click once at each location on the image, and place as many anchor points as necessary to surround the area you're selecting. Press the **Esc** key if you decide you need to start over.

5 Close the Selection

To define an enclosed area, you can close the selection shape by clicking back on the starting anchor point. Alternatively, you can double-click or **Ctrl**+click (Windows users) or ⌘+click (Mac users) to connect the current point to the starting point. When you do this, the selection process is complete.

Click

End

How-To Hints

Using the Shift Key for Right Angles

Press and hold the **Shift** key to constrain the line segments you draw with the **Polygonal Lasso** tool to increments of 45° angles.

For Organic Selections

Select the **Lasso** tool instead of the **Polygonal Lasso** tool to draw freeform shape selections. You can switch to the **Lasso** tool from the **Polygonal Lasso** tool on-the-fly by pressing and holding the **Alt** key (Windows users) or the **Option** key (Mac users) as you drag freeform shapes. Release the **Option/Alt** key to go back to dragging straight lines.

A Geometric Alternative

If you want a little help with geometric selections, try the **Magnetic Lasso** tool, found in the pop-out menu of the **Lasso** tool in the toolbox. Click and drag the tool around the selection area—the selection snaps to the nearest contrast edge. The settings in the **Options** bar allow you to control the snap-to qualities of the tool, which you can adjust as necessary.

How to Select by Color Range

When the area you want to select is predominantly one color, try using the color range as a selection criterion. This approach selects all the pixels in an image based on a specified color value. The color range controls let you designate the exact range so you can fine-tune the selection to a specific set of colors.

Begin

1 Open the File

Select **File**, **Open** to launch the desired file, or click the **Go to Bridge** icon in the **Options** bar to open **Bridge** and then double-click the image thumbnail to launch it.

Double -click

2 Select the Color Range Command

Choose **Select**, **Color Range** to launch the **Color Range** dialog box.

Click

3 Configure the Dialog Box

Click the arrow to the right of the **Select** field to access the menu and drag to select **Sampled Colors**. Start with the **Fuzziness** slider set to **40**, enable the **Selection** radio button, and set the **Selection Preview** option to **None**.

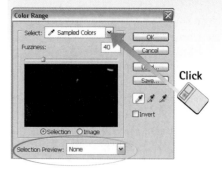

Click

4 Sample a Color

Move the mouse pointer onto the image; notice that the pointer changes to an eyedropper as it moves over the image. Click the color you want to select. In this example, I clicked to select the yellow petal color. The preview in the dialog box shows how much of the image has that color. You can control how much variation of that color is selected by adjusting the **Fuzziness** slider.

Click

5 Adjust the Fuzziness Slider

Increase or decrease the **Fuzziness** slider to include more or less of the color in the selection. If desired, you can select the **Black Matte** and **White Matte** options in the **Selection Preview** list in the **Color Range** dialog box to evaluate the selection area. See the How-To Hints for details on how and when to use the preview options.

 Drag

6 Add Additional Colors

Select the **Plus Eyedropper** from the dialog box and click the image to add more colors to the selected range. Select the **Minus Eyedropper** and click the image to remove colors from the selected range. Click **OK** to close the dialog box and make the selection. If the selection is not to your satisfaction, adjust the **Fuzziness** slider and try again.

End

How-To Hints

Image Previews

To check the selection in more detail, either select **Grayscale**, **Black Matte**, **White Matte** or select **Quick Mask** from the **Selection Preview** drop-down list to show the selection results in the main image window. **Grayscale** shows selected areas in white and unselected areas in black, whereas **Black Matte** shows selected areas as normal and unselected areas as flat black. **White Matte** shows selected areas as normal and unselected areas as white. **Quick Mask** places a mask over the selected or unselected areas, depending on how the **Quick Mask Options** are set (see the following task for details). To select all of a particular color or tonal range in an image, select the desired color from the **Select** drop-down list. You also can select **Out of Gamut** to show which colors would be lost in an RGB-to-CMYK file conversion.

How to Use Quick Mask

Quick Mask is an intuitive way of selecting complex image areas using Photoshop's paint tools to define the selection area. The area is painted in as a mask, and you can erase or add to the mask to define the exact area you want to select. After you define the area, you exit Quick Mask to select the area. When you use Quick Mask with Photoshop's other painting tools (such as the Brush tool), you can literally paint a mask or selection using the actual image as a guide-line. In fact, you don't have to worry about staying within the lines because you can easily reverse the painting by switching the color you're painting with.

Begin

1 Open the File

Select File, Open to launch the desired file.

Click

2 Make a Basic Selection

Although you can start the selection process with Quick Mask, I find it's easier to make an initial selection first, just to set up a relationship between the mask and the rest of the image. Use any of Photoshop's selection tools and select the general area you want to define. Here, I used the Magic Wand tool to select a portion of the boy's arm.

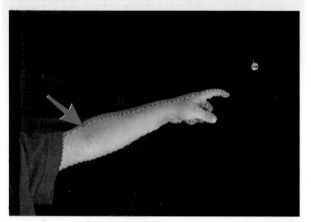

3 Set Quick Mask Options

Double-click the Quick Mask button in the toolbox to launch the Quick Mask Options dialog box. Select Masked Areas or Selected Areas to specify whether the mask represents the selection or the protected (masked) area. I find Selected Areas the more intuitive choice because the area you paint is the selection. If you use Masked Areas, you paint everything that *won't* be included in the selection. The default mask color is red, but you can click the color swatch and select another color. You can also increase or decrease the opacity of the mask by increasing or decreasing the Opacity percentage. Click OK to see the results of your settings. Reopen the dialog box at any time to change these options.

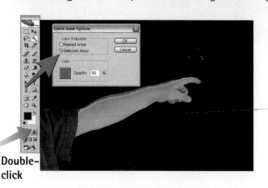

Double-click

4 Draw or Paint the Selection

Use the Photoshop paint tools to fine-tune the mask. See Part 7, "Drawing and Painting with Color," for details. Use the default colors for painting: Black paints more mask and white removes (or undoes) the mask. You can select smaller or larger brushes or zoom in to follow the lines of your image more closely. As you'll see in the next step, you also can easily erase any areas where you painted outside the lines.

Drag

5 Erase Unwanted Areas

Press the **X** key to make white the foreground color (to switch foreground and background colors), and paint with white to erase the mask or reduce the selection area as necessary. When finished correcting unwanted areas, press **X** again (if necessary) to make black the foreground color once more and continue to fine-tune the Quick Mask selection area.

Drag

6 Exit Quick Mask

Click the **Standard Mode** button in the toolbox to exit **Quick Mask** and convert the mask to a selection. Alternatively, press the **Q** key to toggle between standard mode and **Quick Mask** mode to ensure that the selection is correct for the work you're doing to the image.

Click

How-To Hints

Filtering for Graphic Effects

While still in **Quick Mask** mode, you can use any of Photoshop's filters to apply unique textures to the mask. When you switch to standard mode, the texture of the selection is reflected as you edit the image.

Using the Type Tool for Text Selections

You can use the **Type Mask** tool to define a text selection before entering **Quick Mask**. If you're already in **Quick Mask** mode, you can use the regular **Type** tool to create text selections. You can also modify the text selection mask further with filters or other tools.

End

How to Convert Selections to Paths

Because *paths* and selections both define the edges of an area, it's only natural that you would want to convert a selection to a path. This is a good technique if you're one of those people who prefer using the **Brush** or selection tools instead of the **Pen**. Simply make a selection and convert it to a path. To convert a path back to a selection, see Part 9, Task 4, "How to Convert a Path to a Selection." If you want to know more about paths in general, Part 9, "Using Paths," goes to great lengths to describe how to work with paths.

Begin

1 Open the File

Click the **Go to Bridge** icon in the **Options** bar to launch **Bridge**. Navigate to the desired file and double-click its thumbnail to launch it.

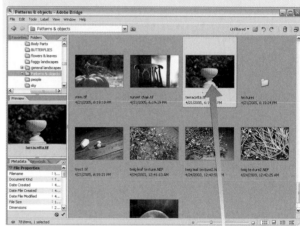

Double-click

2 Make a Selection

Use any combination of selection methods described in this part to select the area to be converted to a path.

3 Open Paths Palette

Select **Window**, **Paths** to open the **Paths** palette.

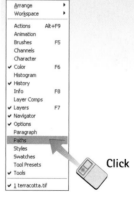
Click

4 Make a Work Path

Select **Make Work Path** from the **Paths** palette menu. This option creates a temporary working path (the *work path*) that has not yet been saved. After a path is saved, it is no longer a work path.

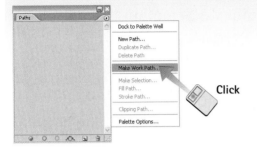

Click

5 Set the Tolerance

Set the **Tolerance** level in the window that appears. The **Tolerance** value determines how many points are used in the path. If the setting is too low, the path will be cluttered with too many extra points; if it's too high, the path will not conform to the selection. Experiment with values between 1.0 and 3.0 for most selections.

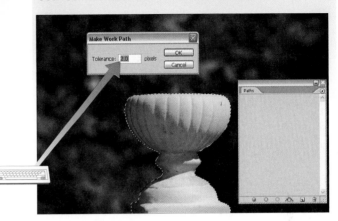

6 Save the Path

When the path is completed, double-click the work path in the **Paths** palette to launch the **Save Path** dialog box. Name the path and click **OK** to save it.

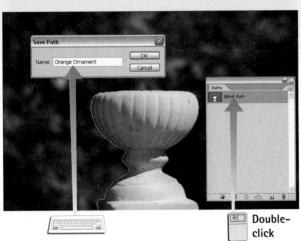

Double-click

End

How-To Hints

Cleaning Up the Selection and Path

Before converting the selection to a path, be sure that no stray pixels are selected. Stray pixels are converted to tiny paths if they are not removed from the selection ahead of time. After the path is selected, select View, Actual Pixels to see the image at full size. Add, delete, or move points as needed to complete the path.

Using Paths Instead of Saving Selections

Paths are a smart alternative to saving selections. Paths add very little to the file size and can be modified and resized infinitely. Selections, on the other hand, are saved as channels, which can quickly bloat overall file size.

Note that there's a difference between *making* a selection and *saving* a selection. Saving a selection creates a separate channel that is masked to show the selection area. This channel is used as a base when the selection is reloaded. It's the channel itself that adds to the file size, not the ability to select the channel.

How to Modify Selections

To select complex shapes and areas, you must sometimes combine multiple selection methods. Adding or subtracting from a selection is only the beginning. You also can shrink or grow a selection, smooth out sharp corners, and tweak or skew the selection area in any direction. This task shows the top 12 shortcuts for working with selections. Combine them as you see fit to select exactly the right area of your image.

Begin

1 Adding to Selections

To add to a selection, hold the **Shift** key as you're using any of the Photoshop selection tools. Alternatively, click the **Add to Selection** button in the **Options** bar. A plus sign appears next to the mouse pointer to show that you're adding to the current selection.

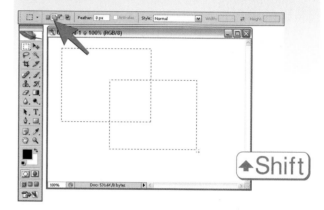

2 Subtracting from Selections

To subtract from a selection, hold the **Alt** key (Windows users) or the **Option** key (Mac users) as you're using any of the Photoshop selection tools. Alternatively, you can click the **Subtract from Selection** button in the **Options** bar. A minus sign appears next to the mouse pointer to show that you're subtracting from the current selection.

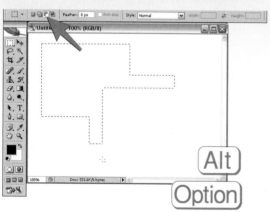

3 Intersecting Selections

With an area selected, you can introduce a second, overlapping selection so that the final selection is made up of only the common, intersecting areas. First, select an area. Then press **Shift+Alt** (Windows users) or **Shift+Option** (Mac users) as you draw a second selection that overlaps the first. Alternatively, click the **Intersect with Selection** button in the **Options** bar. An × appears next to the mouse pointer as you do this. After you release the mouse and the keyboard keys, only the intersecting area remains selected.

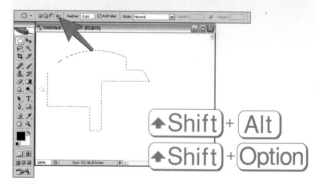

4 Nudging a Selection

After you select an area, you can nudge the selection area up, down, left, or right one pixel at a time. Select any of the selection tools in the toolbox and press the arrow keys on your keyboard.

5 Inverting Selections

To invert an active selection, choose **Select, Inverse**. This action selects the exact opposite of the current selection. In this example, after you select the menu command, everything on the image area will be selected *except* the areas that are currently selected.

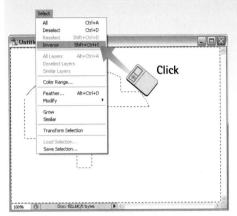

Click

6 Smoothing Selections

Smoothing a selection involves a gradual rounding of corners or sharp edges. To smooth an active selection, choose **Select, Modify, Smooth**. In the **Smooth Selection** dialog box that appears, enter a value from 1 to 100 pixels to determine the degree of smoothing. Click **OK** to modify the selection. Repeat this step as desired to smooth the selection even more.

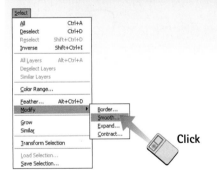

Click

7 Expanding Selections

Expanding a selection means just what it says: expanding the overall area of a selection by a specific number of pixels. To expand an active selection, choose **Select, Modify, Expand**. In the **Expand Selection** dialog box that appears, enter a value from 1 to 100 pixels to determine the degree of expansion. Click **OK** to modify the selection. Repeat this step as desired to expand the selection even more.

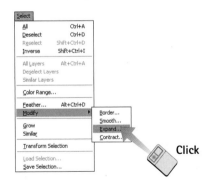

Click

Continues

8 Contracting Selections

Contracting a selection makes the overall selection area smaller. To contract an active selection, choose **Select, Modify, Contract**. In the **Contract Selection** dialog box that appears, enter a value from 1 to 100 pixels. Click **OK** to modify the selection. Repeat this step to contract the selection even more.

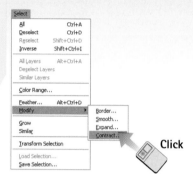

Click

9 Isolating Selection Borders

When you're working with geometric selections, there might be times when you want to apply an effect only to the *border* of a selected area. Choose **Select, Modify, Border**. In the **Border** dialog box that appears, enter a value from 1 to 200 pixels to specify the width of the border. This option thickens the selection line to the width you specify and makes that line the active selection area. Click **OK** to modify the selection.

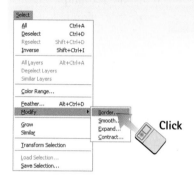

Click

10 Feathering a Selection

Feathering a selection involves vignetting the selection edges, softening any effects that are applied to the selected area. To feather a selection, choose **Select, Feather**. In the **Feather Selection** dialog box that appears, type a feather value from 0.2 to 250 pixels and click **OK**. To set the feather amount before making a selection, enter a pixel value in the **Feather** field of the **Options** bar.

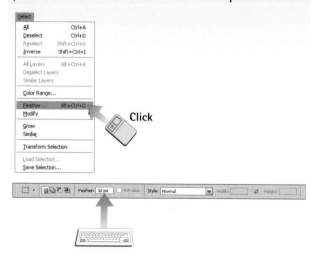

Click

11 Selecting Similar Colors

After you select an area, you can select all other pixels in the image that have the same color value. This capability can be effective if you want to select multiple colored objects or areas. To do this, select a color or range of colors and then choose **Select, Similar**. All pixels with similar pixel values are selected.

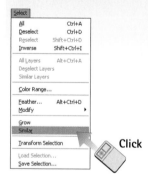

Click

12 Transforming Selections

You can distort or skew a selection using any of the **Transform** options described in Part 10, Task 6, "How to Transform Layers." To transform an active selection, choose **Select, Transform Selection**. A bounding box appears around the selection; drag the handles to modify the selection area. Alternatively, right-click (Windows users) or **Ctrl**+click (Mac users) to view a context menu of transforming options. The **Options** bar also provides a variety of methods to help in transforming the selection. Double-click inside the bounding box or press **Enter** (Windows users) or **Return** (Mac users) to apply the transformation. Press the **Esc** key to cancel the transformation changes.

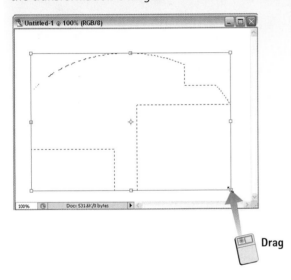

Drag

End

How-To Hints

Smoothing Selections to Make Rounded Corners

Use the **Smooth Selection** technique from step 6 to create rounded-corner rectangular selections. A 16-pixel rounding value works very well with 72dpi web images. The result is ready to be stroked or filled to create a rounded-corner box shape.

Using Tolerance with Select Similar

The **Select Similar** command in step 11 uses the **Tolerance** setting from the **Magic Wand Options** palette to determine how it selects similar colors. If you set the **Tolerance** value high, more similar colors are selected; if you set the **Tolerance** value low, a more narrow range of colors is selected.

How to Save and Load Selections

After you've gone to the trouble of making the perfect selection, you might want to save that selection for future use. This is especially true if you've selected an object or area you know you're going to need or reference again as you work with the image. Photoshop lets you save selections as *alpha channels*, which preserve the exact area and transparency levels and can be reloaded at any time.

Begin

1 Open the File

Select **File**, **Open** and launch the desired file.

2 Make the Selection

Select the desired area using any of Photoshop's selection tools. In this example, I used the **Color Range** dialog box to select the green blades of grass. (Sample the color and click **OK** to make the selection.)

3 Select Save Selection

Choose **Select**, **Save Selection**. The **Save Selection** dialog box opens.

Click

4 Name the Selection Channel

In the **Name** field, type a name for the selection. This is the name Photoshop gives to the alpha channel, which is where the selection is saved. Click **OK** to save the selection.

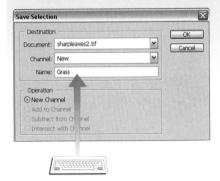

5 Load the Selection

To load a saved selection, choose **Select**, **Load Selection**. In the **Load Selection** dialog box that appears, select the selection name from the **Channel** drop-down list and click **OK** to activate the selection. Note that you can load a selection from any open document; you don't necessarily have to open the selection in the same document in which you saved the selection.

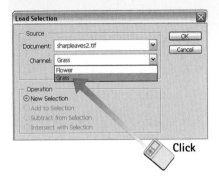

Click

End

How-To Hints

PSD or TIFF?

To preserve the channel along with the saved file in step 4, you must use either the native Photoshop format (PSD) or the TIFF format. The PSD format is recommended.

Viewing Saved Selections

All saved selections are visible in the **Channels** palette, listed by the name you entered in step 4. To review saved selections, select **Window, Channels** to open the **Channels** palette and examine all saved selections. You can also **Ctrl**+click (Windows users) or ⌘+click (Mac users) the **Channel** title to load the selection.

File Size Caution

Although saving selections is easy and convenient, selections can dramatically increase file size if you're not careful. This is especially true if you're saving multiple selections in one file, your selections are large, or they include transparent areas. To monitor file size as you work, select **Document Sizes** from the pop-up menu on the status bar at the bottom of the image window. The value on the left shows the current image's file size if the image were to be flattened; the value on the right shows the image's file size saved with any additional layers and channels.

Task

4

Working with Tone

*T*he tasks in this part look at how to work with image tonality. As far as digital images are concerned, *tonality* refers to the grayscale values from 0 to 255 that differentiate the image pixels. Tonality is black and white and shades of gray; tonality is a histogram, a halftone, salt and pepper, the *I Love Lucy* show, and a dark foreboding sky hanging low over the concrete streets of New York.

I'm using this somewhat poetic introduction to emphasize the fact that tonality is one of the most expressive elements of an image. It can establish a full-contrast range, create a feeling of darkness and danger, or obliterate outlines in the form of fog or mist. If you want to create a strong feeling in an image, consider exaggerating the tonality in some way.

In addition to its expressive qualities, tonality also helps to sharpen an image, even as it increases the contrast. Sharp details, rich and complex color, and the look of texture are all created by manipulating black, white, and shades of gray.

The tasks that follow help you to optimize any given file, making it the best it can be. You can take a dark or underexposed image and make it useable with a few commands and filters. Even better, you can take an image that already looks pretty good and make it a real winner. ●

How to Measure and Compare Pixel Values

Knowing how to accurately measure pixel values is an important first step in being able to evaluate and correct digital images. Many times, you have to determine the tonal value of an image area or compare the value of two different areas. It is important to measure these values numerically because pixel values change from monitor to monitor based on contrast settings, ambient light, and monitor brands. Photoshop uses the **Info** palette to measure pixel values; the **Eyedropper** and **Color Sampler** tools also are helpful aids.

Begin

1 Open the Info Palette

With the image open, select **Window, Info**. The **Info** palette opens on the desktop.

Click

2 Select a Color Model

The upper-left section of the **Info** palette represents the color value of the currently selected pixel. Click and hold the **Eyedropper** icon to display a menu of color modes from which you can select to see the pixel's color specified. (Refer to Part 1, Task 6, "How to Select a Color," for information about color modes.) The **Actual Color** option refers to the document's current mode. If you want to measure the degree of transparency in a given layer, select the **Opacity** option from this menu.

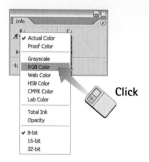

Click

3 Select a Variable Color Model

The upper-right section of the **Info** palette tracks a second set of color values, which allows you to compare the same pixel value with two different modes. Click and hold the **Eyedropper** icon, and select the desired color mode from the list. Move the mouse cursor over the image (don't click) and watch the corresponding readings appear in the palette.

4 Enter Coordinate Units

With so many pixels in an image, it can be hard to sample the same one more than once. The pixel coordinates section in the lower-left corner of the **Info** palette tracks the exact cursor position based on the x,y axis. Click and hold the cursor icon to select the units of measure.

Click

5 Create Sample Points

To accurately track the same value through the course of your imaging session, use eyedropper sample points. Click the **Eyedropper** tool in the toolbox; a submenu of two eyedroppers appears. Select the **Color Sampler** tool (the second tool). Click the tool on the image to place a sample point. A new section is created in the **Info** palette for each sample point you create.

6 Track Sample Values

Drag the sample point to move it; drag the point off the image to delete it. Alternatively, hold down the **Alt** key (Window users) or the **Option** key (Mac users), hover the pointer over the sample point, and click to delete the point from the image (the pointer changes to a scissors when it's on top of the sample point). Remove all sample points by clicking the **Clear** button in the **Options** bar; hide all sample points without removing them by selecting **View**, **Extras**. Each image supports up to four sample points, which can be saved with the image (if you use a file format such as PSD). If you want, set a color mode for each point area in the palette, just as you did in steps 2 and 3.

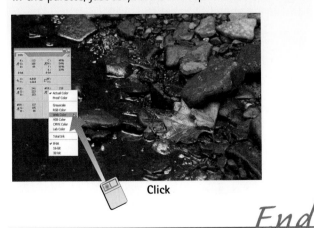

Click

How-To Hints

Selection Dimensions

Use the width/height section in the lower-right corner of the **Info** palette to measure the exact size of an active selection. This capability is especially valuable with the **Marquee** tool, which gives real-time dimensions as you drag. For more information on selections, refer to Part 3, "Selection Techniques."

End

How to Optimize the Tonal Range

When you capture an image with a digital camera or scanner, chances are that the tonal range in your image is lacking in highlights or shadows. An *optimized tonal range* is one in which the darks are completely black, the highlights are white, and the other tones are well distributed. In Photoshop, you adjust the tonal range of an image with the **Levels** option. Not only does adjusting tone ensure good contrast and detail, but it also can correct any unwanted color casts. Even if the image looks pretty good to start with, optimizing the tone can improve things even further.

Begin

1 Open the Info Palette

Open the image for which you want to adjust the tonality. Select **Window**, **Info** to open the **Info** palette.

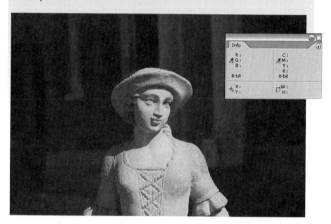

2 Open Levels

Select **Image**, **Adjustments**, **Levels** to open the **Levels** dialog box.

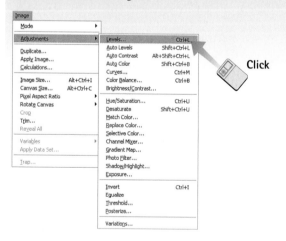

Click

3 Select the Black Point

Click the black **Eyedropper** icon in the lower-right corner of the **Levels** dialog box. Move the cursor over the image; the pointer changes to an eyedropper as it enters the image. Using the readings from the **Info** palette, find the darkest area of the image and click to set the black point.

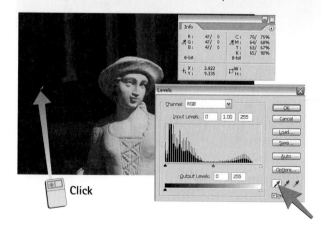

Click

4 Select the White Point

Click the white **Eyedropper** icon in the lower-right corner of the **Levels** dialog box. Move the cursor over the image; the pointer changes to an eyedropper as it enters the image. This time, find the lightest area of the image and click to set the white point.

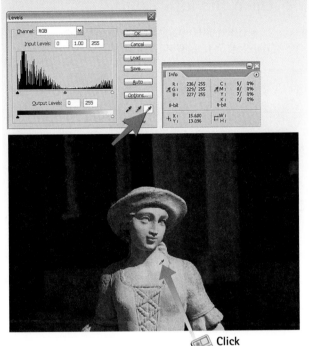

Click

5 Click OK

Click **OK** to apply the effect. By setting the black and white points for the image, you are telling Photoshop what the darkest shadows and brightest highlights in the image are. Doing so establishes the tonal range of the scanned image. You can experiment with setting a black point that is not the darkest area of the image or a white point that is not the brightest area of the image to see what effect this skewed tonal range has.

End

How-To Hints

Reselecting the Darkest or Lightest Area

Take your time when looking for the lightest and darkest points in the image. Selecting a pixel that is not close enough to the light or dark point can result in blowing out the highlights or shadows. If you make a mistake, press the **Alt** key (Windows users) or the **Option** key (Mac users) and click the **Reset** button in the **Levels** dialog box (the **Cancel** button changes to the **Reset** button) to make another attempt.

How to Improve Contrast with Curves

Task 2 showed how to use the **Levels** dialog box to set the white point and the black point of an image, thus optimizing the tonal range for the image. You can use the **Curves** dialog box to increase the contrast in the image, allowing you to selectively enhance image details. If the image seems flat or lacking in contrast, curves can make a dramatic improvement. Curves provide complete control over every color and tonal area of your image, as opposed to the **Levels** command (see the preceding task) or the **Shadow/Highlight** command (see the next task), which automates edits to specific tonal areas.

Begin

1 Open the Info Palette

Open the image you want to affect. Select **Window**, **Info** to open the **Info** palette.

Click

2 Open the Curves Dialog Box

Select **Image**, **Adjustments**, **Curves** to open the **Curves** dialog box.

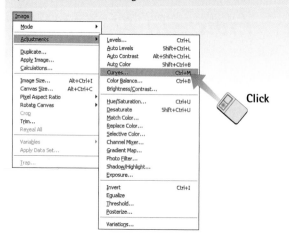

Click

3 Set the Black and White Points

Follow the steps in Task 2 to set the black and white points for the image. Use the **Eyedropper** icons in the **Curves** dialog box rather than those in the **Levels** dialog box.

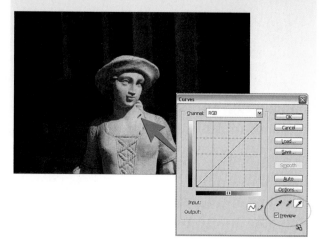

4 Darken Shadows

Click the lower-left portion of the diagonal line in the **Curves** dialog box to place a point on the line. If necessary, slowly drag the point you placed downward to darken the shadow areas in the image.

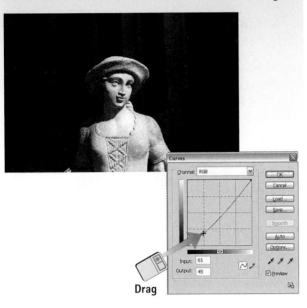

Drag

5 Brighten Highlights

Click the upper-right portion of the diagonal line in the **Curves** dialog box to place a point on the light-areas portion of the line. Slowly drag the point up to lighten the highlights, increasing the overall contrast, especially in the midtones. Click **OK** to apply the effect.

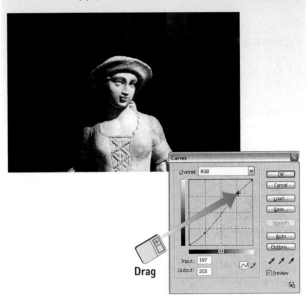

Drag

6 View Results

Compare the final result of the **Curves** adjustment shown here to the image from step 1. Notice the improved detail and clarity in the adjusted image.

How-To Hints

Checking Input and Output Values

In the **Curves** dialog box, watch the **Input** and **Output** values to understand exactly what changes you're making to the curve. The **Input** value refers to the original pixel value (for example, a midtone value of 128). Clicking at an **Input** value of 128 and dragging up to an **Output** value of 160 means that all pixels originally valued at 128 are now a lighter value of 160. In addition, all pixel values around the input value are lightened so that the effect is applied smoothly. Keep the curve shape smooth, and the effect will look natural.

End

How to Improve Contrast with Shadow/Highlight

Shadow/Highlight is an extremely smart set of controls that enables you to brighten shadows and darken highlights simultaneously, controlling the tonal range affected and the overall intensity of the effect. With these controls, you can increase image contrast in the shadows or highlights without significantly sacrificing contrast in the other tonal regions.

Begin

1 Open the Image

Open the image you want to affect. In this example, a white stone monument and a bright sky have overwhelmed the darker values in the image. The goal is to add contrast to the shadows without losing contrast in the sky.

2 Launch Shadow/Highlight

Select **Image, Adjustments, Shadow/Highlight** to open the **Shadow/Highlight** dialog box. Enable the **Preview** and **Show More Options** check boxes to display all the options in the dialog box. The default settings often create dramatic results right away. In this case, the default settings have lightened the shadow areas, bringing out details in the grass.

3 Tweak the Shadows

In the **Shadows** section of the dialog box, use the **Amount** slider to control the degree of change to each shadow pixel; the higher the number, the more the shadows are brightened. The **Tonal Width** slider controls the range of tone to be modified; lower values restrict the effect to just the shadows, and higher values modify lighter tones. The **Radius** slider averages neighboring pixels and controls the overall contrast within the tonal range. For this image, I set the **Amount** to 33, the **Tonal Width** to 40, and the **Radius** to 16.

4 Darken the Highlights

The **Highlights** section enables you to darken the highlight areas using the same control options described in step 3. To bring out the available sky detail, I set the **Amount** to **20**, the **Tonal Width** to **33**, and the **Radius** to **18**.

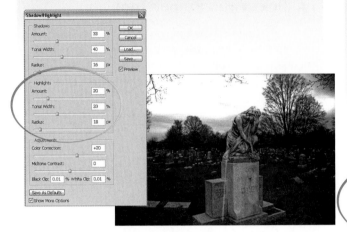

5 Make Further Adjustments

The **Adjustments** section allows you to tweak the **Color Correction** and **Midtone Contrast**. Increase the **Color Correction** value to bump up the color saturation globally. The **Midtone Contrast** slider lightens or darkens the middle tones in the image. In this example, **Color Correction** was set to **+58** and **Midtone Contrast** was set to **−11**.

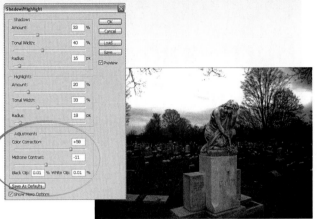

6 View Results

Compare the final result of the **Shadow/Highlight** adjustment shown here to the image from step 1. Notice the improved detail and clarity in the adjusted image.

End

How-To Hints

Understanding the Radius Slider

Every pixel is modified by the **Radius** slider depending on the tonal value of its neighbors. For each pixel in the image, a luminance value for the surrounding neighborhood pixels is determined by the **Radius** control. The size of the neighborhood over which the luminance is averaged depends on the **Radius** setting. Photoshop applies the calculations based on the average values of the pixel's neighborhood. In general, the larger the radius, the larger the extent over which the neighborhood luminance is averaged. If the **Radius** value is too large, the result can be an over-average of luminance values, displayed as unnatural image halos.

How to Use the Dodge, Burn, and Sponge Tools

At times, you will want to lighten or darken an image only in selected areas. Although you could select an area and make changes only to that area (refer to Part 3), you might find the **Dodge**, **Burn**, and **Sponge** tools more effective. These tools allow you to brush your corrections onto an image: The **Dodge** tool lightens the image, the **Burn** tool darkens it, and the **Sponge** tool lets you saturate or desaturate the color intensity.

Begin

1 Select the Proper Tool

Open the image you want to affect. Click and hold the **Dodge** tool in the toolbox. A pop-out menu appears from which you can select the **Dodge**, **Burn**, or **Sponge** tool. Point to the desired tool and release the mouse button to select it.

Click

2 Set the Options Palette

If you're using the **Dodge** or **Burn** tool, from the **Options** bar, select **Shadows**, **Midtones**, or **Highlights** from the **Range** menu, depending on the tonal area of the image you want to modify. For the **Sponge** tool, select **Saturate** or **Desaturate** to increase or decrease the color intensity.

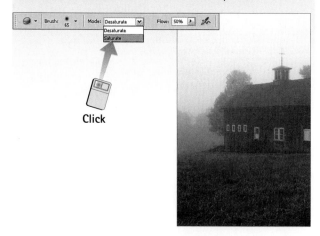

Click

3 Set the Exposure or Flow

The **Dodge** and **Burn** tools use an **Exposure** slider to control the intensity of the effect as you brush it in. The **Sponge** tool uses a **Flow** slider to accomplish the same thing. In the **Options** bar, click and drag to adjust the **Exposure** or **Flow** slider. Select a higher percentage number for a dramatic effect; select a lower number for subtle changes.

4 Select a Brush

From the **Brushes** palette (located in the palette well on the right end of the **Options** bar), select a suitable brush size for the tool you're working with and the image you're editing. To avoid hard-edged brushstrokes, select a feathered brush.

5 Begin Brushing in the Effect

Begin with a very low **Exposure** or **Flow** setting and a feathered brush that is large enough to cover the desired area in just a few strokes. Repeatedly brush over the area, building up the effect intensity as you go. If a pronounced brushstroke appears, undo the stroke (select **Edit**, **Undo**) and lower the intensity. Click and drag lightly to apply the effect, instead of dragging back and forth.

Drag

6 Change Brush Size and Exposure

As you work, select a smaller brush size as needed to work into smaller areas. If you change the brush size, consider decreasing the **Exposure** or **Flow** setting to hide the brushstrokes. This might be necessary because smaller brushstrokes are more visible when repeatedly applied.

How-To Hints

Undoing the Effect

Because these effects are applied with repeated brushstrokes, selecting **Edit**, **Undo** does not revert the image to its appearance before you began. Give yourself a safety net by opening the **History** palette and creating a snapshot before you begin. (Refer to Part 2, Task 2, "How to Undo with the History Palette," for more information.) After the effect is applied, click the snapshot to revert to the previous state or to compare the result.

Brushing in a Straight Line

To brush the effect along a straight line, click once at the start of the line, press and hold the **Shift** key, and click at the end of the line. Photoshop applies the effect in a straight line between the two points.

End

How to Sharpen Images

Sharpening images with Photoshop is a common and useful task. Photoshop can't actually restore lost image detail, but it can enhance the edge contrast of detail that is present. If your image appears soft or blurry, sharpening can bring back the appearance of detail and clarity. A good way to add overall sharpness to an image is to use the **Unsharp Mask** filter. Be careful not to oversharpen, which results in an unnatural halo around the objects in the image, flattening the space. If this occurs, select **Edit, Undo** and reapply the effect.

Begin

1 Select the Unsharp Mask Filter

With the image open, select **Filter, Sharpen, Unsharp Mask**. The **Unsharp Mask** dialog box opens.

Click

2 Set the Amount Slider

Enable the **Preview** check box and set the thumbnail magnification view to **100** by clicking the + or − button. The **Amount** slider controls the degree of sharpening applied to the image. Adjust the slider as needed, noting the changes in the preview window in the dialog box.

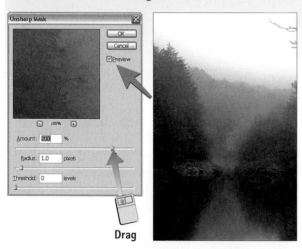

Drag

3 Set the Radius Slider

The **Radius** control determines the width of what Photoshop considers to be an edge. A higher **Radius** value increases apparent sharpness as it lowers image detail. For most naturalistic images, begin by setting this option to **1**—and don't let it rise above **3**.

Drag

4 Set the Threshold Slider

The **Threshold** setting determines how tonally different two pixels must be before qualifying as an "edge." Leave it at **0** to apply the effect globally; move it higher to exclude smaller tonal transitions from sharpening. A setting from **2** to **20** is usually enough to prevent the introduction of noise into gentle gradations.

Drag

5 Apply the Effect

To zoom in on the image window while the **Unsharp Mask** dialog box is open, select **View, Zoom In** from the main menu as many times as necessary. If the image is larger than the image window, you can use the scrollbars to scroll to different areas in the image window (or hold down the **spacebar** to toggle to the **Hand** tool and drag to various parts of the image). Check the image carefully to ensure that all areas are sharpened to the proper level. When you are satisfied with the image, click **OK** to apply the effect.

6 Fade the Result As Necessary

Select **Edit, Fade Unsharp Mask** to open the **Fade** dialog box. Move the **Opacity** slider to the left to gradually decrease the sharpen effect as necessary. To soften the effect, set the slider accordingly and click **OK**, leaving the **Mode** setting at **Normal** (see Part 13, Task 1, "How to Use Blending Modes," for details on other mode options). If you determine that the initial effect is acceptable, click **Cancel** to close the **Fade** dialog box and leave the image unchanged.

Drag

How-To Hints

Don't Forget About Color

Sharpening an image is as much about color as it is about tone. Be sure to color balance your images to maximize overall contrast and color vibrancy.

Sharpen Wisely

Sharpening is generally the last thing you do to an image. The amount of sharpening is determined by the subject matter (faces tend to need more, backgrounds usually the least) and the size of the final output (images for screen need very little sharpening, prints need more, and very large prints need the most).

End

How to Use Smart Sharpen

New with Photoshop CS2, the **Smart Sharpen** filter offers more control than the **Unsharp Mask** filter. For example, **Smart Sharpen** allows you to sharpen more in the shadows than the highlights, or vice versa. In addition, **Smart Sharpen** includes alternative sharpening methods that go beyond anything **Unsharp Mask** could ever do.

Begin

1 Open the Smart Sharpen Filter

With your image open, select **Filter, Sharpen, Smart Sharpen**. The **Smart Sharpen** dialog box has a much larger preview pane than does **Unsharp Mask**, so you can safely disable the **Preview** check box if it slows down the preview refresh time. Set the **Zoom** to at least **100%** using the + and − buttons located under the preview pane.

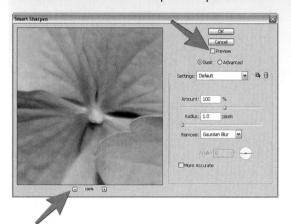

2 Set the Amount Slider

The **Amount** slider determines how much sharpening is applied. As you increase this value, you increase the edge contrast added to the image. This is how the sharpening effect is achieved. However, higher values can also exaggerate noise and image grain.

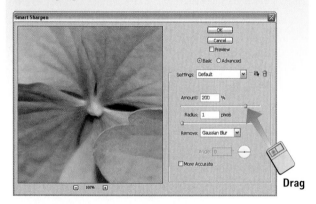

Drag

3 Set the Radius Slider

The **Radius** slider determines the width of what Photoshop considers to be an edge (remember that sharpening works by adding contrast to edges). You should be as conservative as possible with the **Radius** slider because higher values add halos around image details. Lower is better here.

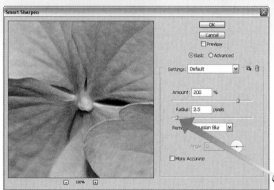

Drag

4 Set the Remove Method

Smart Sharpen provides three blur-removal methods, available from the **Remove** drop-down menu. **Gaussian Blur** works exactly like **Unsharp Mask**, whereas **Lens Blur** uses a more sophisticated algorithm to provide finer sharpening. **Motion Blur** assumes that the blur was caused by camera shake or subject movement and sharpens at an angle you specify. Although the **More Accurate** option increases the accuracy of all sharpening methods, it can be a drain on computer resources.

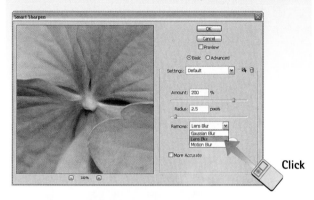

Click

5 Set the Advanced Controls

When you click the **Advanced** option, the sharpening controls area displays three tabs. The **Sharpen** tab has the controls used in steps 2–4. The **Shadow** and **Highlight** tabs provide controls to fade the sharpening effect in their respective tonal ranges. On each tab, you can specify the **Fade Amount** from 0% (no fade at all) to 100% (no sharpening at all). The **Tonal Width** slider sets how much of the highlight or shadow range to fade. **Radius** defines the area used to identify a pixel as a highlight or a shadow.

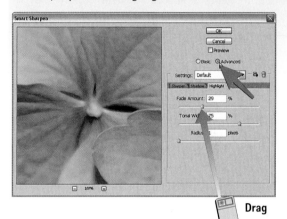

Drag

6 Apply the Effect

Smart Sharpen uses navigation techniques common to most Photoshop filters, so clicking and holding inside its preview pane shows the unsharpened version. Releasing the mouse button restores the sharpened preview. Toggling this before/after view can be helpful. Click and drag inside the preview pane to shift the area displayed, or click in the actual image to center that section in the preview pane. When you've inspected the entire image, click **OK** to apply the effect.

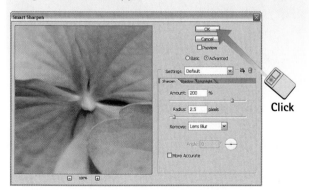

Click

How-To Hints

Selectively Sharpen

Smart Sharpen (or any sharpening method) can be constrained by selecting the area to be sharpened first with any standard selection technique. Alternatively, sharpen a duplicate layer and then use the **Eraser** tool or a layer mask to hide the areas you don't want sharpened.

Sharpen to a New Layer

Sharpening a duplicate image layer offers multiple advantages: It protects the original version so you can return to it later and allows multiple sharpness settings to be saved for different output purposes. And on severely sharpened images, the blending mode of the sharpened layer can be set to **Luminance** to eliminate color shifts along edges.

End

How to Use Blur to Sharpen

Although it might sound paradoxical, you actually can use the **Blur** filter to *sharpen* an image. Specifically, you can blur one area of your image to make the other area look sharper. In this task, you intentionally soften the background areas of an image, making the subject appear sharper in comparison. This is a good approach for images that are too soft to be remedied using the **Unsharp Mask** or **Smart Sharpen** filter alone.

Begin

1 Open the File in Photoshop

Select **File, Open** or click the **Go to Bridge** icon on the **Options** bar to open **Bridge** and double-click to open the file you want to modify.

Click

2 Apply Sharpening

Begin by sharpening the image as best as you can. Select **Filter, Sharpen, Unsharp Mask** or **Filter, Sharpen, Smart Sharpen** and follow the directions in Task 6 or 7 to sharpen the image.

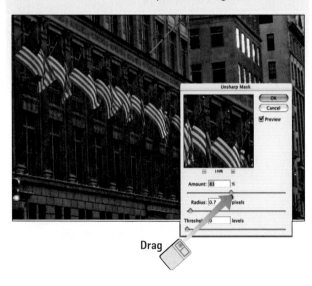

Drag

3 Select Area to Blur

Using Photoshop's selection tools, select the area to which you want to apply the blur. For more on making selections in Photoshop, refer to Part 3. In this example, I've selected the grass and trees on the either side of the boy.

4 Feather the Selection

Feathering softens the edges of a selection, helping it to blend with unselected areas. If you did not specify a feather before you made the selection, choose **Select, Feather**. In the **Feather Selection** dialog box, specify the desired pixel value. The amount of feathering you select depends on the overall resolution of the image and the subject matter. The selection in this example is approximately 2000 × 3000 pixels, and it uses a 32-pixel feather.

Click

5 Apply Gaussian Blur

Select **Filter, Blur, Gaussian Blur** to open the **Gaussian Blur** dialog box. (Gauss was a mathematician; the Gaussian blur effect is based on his mathematical formulas.) Adjust the **Radius** slider until the proper blur amount appears in the window. Click **OK**.

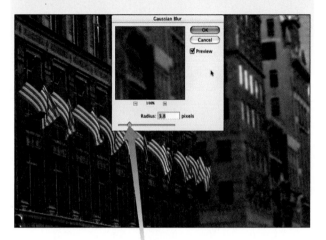

Drag

6 Touch Up with the Blur Tool

After deselecting the selection (press **Ctrl+D** in Windows or **⌘-D** on the Mac), select the **Blur** tool from the toolbox and brush in the smaller areas to complete the blur transition.

Click

End

How-To Hints

Don't Overdo It

The blur effect works best when it is subtle and subliminal. Resist the urge to knock the background way out of focus.

Building Up the Blur Effect

In the **Options** bar for the **Blur** tool, keep the **Strength** setting relatively low so you can build the effect with multiple brushstrokes. This gives you more control and accuracy.

How to Convert Images to Grayscale

If you are going to print a color image in black and white, you should convert a copy of it to grayscale first. At first glance, converting an image to grayscale seems like an easy task: You select **Image**, **Adjust**, **Desaturate** to remove all the color (or better yet, let the printer force the image to gray). What could be easier? The problem with this approach is that the proper tonal range for all image areas might not be emphasized. In this task, you optimize the tones so there is detail everywhere, ensuring that the central subject is well represented.

Begin

1 Open the File in Photoshop

Select **File**, **Open** or click the **Go to Bridge** button on the **Options** bar to open **Bridge** and double-click the color image you want to open.

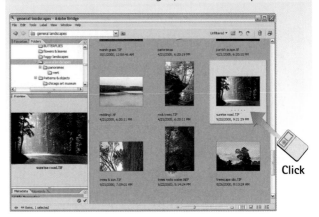

Click

2 Convert to Lab Color

Select **Image**, **Mode**, **Lab Color** to convert the image to the Lab color space. Lab color maintains a larger range of tones in the image than does any of the other color models.

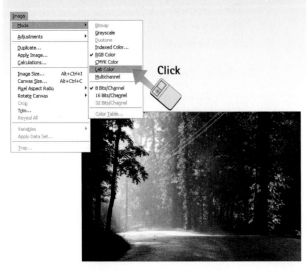

Click

3 Open Channels

Select **Window**, **Channels** to open the **Channels** palette. Click the **Lightness** channel to make it visible and to make it the active channel. In Lab color mode, the **Lightness** channel preserves all the luminance data in the image, separate from any color information, giving you more control over tone distribution. Other grayscale options interpret color information as grayscale data, distorting the tonal range.

Click

4 Modify with Curves

Select **Image**, **Adjustments**, **Curves** to open the **Curves** dialog box. Modify the curves as described in Task 3 to enhance the contrast and range for your image as necessary.

5 Duplicate Channel

With the **Lightness** channel still selected, open the **Channels** palette menu and select **Duplicate Channel**. In the dialog box that appears, name the new file and select **New** from the **Destination** pop-up menu. This action saves the **Lightness** channel to a new file that you can modify further.

Click

6 Close the Original File

Close the original file by selecting **File**, **Close**. Click **No** when asked whether you want to save changes to leave the original color file untouched.

Click

End

How-To Hints

Another Approach

As an alternative to converting the file to Lab color as explained here, you can keep the file in RGB mode. In this approach, click each channel in the **Channels** palette to view a grayscale rendition of each channel. You will see a wide range of grayscale variations based on the color in the image. If you see one with the tone and contrast you like, select and copy the grayscale channel and paste it in a new file.

Yet Another Approach

Working from a *copy* of your color image, select **Image**, **Adjustments**, **Channel Mixer**. In the **Channel Mixer** dialog box, enable the **Preview** check box and the **Monochrome** option. You can now create an almost infinite variety of new grayscale versions by combining the color channels in various proportions using the **Red**, **Green**, and **Blue** sliders. The **Constant** slider provides overall lightening and darkening.

Task

Working with Color

*F*or some people, color corrections are very intimidating. They see the RGB or CMYK conversion curves and tables and talk to prepress guys who emphasize perfect flesh-tone balance, and then decide that color correction is something to be left to the "experts."

Although it's true that you can mess up the color in an image, it's also true that you can do quite a bit on your own. This is especially true if you're designing for the Web as opposed to print because the monitor is much more representative of the way the final image will look on the Web as opposed to its appearance on paper.

The tasks in this part explain the basics of color correction and show what a huge difference color can make in an image. Although you won't become a prepress expert, you should learn to trust your eye a bit more and to have confidence in correcting the color in your own images. ●

How to Make Global Color Corrections

Global color corrections can fix an image that appears to have a color cast or overall tint. This color cast could have been caused by an input device (such as a scanner or digital camera) or by a light source (such as fluorescent lighting). This task shows you how to correct the tint of an image so the image appears natural to the eye. You can apply this technique to images of natural subjects (such as trees and sky) as well as to more abstract projects.

Begin

1 Open the File

Select **File, Open** (or click the **Go to Bridge** icon) and select the image file you want to edit.

Click

2 Open the Info Palette

Select **Window, Info** to display the **Info** palette.

3 Set the Black and White Points

If you haven't done so already, set the black point and white point, as explained in Part 4, Task 3, "How to Improve Contrast with Curves." In brief, open the **Curves** dialog box by selecting **Image, Adjustments, Curves** and use the black and white eyedroppers in the **Curves** dialog box to set the points. Click **OK** to apply the effect.

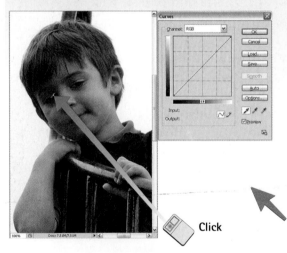
Click

4 Measure Values

Look at the image onscreen and search for areas that appear to have a color cast. Move your mouse pointer over these areas and measure the results in the **Info** palette. Generally, a cast is especially evident in parts of the image you know are supposed to be white or gray (a white area should have equal values for the R, G, and B measurements). In this example, a slight red cast is evident on the gray metal.

5 Evaluate the Results

In comparing the numbers for a white or gray value, look for a number that is much higher or lower than the other two. In this case, the red is slightly higher than the green or blue, indicating that the sample area has a red cast. If a number is low, its inverse is dominant; you must add the low color to balance the color cast. (Red's inverse is cyan, green's inverse is magenta, and blue's inverse is yellow.)

6 Select a Channel Color

This step corrects a specific color channel based on the evaluations made in the previous step. Reopen the **Curves** dialog box, click the arrow next to the **Channel** drop-down menu, and select the color you want to modify based on your readings in steps 4 and 5. This action launches a curve that corresponds to that color channel only.

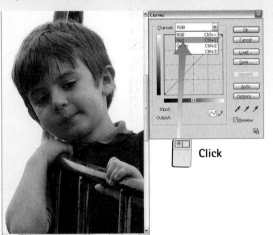

Click

7 Modify the Color

Click and drag the curve up or down, adding or subtracting the target color to eliminate the color cast from the image. Click **OK** to apply the change.

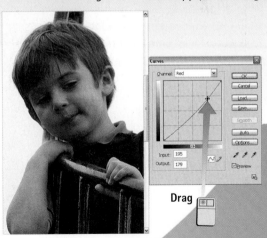

Drag

End

How to Use the Match Color Command

The **Match Color** feature enables you to apply the color characteristics from a source image or layer onto a target layer or file. For example, if you're pulling together a series of headshots from different sources, **Match Color** can make them look like a more cohesive group, with consistent flesh tones, light temperatures, and color saturation.

Begin

1 Launch Match Color

With the target and source images open, select **Image, Adjustments, Match Color**. The **Match Color** dialog box opens.

Click

Target —

2 Set the Source Layer or File

The source file or layer sets a correction baseline for color changes that are applied to the target file or layer. Select the open image from the **Source** pull-down menu in the **Image Statistics** section. To select a layer from the target image as a source, select it from the **Layer** pull-down menu. If the **Preview** check box is enabled, the image shifts color to reflect the source.

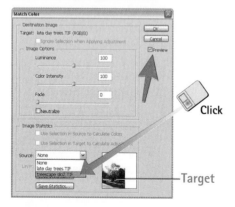

Click

—Target

3 Modify Luminance

Drag the **Luminance** slider to adjust the tonal brightness to suit the subject matter in the target image.

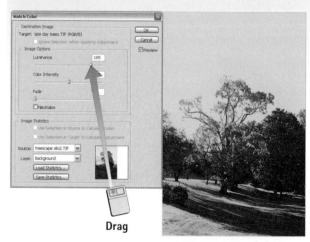

Drag

4 Modify Color Intensity

Drag the **Color Intensity** slider to adjust the color saturation in the target image.

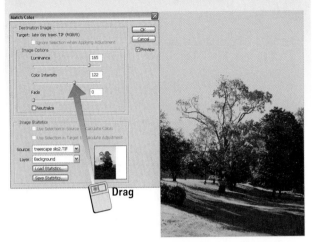

Drag

5 Fade the Effect

Increase the **Fade** slider to reduce the cumulative effect on the target image or layer. You can also enable the **Neutralize** check box to neutralize any color casts in the image. This option is good if you are making slight color modifications; it works less well in images that have a predominant color or light source.

Drag

6 Apply the Effect

Click **OK** to close the **Match Color** dialog box and apply the final effect. In this case, the blown-out sky and harsh highlights of the target image have been tamed, picking up the soft, muted landscape colors of the source image.

Target   Source

End

How-To Hints

Using Selections to Calculate Results

Selections are an effective way to modify the tonal set used in the **Match Color** calculations. In the source image, select a specific area to limit the source color information to the tonal range of only that area. With the area selected in the open source image, enable the **Use Selection in Source to Calculate Colors** check box in the **Image Statistics** section of the dialog box.

Color information from the source is applied using the tonal range of the target image. To restrict the tonal range of the target image, make a selection in the target image before launching the **Match Color** command. With an area selected in the target image, the final effect is applied to only the selection. To use the selected area as a calculation while applying the result to the entire image, enable the **Ignore Selection when Applying Adjustment** check box at the top of the **Match Color** dialog box.

How to Correct a Range of Colors

At times, you might want to change a range of colors within an object or area. You might want to make a red ball yellow, for example, or a blue car green. This involves changing more than just one color shade because numerous values represent the highlights and shadows across the form. At the same time, you don't want to change any areas outside the desired object. Photoshop offers the perfect set of tools for making these types of changes: the **Select Color Range** and the **Hue Saturation** controls. This task shows you how to specify a range of colors and globally change them to another color.

Begin

1 Open the File

Select **File**, **Open** and select the image file you want to modify.

2 Select Color Range

Select **Select**, **Color Range** to launch the **Color Range** dialog box. From the **Select** drop-down list box, select **Sampled Colors** so you can select the colors in the image that you want to change.

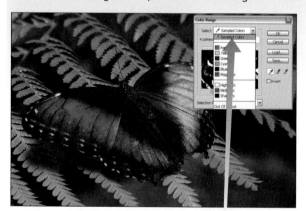

Click

3 Sample the Color Range

The **Eyedropper** icon should be selected by default. If it's not, click it in the dialog box and then click in the thumbnail or main image to select a color. Select **White Matte** from the **Selection Preview** pop-up menu to preview the colors selected against a white background within the main image window. The selected color is shown in the main image window against a white background so you can see exactly what is included in the sampling. If necessary, switch to the **Add to Sample** tool and click other areas to include them in your sample. Drag the **Fuzziness** slider to increase or decrease the range of colors selected. Click **OK** to create a selection of the color range as shown.

Click

4 Change the Hue

Select **Image, Adjustments, Hue/Saturation** to launch the **Hue/Saturation** dialog box. Drag the **Hue** slider to shift the color range as desired. Here, I changed the blue butterfly to an orange one.

Drag

5 Check the Brightness

If the color range selected is very dark or very light, moving the **Hue** slider might not change anything. In this case, drag the **Lightness** slider and then modify the **Hue** slider as needed to achieve the desired effect.

Drag

End

How-To Hints

Enabling the Colorize Check Box

If you want the selected area to change to all one hue, enable the **Colorize** check box in the Hue/Saturation dialog box. This option lets you select a single hue for the selected range by moving just the **Hue** slider.

Selecting a Target Area First

As you specify a color range, it is normal for stray pixels from other areas, such as the background, to creep in and add noise to the image. To keep stray pixels to a minimum, select the object with any of Photoshop's selection tools before you sample a color range (refer to Part 3, "Selection Techniques"). You also can use the **Image, Adjustments, Color Balance** command to apply this same kind of effect.

How to Use the Color Replacement Tool

The **Color Replacement** tool works like a combination of the **Background Eraser** and the **Clone Stamp** or **Healing Brush** in that it samples color information from one area of the image and paints it into another area. Options for data sampling are **Hue**, **Saturation**, **Color**, and **Luminosity**. The **Color Replacement** tool transfers only one data option per application (such as **Saturation**, for example), while leaving the other variables untouched. You can reapply the tool and select a different data option to add that information as well.

Begin

1 Open the File

Select **File**, **Open** and launch the image file you want to modify.

2 Select Color Replacement Tool

Select the **Color Replacement** tool from the toolbox. If it's not visible, click and hold the **Brush** or **Pencil** tool and select the **Color Replacement** tool from the pop-out menu.

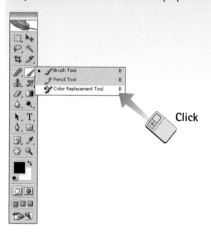

Click

3 Select Brush and Mode

In the **Options** bar for the **Color Replacement** tool, select a brush size and select **Hue**, **Saturation**, **Color**, or **Luminosity** from the **Mode** menu. This selection transfers the characteristics of the sample value onto the pixels you paint over.

Click

4 Select Replacement Color

Click the **Foreground** color swatch in the toolbox and use the **Color Picker** to select the color you want to paint into the image. Alternatively, hold down the **Alt** key (Windows users) or the **Option** key (Mac users) to change to the **Eyedropper** tool, which you can use to sample a color from the image.

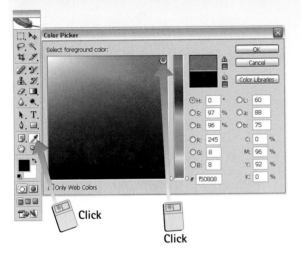

Click

Click

5 Set Sampling Option

The **Color Replacement** tool works by replacing the pixel value of the sample point (the point where you click to start painting) with the replacement color you chose in step 4. The **Sampling** icon choices in the **Options** bar control how the sample point is managed as you paint. The **Continuous** option resamples the sample point continuously as you paint; the **Once** option modifies the pixel value of the first point you click; and the **Background Swatch** option enables you to replace only the pixels that match the **Background** color.

Continuous   Once   Background
Swatch

6 Set the Limits Option

The **Limits** option in the **Options** bar controls how the color spreads as you paint. Select **Discontiguous** to replace the sampled color wherever it occurs under the brush; select **Contiguous** to replace areas that contain the sampled color and are connected to one another; or select **Find Edges** to replace connected areas containing the sampled color while preserving the sharpness of shape edges. Finally, set a **Tolerance** percentage, which determines the range of colors associated with the sample value.

Click

7 Brush in the Effect

Brush the effect into the image. You can modify settings as you paint, changing the **Tolerance**, **Limits**, or **Mode** setting as dictated by the subject matter. You can also use the **Fade** command to soften the effect of the last stroke after it's applied. Select **Edit, Fade Color Replacement Tool** and lower the slider in the dialog box that appears.

Click

End

How to Build Duotones for the Web

Duotones are grayscale images printed with two colors of ink. Although they originally were designed to push the tonal range of standard grayscale images, designers have embraced duotones for their graphic look and feel. This task shows you how to set up a pseudo-duotone effect for the Web, adding a second color to tint a grayscale image. Task 8 addresses setting up actual duotone plates for print.

Begin

1 Open the File

Select **File, Open** to launch the desired image. Open the **Layers** palette by selecting **Window, Layers**.

2 Create a New Adjustment Layer

Select **Layer, New Adjustment Layer, Gradient Map** to create a new adjustment layer that will generate the duotone effect. If you want, change any of the settings in the **New Layer** dialog box and click **OK** to create the new layer. You can also make these modifications from the **Layers** palette at any time.

Click

3 Launch the Gradient Editor

After you click **OK** in the **New Layer** dialog box, the **Gradient Map** dialog box opens. With the **Preview** check box enabled, click the gradient to launch the **Gradient Editor**.

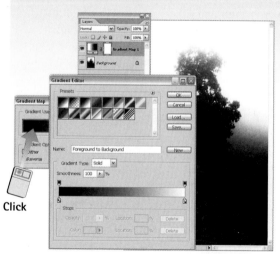

Click

4 Select the Duotone Colors

Click the color stop on the lower-left of the gradient to select it, and then click the **Color** swatch to launch the **Color Picker**. From the **Color Picker**, select the first color you want to use in the duotone and then close the **Color Picker**. Repeat this step with the color stop on the lower-right of the gradient to select the second color in the duotone.

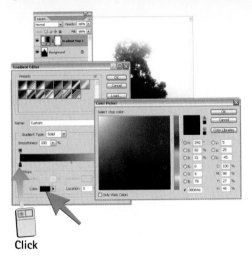

Click

5 Add Tritone and Quadtone Colors

To create a tritone image, click anywhere in the color stop row, just below the gradient bar, to create a third color stop. Click the **Color** swatch to select the color from the **Color Picker** and drag the stop to the left or right to control where the third color is applied to the image. To create a quadtone image, repeat this step to add a fourth color.

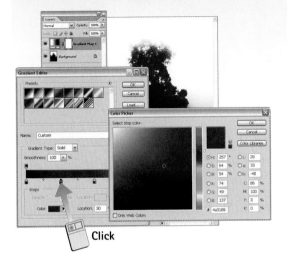

Click

6 Save the Gradient

Click the **New** button in the **Gradient Editor** window to add the gradient to the palette for future use (use the **Name** field to provide an appropriate name for the swatch). Click **OK** in the **Gradient Editor** window and again in the **Gradient Map** dialog box to complete the effect.

How-To Hints

Electric Color Effects

Change the gradient to a **Noise** gradient to shake things up even more. In the **Gradient Editor** dialog box, select **Noise** from the **Gradient Type** menu. Change any of the RGB sliders or select the **Randomize** option to experiment with different effects.

Reversing the Effect

Close the **Gradient Editor** dialog box and click the **Reverse** check box in the **Gradient Map** dialog box to reverse the color mapping and create a negative effect.

End

How to Build Duotones, Tritones, and Quadtones for Print

Whereas a duotone adds one color to the black plate, a *tritone* adds two colors to the black plate, and a *quadtone* adds three colors to the black plate (for totals of three and four colors, respectively). Work closely with your printing specialist to create a plan for setting percentages and proofing the image before printing. This task shows you how to apply the settings and set up the file for the printing specialist, who should help you define the settings.

Begin

1 Open the File

Select **File, Open** and launch the image file you want to modify. If you worked with an image in Task 5 to create a duotone for the Web, note that you should use the *original* image for this task, not the already converted image.

2 Convert to Grayscale

If you started with a color image, select **Image, Mode, Grayscale** to convert the color model from its original color set to a true grayscale image.

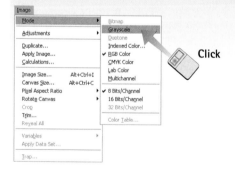

Click

3 Optimize the Tonal Range

Set the white and black points as explained in Part 4, Task 2, "How to Optimize the Tonal Range." Select **Image, Adjust, Curves** and select the black or white eyedropper from the **Curves** dialog box to set the black or white point and optimize the tonal range. Click **OK** to close the dialog box. Now you have an optimized black-and-white monotone image with which to work.

4 Open the Duotones Dialog Box

Select **Image, Mode, Duotone** to open the **Duotone Options** dialog box. This dialog box does not open unless you are using a grayscale image. Click the **Type** pop-up menu and select **Duotone**.

Click

5 Apply the Color

Click the color swatch below the black color swatch to launch the **Color Libraries** dialog box, which defaults to the **Pantone Coated** standard. (You can select a different color set from the list if you want.) Scroll through the colors and click a swatch to see it applied to your image. After you find the color you want, click **OK** to return to the **Duotone Options** dialog box. (You can also select a color other than black. To do this, click the black color swatch and select a color.)

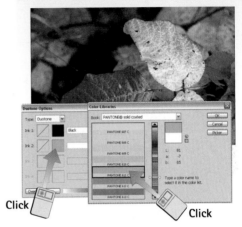

Click   **Click**

6 Set the Tonal Curve

The *tonal curve* determines which areas in the image are affected by the second color. Click the **Curve** button next to the **Ink 2** label to launch the **Duotone Curve** dialog box. Click the diagonal line in the curve grid and drag it up or down to add or subtract the color in that area. The image updates as you do this, so trust your eyes more than the numbers unless you are following required specs from your printer. Remember that you can also change the curve for the black plate, represented by the **Ink 1** label.

Drag

Click

7 Add Additional Colors

If you select **Tritone** or **Quadtone** from the **Type** box in the **Duotone Options** dialog box in step 4, Photoshop creates one or two additional ink sets. Select colors and set the curves as described in steps 5 and 6 for each of the ink sets. Click **OK** to apply the effect.

End

Task

Image Editing Basics

*I*t is inevitable that you will have to resize, rotate, flip, or silhouette almost every image with which you work. These basic tasks are important because you must know how to do them before you can apply more advanced processing. In addition, if you do not properly perform tasks such as silhouetting and resizing, you can destroy image resolution or create less-than-desirable results.

These *preprocessing tasks* or *image prep tasks* are fundamental skills every Photoshop user must master. Exercising these skills with speed and precision will bring a high level of consistency and quality to all your work.

You should pay special attention to resizing images safely to minimize loss of image quality. Images are made up of small building blocks called *pixels*; the number of pixels in an image's width and height determines the image's resolution. Consider an image that is 500 pixels high and 700 pixels wide. If you ask Photoshop to increase the image size to 700 high by 900 wide, you are asking it to add pixels. Where do these pixels come from? Photoshop makes them up, using a process called *interpolation*.

When adding a new pixel, Photoshop looks at the surrounding pixels to determine the value of the pixel it will add. When Photoshop interpolates an image, it can use one of five methods: Bicubic, Bicubic Smoother, Bicubic Sharper, Bilinear, and Nearest Neighbor. Select the method Photoshop uses from the **Preferences** dialog box by selecting **Photoshop, Preferences, General**. With the Bicubic methods, Photoshop looks at the pixels on all four sides as well as on all diagonals to con-textualize what the new pixel's value should be. When enlarging an image, use Bicubic Smoother; when reducing an image, use Bicubic Sharper. Adobe has also left the Bicubic setting, which has always been the default quality standard, in case you'd rather keep using what you're used to. With the Bilinear method, Photoshop looks only at pixels vertically and horizontally. With the Nearest Neighbor method, Photoshop looks only from side to side. As you can imagine, the Bicubic methods deliver the highest level of quality for most photographic images, although they take the longest to process. The Nearest Neighbor method generally provides the lowest quality for photos, but it does a great job on hard-edge, graphic shapes and is also the fastest method of interpolation. ●

How to Resize Images

The size of a Photoshop image is measured in width and height, combined with a resolution value expressed as *pixels per inch (ppi)*. For example, you could have an image 4" × 5" at 300ppi. When resizing images, it is important to understand your minimum target resolution and never go below it. (For example, in the print world, 300ppi is generally a target resolution. For web images, 72ppi is sufficient.)

Begin

1 Open the Image in Photoshop

Select **File, Open** or click the **Go to Bridge** button on the **Options** bar and select the image file with which you want to work.

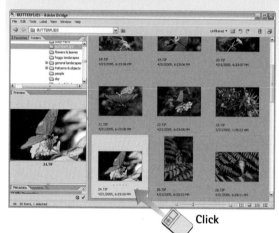

Click

2 Check the Image Size

Select **Image, Image Size** to open the **Image Size** dialog box. Make sure that the **Constrain Proportions** check box is enabled. This option ensures that the width-to-height ratios are maintained and prevents you from distorting the image as you resize it.

Click

3 Deselect Resample Image

Make sure the **Resample Image** check box is disabled. Deselecting this option keeps you from accidentally degrading image quality, especially if you plan to enlarge the image. Resampling works well when you want to resize and shrink the image, but resampling can be disastrous when you're trying to increase the dimensions.

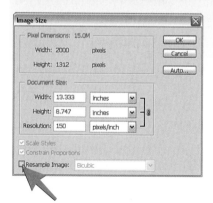

4 Enter Target Resolution

Resolution refers to the number of pixels per inch. For printing, the image resolution should typically be between 225ppi and 300ppi; in contrast, images for the Web need to be only 72ppi. Type the target resolution for this image in the **Resolution** field. As you do this, the dimensions (the **Height** and **Width** fields in the **Document Size** area) change, ensuring that image quality is not sacrificed. In this case, typing **300** in the **Resolution** field changed the dimensions from 13 × 8 to approximately 6 × 4. Notice that the actual width and height in pixels doesn't change. No pixels are added or deleted by interpolation because **Resample Image** is turned off.

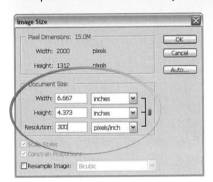

5 Enter Target Dimensions

Because resolution is tied to image dimension, changing the dimension values modifies the target resolution you entered in step 4. To change dimensions without altering resolution, enable the **Resample Image** check box and select **Bicubic**, **Bicubic Smoother**, or **Bicubic Sharper** as the interpolation method (remember that image quality degrades if you enable the **Resample Image** check box; see the How-To Hints). If you are designing for the Web, enter the dimension size in the fields in the **Pixel Dimensions** area; if you are designing for print, use the **Document Size** section. Specify the units of measurement using the pop-up menus, enter the desired dimensions, and click **OK** to resize the image.

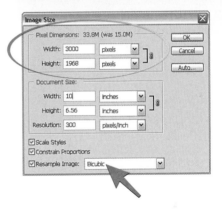

End

How-To Hints

Resizing Graphics

When enlarging an image, try selecting **Bicubic Smoother** from the **Resample Image** pop-up menu. When reducing, try **Bicubic Sharper**. When resizing graphics with hard edges and flat color, select **Nearest Neighbor**, which creates very crisp lines and hard edges, preserving more of the original look of the design.

Enlarging Size and Reducing Resolution

You should avoid enlarging an image without decreasing resolution. For example, to enlarge a 4 × 5 image at 600ppi to 5 × 7, you should reduce the resolution to approximately 425ppi. This precaution keeps you from interpolating the image and losing detail. If you deselect the **Resample Image** check box in the **Image Size** dialog box, Photoshop automatically makes these adjustments for you.

How to Add Canvas

Task 1 looked at how to scale an image up or down by increasing the resolution or dimensions of the image itself. In contrast, this task explains how to keep the image the same size and just add more workspace around it. Photoshop calls this extra work-space *canvas* and enables you to specify exactly how much is added. Adding canvas is important when adding and combining images, when adding flat color for text, or anytime you need to increase the image dimensions without enlarging the image data.

Begin

1 Open the Image

Open the image file with which you want to work. By default, all files have a canvas that is identical to the image dimensions.

2 Open the Canvas Size Dialog Box

Select **Image**, **Canvas Size** to open the **Canvas Size** dialog box.

Click

3 Specify Anchor Placement

The **Anchor** diagram lets you specify where the extra canvas is added. The highlighted box represents the current image; the remaining grid represents the canvas to be added. Click in the diagram to move the highlighted box and control where the extra canvas will be placed.

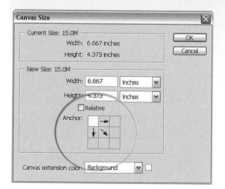

4 Specify Dimensions

Note the current size of the image at the top of the dialog box. Type values for the new image size in the **Width** and **Height** fields in the **New Size** area. Use the drop-down menus to specify your preferred unit of measurement. The **Percent** option can be handy if you simply need some extra working space; use the **Pixels** option to make room for another image. Enable the **Relative** check box if you prefer to specify the added canvas size rather than the total canvas size.

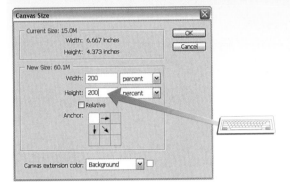

5 Set the Background Color

When you add canvas to an image, the canvas is filled with the current background color by default. To change this color, use the **Canvas Extension Color** drop-down menu. Along with **Background** and **Foreground**, you can select from **White**, **Black**, **Gray**, or **Other**. If you select **Other**, the **Color Picker** dialog box opens; select a color for the background of the canvas you will add. Alternatively, move the dropper into the image area to sample a color from the image itself. Click **OK** to apply the new background color.

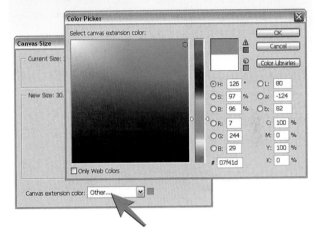

6 Observe the Results

When you're satisfied with all your new canvas size settings, click OK to apply them to your image. This example shows the canvas that was added when I moved the **Anchor** box to the upper-left corner of the grid and increased the width and height of the canvas **200%**. Notice that the extra space appears as blank canvas around the original image.

End

How-To Hints

Transparent Background

When a multilayered image has no background layer, adding canvas always places transparent canvas rather than canvas that has the background color. To force the added canvas to have a white background, select **Flatten Image** from the **Layers** palette menu.

Resizing Versus Adding Canvas

Remember that adding canvas creates extra space around an existing image but does not alter the appearance or quality level of the image. Adding canvas is not the same as enlarging the image, which can degrade the quality. However, adding canvas can dramatically increase the size of your image file.

How to Crop an Image

Cropping an image involves cutting an image down to a specific square or rectangular section, excluding all other unwanted areas. You can crop an image to fit a specific dimension or to enhance its composition. Sometimes cropping involves trimming away a little detail around the edges. At other times, cropping can isolate a small component of an image and discard everything else. Cropping an image does not change the resolution or image quality; it only shrinks the canvas size as unwanted areas are eliminated.

Begin

1 Open the Image

Select **File, Open** or click the **Go to Bridge** button on the **Options** bar and double-click to open the desired image file.

Click

2 Select the Crop Tool

Select the **Crop** tool from the toolbox. Click and drag the **Crop** tool over the image to specify the area to be cropped. A dotted line appears, showing what has been selected.

Click

3 Define the Crop Area

If the **Shield** check box is selected in the **Options** bar, the area outside the crop area is covered with a mask color (click the color swatch in the **Options** bar to change the color). Everything outside the dotted rectangular area *will not* appear in the finished image area. If the selection is wrong, click the **Cancel** button (the circle-with-a-slash button) in the **Options** bar to deselect and then drag again to specify the area.

Drag

4 Modify the Crop Area

Notice that the crop area has handles at the corners and on the sides. To modify the crop area by extending a side, drag a side handle. To extend the crop area from two adjoining sides, drag a corner handle. To move the entire crop area, click inside the selected crop area and drag the box to a new position.

Drag

5 Rotate the Crop Area

You can even rotate the crop area. To do this, position the cursor outside of a corner handle until it changes to a rotate icon. Click and drag to rotate the crop box.

Drag

6 Crop the Image

When the rotated crop selection is where you want it, double-click in the selection to crop the image, press **Enter** in Windows or **Return** on the Mac, or click the check mark button in the **Options** bar.

Double-click

End

How-To Hints

Crop Perspective

To create an angled, perspectival crop effect, enable the **Perspective** check box in the **Options** bar for the **Crop** tool. As you move the mouse pointer into the image area, it changes to an arrow icon, indicating that the perspective option is active. You can then click and drag each crop handle independently. As you can guess, this option lets you create crops that aren't rectangular, regardless of whether the crops create accurate perspective.

Crop to Fit

If you want to crop to a specific width/height ratio, you can type the settings on the **Options** bar before dragging with the **Crop** tool. As you drag, the **Crop** tool is constrained to match your settings. To create a freehand crop, leave these setting fields blank or click the **Clear** button to blank (reset) them.

How to Flip and Rotate an Image

You might want to reverse the orientation of an image for compositional or aesthetic reasons. This is relatively simple to do in Photoshop (provided that there is no text that would be reversed). In addition to reversing an image, you can rotate the entire image canvas, reorienting it to a new position. This is a common requirement for optimizing scans that were set up in the wrong direction. This process is similar to the **Free Transform** command discussed in Part 10, Task 6, "How to Transform Layers." The main difference is that **Free Transform** operates on individual layers rather than the entire image (so that your text, on a separate layer, isn't affected).

Begin

1 Open the File

Open the image you want to flip or rotate.

2 Rotate the Image

Select **Image, Rotate Canvas**. From the submenu, select **90° CW** (clockwise), **90° CCW** (counterclockwise), or **180°**. In this example, I select **90° CW**. The command is executed as soon as you select it from the menu.

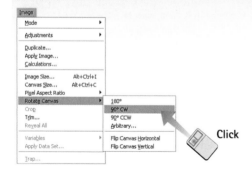

Click

3 Apply Arbitrary Rotation

Select **Image, Rotate Canvas, Arbitrary** to open the **Rotate Canvas** dialog box. Use this dialog box to specify the precise degree and direction of rotation. In this example, I want to rotate the image an additional **15°** clockwise (**CW**). Click **OK** to rotate the canvas, which enlarges to accommodate the angled image.

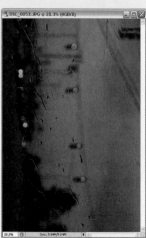

4 Flip the Image Horizontally

Select **Image, Rotate Canvas, Flip Canvas Horizontal** to flip the image horizontally.

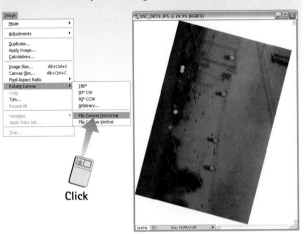

Click

5 Flip the Image Vertically

Select **Image, Rotate Canvas, Flip Canvas Vertical** to flip the image vertically.

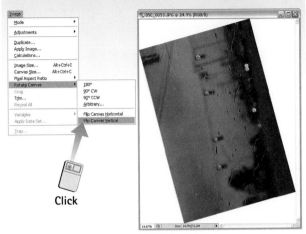

Click

6 Observe the Results

As you can see, rotating and flipping an image can greatly affect how the image is perceived. Although you haven't really changed anything about the image other than the way it is presented to the viewer, you can see that presentation is important.

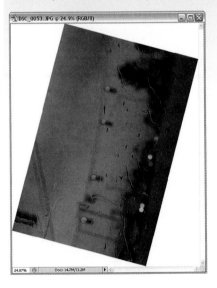

How-To Hints

Rotating and Flipping

When you *rotate* an image, it's as if you placed a print of the image on the desktop and spun it—nothing about the image changes except the orientation. When you *flip* an image, however, it's as if you created a mirror image. Any lettering is now backward and left hands look like right hands. When you flip an image, be sure that there is no text, cars on a road, or other telltale signs that could give this manipulation away.

End

How to Warp an Image

One of the most requested features for Photoshop has finally been added to Photoshop CS2: the ability to freehand warp an image. Although we've had the ability to use various rectangular transformations for several versions now (**Scale**, **Skew**, **Rotate**, and so on—see Part 10, Task 6, "How to Transform Layers"), the new **Warp** command lets you push around pixels like so much modeling clay.

Begin

1 Open the File

Select **File**, **Open** or click the **Go to Bridge** button on the **Options** bar and select the image you want to warp.

Click

2 Select the Area to Warp

Use the **Rectangular Marquee** tool or any other selection method to select the area you want to warp. In this example, my goal is to straighten the tree, so I dragged a rectangular selection around it.

Drag

3 Select Warp

Select **Edit**, **Transform**, **Warp** to activate the warp mesh.

Click

4 Examine the Warp Mesh

The selected area is overlaid with a rectangular warp mesh made up of perpendicular straight lines. The mesh provides a visual cue as an aid in the transformation of the image.

5 Begin Warping

Click and drag inside the warp area to begin warping the image. The warp mesh distorts as you warp, letting you know the degree and distance of your transformation. The corners of the mesh have handles you can drag to warp the sides. If you are unhappy with the results, press the **Esc** key or click the **Cancel Transform** button on the **Options** bar to leave the **Warp** mesh and then start over. When you're satisfied with the result, either press the **Enter** key in Windows or the **Return** on the Mac or click the **Commit Transform** button on the **Options** bar.

Drag

6 Examine the Results

Carefully examine your image for clues that might give away your transformation. Be particularly watchful for warped lines that must remain straight, such as architectural details. If your warped area is smaller than the original, you might have areas where the canvas shows through. If you're not happy with the results, select **Edit, Undo** or use the **History Palette** to remove the transformation and try again.

How-To Hints

Warp Styles

The same **Warp** styles (**Arch, Arc, Flag,** and so on) that were previously been available only for type (see Part 8, Task 5, "How to Warp Text") can now be applied to any image. Just select one of these styles from the drop-down menu on the **Options** bar after you've activated the warp mesh. You can then modify the style by dragging the mesh control handles or by entering percentage values directly into the **Set Bend, Set Horizontal Distortion,** and **Set Vertical Distortion** fields on the **Options** bar.

Warping Wisdom

As with any transformation, warping can degrade image quality. Therefore, it's better to warp all at once than to warp in several stages. If you're going to be doing additional transformations such as **Skew** or **Rotate,** you can switch from **Warp** to **Free Transform** and back using the **Switch** button on the **Options** bar. Any transformations you do before committing are calculated as a single transformation, limiting image degradation.

End

How to Silhouette an Image

Silhouetting (also called *knocking out*) an image refers to isolating part of an image against a white background, cutting it out from the rest of the frame. This task uses the **Extract** command to silhouette an image cleanly and easily. The **Extract** command asks you to define the edge of the object and then cuts it away from the background. Then you can smooth and modify the silhouette edges endlessly before you accept the final result.

Begin

1 Open the File

Open the desired image file. Then select **Filter, Extract** to open the **Extract** dialog box.

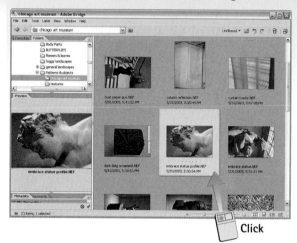

Click

2 Select the Edge Highlighter Tool

In the **Extract** dialog box, select the **Edge Highlighter** tool from the mini-toolbox on the left. In the **Tool Options** area, click the **Brush Size** drop-down arrow to set an appropriate brush size. (Use a smaller brush size to define sharper edges more accurately; use a larger brush to highlight wispy, intricate edges, such as hair or trees.) Then select highlight and fill colors from the pop-up menus, choosing colors that give a clear view of both the mask and the underlying image.

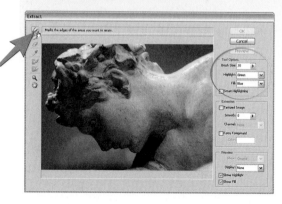

3 Define a Silhouette Edge

Leave the **Smooth** setting at 0 and drag along the edge between the object and the part of the image to be erased. Be sure that the line overlaps both the object and the background. Don't be concerned with other object areas that touch the edge of the image you're tracing around. Use the **Zoom** and **Hand** tools if necessary to do an accurate job.

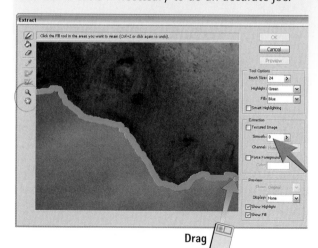

Drag

4 Fill the Object

Select the **Paint Bucket** tool and click within the outlined image area to fill the object. If the entire image area fills instead of just the area you selected, there is a break in your highlighted edge somewhere.

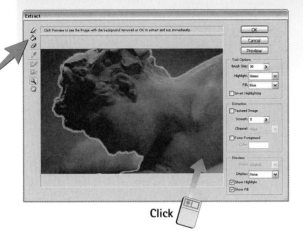

Click

5 Preview the Result

Click the **Preview** button to process a preview of the silhouette. Use the **Show** drop-down list to switch between previews of the **Original** and **Extracted** images.

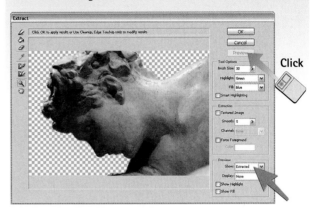

Click

6 Modify the Preview

If artifacts appear in the background, increase the **Smooth** slider and click the **Preview** button again. Use the **Cleanup** tool to completely erase background artifacts and the **Edge Touchup** tool to clean up the boundary edge. When the preview is accurate, click **OK** to extract the image. If necessary, you can then use the **Eraser** tools from the main toolbox to clean up any stray pixels and remaining artifacts, or you can use the **History Brush** to restore anything accidentally erased.

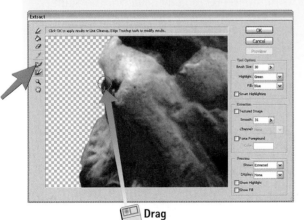

Drag

End

How-To Hints

Forcing the Foreground

If a single, flat color dominates the object, sample it with the **Eyedropper** tool from the **Extract** dialog box and enable the **Force Foreground** check box in the **Extraction** section of the **Extract** dialog box. This action selects all pixels matching the selected foreground color.

Other Methods

Although the **Background Eraser** and **Magic Eraser** tools do similar things as the **Extract** command (see Part 7, Task 3, "How to Erase a Background"), the **Extract** command is especially suited for problem areas, such as smoke and fine-hair details.

How to Use the Healing Brush

The **Healing Brush** is built on the concept and functionality of the **Clone Stamp** tool: It paints using sampled data from a user-specified point. Instead of just moving the pixel information from one spot to the other as the **Clone Stamp** tool does, however, the **Healing Brush** actually blends the two data sets together, blurring information and smoothing the results. The **Healing Brush** does a great job of eliminating spots and scratches from scanned photographs, and it's also superb at touching up blemishes and wrinkles on faces. If you work with portraiture or photo restoration, you'll use this tool a lot.

Begin

1 Open the Image

Open the image you want to touch up using the **Healing Brush**.

2 Select the Healing Brush Tool

Select the **Healing Brush** tool from the toolbox. You'll find it grouped with the **Spot Healing Brush**, **Patch** , and **Red Eye** tools.

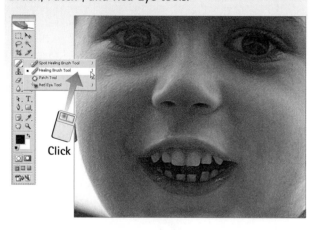

Click

3 Set the Tool Parameters

In the **Options** bar for the **Healing Brush**, set the brush size and blending mode. A hard brush (100% **Hardness**) is recommended. For the **Source**, select either **Sampled** or a preset **Pattern**. If you want the source point to move as you move the mouse pointer, enable the **Aligned** check box. If you're editing a multilayer file, enable the **Sample All Layers** check box so you can sample the composite image.

4 Set the Sample Point

Hold down the **Alt** key (Windows users) or **Option** key (Mac users) and click to set the source point for the brush. If your goal is to smooth a blemish or scratch, select a source point that resembles the area you want to repair.

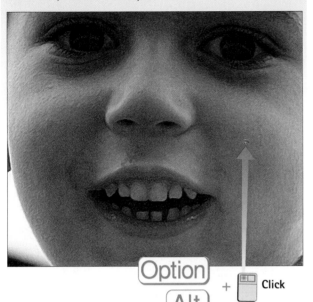

Option
Alt + Click

5 Paint the Corrections

Position the cursor over the area to be repaired and click to paint the corrections. Photoshop briefly displays the sampled information before blending it with the target image. Here, I've eliminated a slight blemish on the boy's lip by sampling a spot an inch or so away from the blemish.

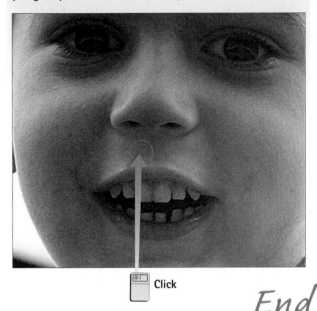

Click

End

How-To Hints

The New Spot Healing Brush

For single spots such as dust specks and skin blemishes, you might find Photoshop CS2's new **Spot Healing Brush** quicker to use. Simply select it from the toolbox, pick a brush size only slightly larger than the blemish, and click once. That's it! Photoshop automatically looks around to find a good sample to use for the healing.

Using the Blending Modes

Remember to use the blending modes to your advantage whenever necessary. For example, if you're trying to clean up darker blotches on an otherwise solid background, use the **Lighten** blending mode and sample the same color and values as the background. These options will correct the dark spots without altering the background.

Healing Brush Versus Clone Stamp

Although the **Clone Stamp** tool is useful for many applications, it occasionally leaves traces of its application, especially when it's used by novices. The **Healing Brush** automatically blends the sample data with the source area, creating an edit that is more easily concealed.

Task

PART 7

Drawing and Painting with Color

Considering that Photoshop is often called a "paint" program, it's surprising how seldom the paint tools are used. Typical users resize images, color correct, or apply a filter, but few people focus on the drawing or painting functions of the program.

Handled properly, the drawing and painting tools can yield predictable and acceptable results—even if your drawing skills are limited. Touching up images, spotting photographs, and erasing an area of a photo all involve the drawing and painting techniques described in the tasks in this part.

The underlying skill for almost all these tasks is the ability to effectively use a brush to apply the effects. When using a brush, the basic rule of thumb is to move from big and light strokes to small and heavy strokes. This means you should start with the largest possible feathered brush set and move toward the lightest possible setting. As you build up the effect, reduce the size of the brush to concentrate the results and slightly increase the pressure by increasing the **Opacity** slider. The one instance when this rule does not hold true is when you are doing line drawings and want to put down a clean brushstroke.

The tasks in this part also look at filling areas with color or gradients. Although filling is certainly not the same as brushing in an effect, it does create a graphic effect that many people associate with digital drawing. ●

TASK 1

How to Paint an Image

Painting an image in Photoshop involves selecting a brush and applying an effect to an image. This task outlines the basic procedure for working with any of Photoshop's painting tools, regardless of the effect you are applying or the kind of file to which you're applying it. Photoshop makes available the **Airbrush, Brush, Rubber Stamp, History/Art History Brush, Eraser, Pencil/Line**, and **Sharpen/Blur** painting tools and the **Dodge/Burn/Sponge** tools.

1 Select the Brush Tool

Open an image file, and then click the **Brush** tool in the Photoshop toolbox.

Click

2 Select a Blending Mode

With the **Brush** tool selected, select a blending mode from the **Mode** menu in the **Options** bar.

Click

3 Set the Opacity

The **Opacity** and **Flow** sliders control the density of the brushstrokes applied by the brush. **Opacity** determines the maximum density that will be applied, whereas **Flow** controls how many passes are needed to reach the maximum density. Click and drag the sliders to a lower setting for more transparent effects; leave them at **100%** to paint with a completely opaque stroke.

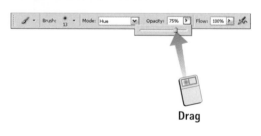

Drag

4 Select a Brush

Click the small arrow next to the **Brush** icon in the **Options** bar to open the **Brush** palette. Move the **Master Diameter** and **Hardness** sliders to fine-tune the brush size and softness, or select a pre-set from the list. To avoid painting the image when you click, click in an empty space in the **Options** bar to close the **Brush** palette. Alternatively, pressing the **Enter** key (**Return** for Mac) also closes the **Brush** palette.

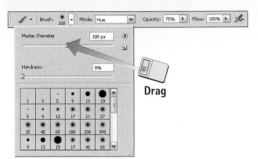

Drag

5 Paint the Image

To apply the paint effect, move the mouse pointer into the image window and click and drag.

Drag

End

How-To Hints

Manage Your Brushes

Remember that you can control the display of thumbnails in the **Brush** palette, load saved brush sets, and save custom brushes as presets. To change the thumbnail display options, click and hold the **Brush** palette menu and select text, thumbnail, or list display options. To save a brush for future use, click the **New Preset** icon located just under the **Brush** palette menu.

Setting Brush Size Preferences

You can set the **Brush** cursor so it appears as the currently selected brush size rather than as a tool icon or a set of crosshairs. This way, you know exactly how large the brush is (its circle icon shows you) in relation to the resolution of the image; you therefore have a better sense of where you will paint the effect. Select **Edit**, **Preferences, Displays & Cursors** and click the **Normal Brush Tip** button in the **Painting Cursors** section of the dialog box.

Photoshop CS2 offers some new **Painting Cursors** options in the **Preferences** dialog box: Use the **Full Size Brush Tip** to add any feathering radius to the diameter of the cursor; you can indicate the degree of softness by thickening the cursor outline. Enable the **Show Crosshair in Brush Tip** option to add a crosshair in the center of the cursor.

How to Erase an Image

Erasing an image is the opposite of painting in the sense that it removes the current pixel values in the image window, based on the brush strokes. When you erase, consider which **Eraser** tool you should use and what you want to erase. The **Eraser Options** bar offers three **Eraser** tool options: **Brush, Block,** and **Pencil.** The **Brush** eraser lets you erase using a brush preset, as described in Part 2, Task 3, "How to Create Custom Tool Presets." The **Block** eraser offers a flat, geometric effect that's perfect for hard-edged erasures, and the **Pencil** eraser lets you erase using hard-edge brush strokes only.

Begin

1 Select the Erase Tool

With the image you want to modify open onscreen, click the **Eraser** tool in the toolbox and drag to select the desired tool. Select the **Eraser, Background Eraser,** or **Magic Eraser** tool.

Click

2 Select an Eraser Type

From the **Mode** menu in the **Options** bar, select the desired eraser type. Your options are **Brush, Pencil,** and **Block.**

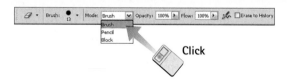

Click

3 Set the Pressure If Necessary

For all brush types except **Block,** click and drag the **Opacity** slider to set the desired opacity of the erasure effect. A low value creates transparency; a high value erases the image more completely. If you want to soften an image rather than erase it, set a low value and brush over it several times.

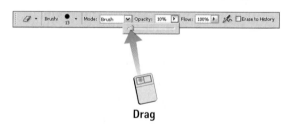

Drag

4 Select a Brush Size

For all eraser types except **Block**, select the desired brush size from the menu in the **Options** bar. Select a preset or drag the **Master Diameter** slider to set the brush size. When using the **Block** eraser, select the **Magnify** tool and click to zoom in; this action creates the desired brush size relative to the image. To zoom out, Windows users can press the **Alt** key (Mac users can press the **Option** key) and click again.

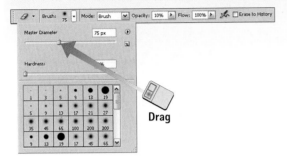

Drag

5 Erase the Image

Move the cursor into the image window and click and drag to erase the image. If you're using the **Block** eraser, you can click once to erase a clean square corresponding to the **Block** eraser size.

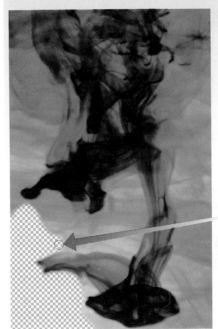

Drag

End

How-To Hints

Zooming for the Block Eraser

Although you cannot select smaller brush sizes for the **Block** eraser, you can click the **Magnify** tool in the toolbox and zoom in to erase tight areas.

Erasing to History

Enable the **Erase to History** check box in the **Eraser Options** bar to erase the image back to the **History** palette state, as specified by the **History Brush** selection setting. See Task 4, "How to Use the History Brush," for more information on using the **History Brush**.

How to Erase a Background

Photoshop offers two ways to erase a background: the **Background Eraser** and the **Magic Eraser**. This task looks at how to use both tools, highlighting the differences between them. The **Background Eraser** erases an image area selectively, based on a pixel's value. It remembers the first pixel value you click and then erases only that value, ignoring other values. This initial value is referred to as a *sample point* because the value of the pixel is used as a sample to determine how the eraser interacts with the image. You use the **Tolerance** slider to determine whether the brush erases the exact value sampled or a range of values based on the sample.

Begin

1 Select Background Eraser

With the image you want to modify open onscreen, select the **Background Eraser** from the toolbox. If necessary, click and hold the active **Eraser** tool and drag to select the **Background Eraser** from the pop-out menu that appears.

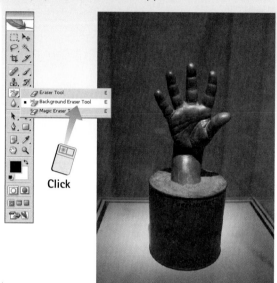

Click

2 Protect Foreground Color

You can protect a specified image color from being erased, making it easier to delete the background. To do this, select the **Eyedropper** tool and sample the color you want to "protect." With the desired color as the current foreground color, enable the **Protect Foreground Color** check box in the **Options** bar.

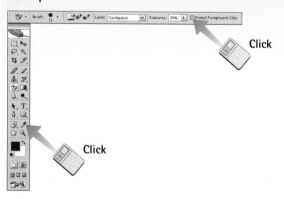

Click

Click

3 Specify Eraser Options

From the **Limits** menu in the **Options** bar, select the **Find Edges** option. This option erases adjacent pixels while maintaining strong edges—the perfect choice for eliminating the area behind the hand sculpture. The **Contiguous** and **Discontiguous** options do not keep as crisp an edge as **Find Edges**, and they do not work as well for this image.

Click

4 Estimate the Tolerance Setting

Always start with a low **Tolerance** value and increase as you erase to keep a crisp edge to the image. The higher the **Tolerance** setting, the more the tool erases. If there is high contrast between the background and object, set the **Tolerance** slider to a higher setting. The result will be a fast and clean erasure with a crisp edge. If the background and object are similar in contrast, use a low **Tolerance** setting and erase the area several times, perhaps using a smaller brush. Each image is unique, so you'll have to experiment to find the right settings. To set the tolerance, drag the **Tolerance** slider in the **Options** bar.

Drag

5 Set the Sampling Option

The **Sampling** icons offer the choices of **Continuous**, **Once**, and **Background Swatch**. Click the **Once** icon to sample only the pixels read when you first click the eraser on the image. As you continue to drag the eraser, only the initial pixel value is erased. Click the **Continuous** icon to sample continuously, allowing you to erase adjacent background areas of different colors. You can cover a wider range of pixels, although you run the risk of erasing the image edge. Click the **Background Swatch** icon to erase only the active color in the background swatch in the toolbox. With this option, you can select a background color and the eraser erases only that specific color.

Continuous   Once   Background
                            Swatch

6 Erase the Background

Move the cursor into the image window and click and drag to erase the background. The exact erasure result depends on the sampling option you chose in step 5.

Drag

Continues

At this point, let's start over with the same image and use the **Magic Eraser** instead of the **Background Eraser** to get the job done. The **Magic Eraser** eliminates broad areas of the background with a single mouse click, in much the same way that the **Magic Wand** tool selects broad areas. When you click in the image, the **Magic Eraser** measures the pixel value you clicked and erases all adjoining pixels as well. For example, if you have a large, flat area of solid color, a single click erases the entire area.

In these next steps, you use the **Tolerance** setting in the **Options** bar to specify how wide or narrow your erasure range will be. Increase the **Tolerance** setting to erase the full area in spite of slight variations in pixel values. Decrease the **Tolerance** setting to erase a narrower range of pixel values. It helps to examine the image carefully and click the "best" spot to select the color you want to erase.

7 Select the Magic Eraser

Select the **Magic Eraser** from the tool-box. If necessary, click and hold the active **Eraser** tool and select the **Magic Eraser** from the pop-out menu that appears.

Click

8 Enable the Anti-Alias Option

In the **Options** bar, enable the **Anti-alias** check box to create a smooth erasure edge. Enable the **Sample All Layers** check box to erase across all visible layers. Enable the **Contiguous** check box to erase all adjoining pixels; leave the **Contiguous** option disabled if you want to erase the pixel value wherever it appears in the image.

9 Erase the Image

Click in the image window to erase a range of pixels. If you don't like the result, select **Edit**, **Undo**; revise the **Tolerance** setting; and try again. Continue clicking to delete the desired area.

Click

End

Switching Tools

To switch quickly among the **Eraser**, **Magic Eraser**, and **Background Eraser** tools, press **Shift+E**.

Adjusting Tolerance Often

Keep an eye on the areas you are erasing and adjust the **Tolerance** setting up or down to optimize the amount of background being erased. Using a low **Tolerance** setting might require you to sample often, erasing the background a chunk at a time. This might be necessary to keep a clean line of separation between the subject and background.

Protecting the Foreground Color

When using the **Background Eraser**, select the **Eyedropper** tool from the toolbox and sample the color in an image, making that color the active foreground color. Then enable the **Protect Foreground Color** check box in the **Options** bar for the **Background Eraser**. Now, when you use the **Background Eraser** on the image, the tool won't delete pixels of the selected foreground color. Also remember to adjust the **Tolerance** slider to get the exact edge effect you want.

How to Use the History Brush

The **History Brush** enables you to selectively paint an iteration of an image from a previous state, as displayed in the **History** palette. Recall that, as you work on an image, previous image states are recorded in the **History** palette. The **History Brush** lets you access these previous states as a source file, brushing them back into an image. The **History** palette stores only a limited number of states as specified in the **General Preferences** box (select **Edit, Preferences, General**). As you add states to the palette, you can convert a state to a snapshot to preserve that state. The basic rules of working with the **History** palette were outlined in Part 2, Task 2, "How to Undo with the History Palette."

Begin

1 Select the History Brush Tool

With the image file you want to modify open onscreen, select the **History Brush** tool from the toolbox. Note that all history states are erased when a file is closed; for this task, be sure you are working with a file that has been modified from its original state since it was opened.

Click

2 Set the Opacity

In the **Options** bar, set the **Opacity** slider to determine the transparency or opacity of the brushstroke. For example, set the **Opacity** slider to **100** to add the history state as a solid area. Lower the value on the **Opacity** slider to make the brush stroke more transparent.

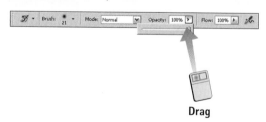

Drag

3 Select a Brush

Select a brush size and a feathered effect from the **Brush** menu in the **Options** bar.

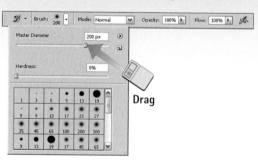

Drag

4 Set the Source

Select **Window, History** to open the History palette. Compare the various available history states and snapshots, and click the left column to place the source icon (a paintbrush) next to the state or snapshot you want to use as a source.

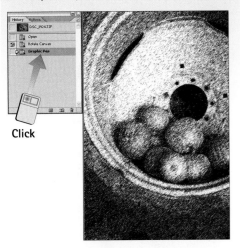

Click

5 Paint the Image

Move the mouse pointer into the image window and click and drag to paint in the source image as it exists in the state you selected from the **History** palette in step 4.

Drag

6 Look at the Results

In this example, the image was modified with a filter; the original image was used as the source to paint back the unfiltered pumpkins. The before and after images are shown here side by side so you can see the differences.

Final version showing original history state painted onto pumpkins

Original version used as history source

End

How-To Hints

Painting in Corrections

The **History Brush** is a great tool for brushing color corrections into an image. Apply any of Photoshop's color-correction commands and then select the previous state from the **History** palette, undoing the effect. While still in the **History** palette, click in the left column next to one of the color-correction commands to set the **History Brush** source icon, as described in step 4 (even though the tile is grayed out, you still can set the icon). Select the **History Brush** and brush the correction into the exact areas you want within the image.

As a wild alternative, you can paint a history state back in with the **Art History** brush. Located in the **History Brush** pop-out menu, this tool paints with expressive brush-stroke patterns that echo the initial history state. With the **Art History** brush selected, modify the **Style, Opacity, Area,** and **Tolerance** options to create a wide range of effects.

How to Use the Clone Stamp

The **Clone Stamp** tool "clones" one area of an image, enabling you to paint it into another area. It can be useful for filling in an open area with a pattern or a color or for duplicating or repeating an object. The basic process for using the **Clone Stamp** tool requires you to set a *source point* (the point from which the pixel values come) in the image and then to paint that value into another area of the image.

Begin

1 Select the Clone Stamp Tool

Open the image file you want to modify and select the **Clone Stamp** tool from the toolbox.

Click

2 Set the Opacity

In the **Options** bar for the **Clone Stamp** tool, click and drag the **Opacity** slider to set the transparency of the effect. For example, if you want to select a part of the image and apply it to another area on the image at the same intensity as the original, set the **Opacity** slider to **100**. Set the slider to **50** if you want the copied area to appear more transparent (lighter) than the original area.

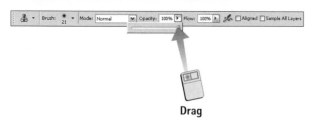

Drag

3 Set the Aligned Option

Enable the **Aligned** check box if you want the reference point to move when you move the brush. For example, if you place the reference point to the left and down 50 pixels from the current brush position, the reference point will always be to the left and down 50 pixels as you paint with the brush. Leave this option disabled if you want the reference point to sample the same area every time you click the brush (the size of the area depends on the brush size you select).

Click

4 Select a Brush

Select a brush size and feather that are appropriate for the image. For the pine cone image, I am cloning a foreground object. A large-size brush with a slightly feathered edge will work to minimize brush strokes while blending with the background. (For the string, I'll use a smaller brush.) Modify the **Flow** slider if you want to start with a lower opacity and be able to build more opacity on top of the initial strokes.

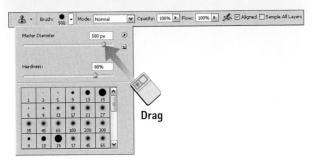

Drag

5 Set the Reference Point

Move the brush into the image window and position it at the desired reference point. Press and hold the **Alt** key (Windows users) or the **Option** key (Mac users) and click to set the reference point. The reference point is the starting point for the area you will clone.

Alt   Option

+

Click

6 Stamp the Image

With the reference point set, click and drag in a new location (away from the original area) in the image. Notice that a crosshair (the reference point) effectively paints a copy of the original area in the new location. If the **Aligned** check box was not enabled, the specific area you referenced in step 5 is the starting point, regardless of where you click.

End

How-To Hints

Sampling All Layers

Enable the **Sample All Layers** check box on the **Options** bar for the **Clone Stamp** tool if you want the tool to sample all the layers as it paints. This is a good way to selectively consolidate material from multiple layers into one layer.

Pattern Stamping

You can paint a predefined pattern into an image with the **Pattern Stamp** tool, located in the **Clone Stamp** pop-out menu. With the **Pattern Stamp** tool selected, select a pattern from the **Pattern** palette in the **Options** bar, select a brush size and other paint options, and paint the pattern into the image.

TASK 6

How to Draw Graphic Shapes

When you are editing images, you might want to draw a flat geometric shape, such as a box or circle. Whether you want to create a screened area to add text, build a web interface, or create an image composite, graphic shapes play a central role in the process. Adobe has made this function even more useful in Photoshop CS2 because you can now draw and edit graphics in the image as you would with any other vector objects.

Begin

1 Open File

Select **File**, **Open** and select the file you want to modify with a graphic shape.

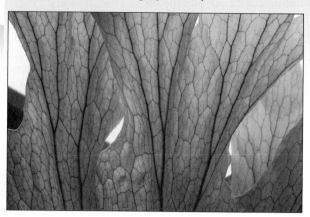

2 Select Shape Color

Click the **Foreground** color swatch in the toolbox to open the **Color Picker**. Select the color you want for the shape you will draw and click **OK**.

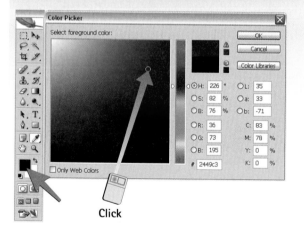

Click

3 Select the Shape Tool

Select the desired shape tool from the toolbox. Click and hold the graphic shape button to see a menu of all the shape options: **Rectangle**, **Rounded Rectangle**, **Ellipse**, **Polygon**, **Line**, and **Custom Shape**. When you drag the selected shape, remember that the **Shift** key constrains rectangles and ellipses into squares and circles.

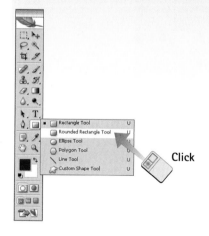

Click

160 PART 7: DRAWING AND PAINTING WITH COLOR

4 Set the Shape Type

In the **Options** bar for the selected shape tool, select the method for drawing the shape. Select the **Fill Pixels** icon to create a flat-filled region on the current active layer. The **Shape Layers** icon creates a separate shape layer with a clipping path. The **Path** icon creates an unfilled work path (on the **Path** palette).

Shape Layers   Paths   Fill Pixels

5 Draw the Shape

Click and drag in the image to draw the desired shape. Remember to use the **Opacity** slider and blending modes in the **Options** bar if necessary. If you selected the **Shape Layers** option in step 4, a new layer appears in the **Layers** palette. If you selected the **Paths** option, an active path appears onscreen.

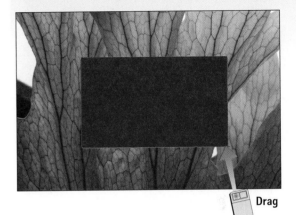

Drag

6 Edit the Shape

If you started with the **Paths** or **Shape Layers** option in step 4, you can edit the shape you've drawn; after you draw the first shape, the edit options are activated and enable you to add to shape areas, subtract from shape areas, intersect shape areas, or exclude overlapping shape areas from the first path drawn. Drag subsequent shapes using these options.

Edit Options

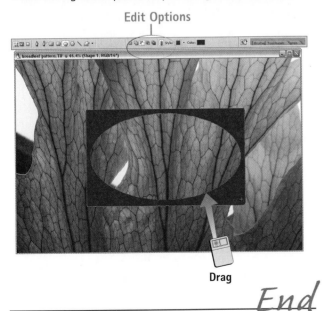

Drag

End

How-To Hints

Setting Shape Options

Each shape tool includes a menu of shape options for specifying how the shapes are drawn. Click the arrow at the end of the second group of icons (after the rounded star icon) in the **Options** bar to open the **Geometry Options** menu; select from parameters such as rounded corners and fixed shape sizes.

Using the Custom Shape Tool

The **Custom Shape** tool allows you to draw unique shapes as selected from a predefined shapes palette. To create a custom shape, create a shape using the path or shape tools. Select **Edit, Define Custom Shape** and enter a name for the shape. It now appears in the list of shapes in the **Options** bar. Be sure to select **Fixed Size** in the Geometry Options menu of the **Options** bar to draw the shape with its original proportions (or hold down the **Shift** key when drawing the object to constrain the original proportions).

How to Build a Custom Brush

Photoshop provides the capability to create custom brushes that feature advanced texture and color control, random stroke variation, pressure sensitivity controls, and much more. These options are controlled through the Brushes palette. In the Brushes palette, brush presets are displayed on the right, above the Master Diameter slider. The full list of settings options appears on the left.

Begin

1 Create a New Scratchpad File

Select **File, New** to create a new file. Set the background to white and set the file-creation parameters as desired in the dialog box that appears. You will use this file to test the results as you build your custom brush.

2 Open the Brushes Palette

By default, Photoshop places the **Brushes** palette in the palette well. Click the **Brushes** tab to open the palette, or select **Window, Brushes**.

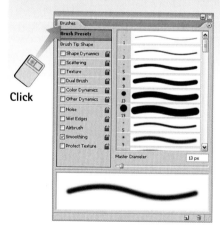

Click

3 Set the Brush Shape

Select the **Brush Tip Shape** option in the left column to load the brush shape options. Adjust the **Diameter** slider to specify the overall brush size in pixels. Specify the **Angle, Roundness,** and **Hardness** settings as desired, evaluating the results in the preview field at the bottom of the palette. You can also set the brush angle and roundness by dragging components of the crosshairs icon. Click and drag the black dots to set the roundness; click and drag the arrowhead to set the angle. Paint in the sample file to fine-tune your results.

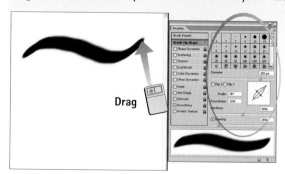

Drag

4 Set Shape Dynamics

Back in the **Brushes** palette, select **Shape Dynamics** from the list on the left to load the shape dynamics options. Shape dynamics provide control over variations within brush strokes, which are referred to as *jitter*. You can set the **Size**, **Angle**, and **Roundness** variations using the associated sliders. The **Control** menu below each slider allows you to set the method for controlling the variation, such as a tablet or stroke fade. You can also specify the brush's minimum diameter and roundness percentage. Paint in the sample file to fine-tune your results.

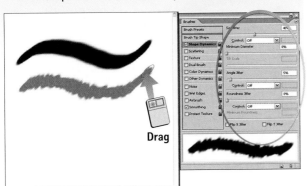

Drag

5 Set Scatter

Select the **Scattering** option in the **Brushes** palette to load the scatter options. *Scatter* refers to the way the brush stroke spreads out from the line drawn by the mouse or pen. By default, the main **Scatter** slider sets a vertical percentage variation; enable the **Both Axis** check box to set both vertical and horizontal variation. The **Count** slider controls the density or flow of the marks, and the **Count Jitter** slider controls variations within the flow. Use the **Control** menus below the sliders to set the controlling method. Paint in the sample file to fine-tune your results.

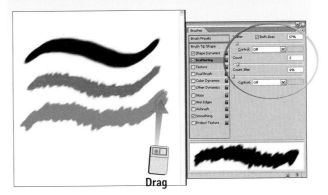

Drag

6 Set Texture Capabilities

Select the **Texture** option in the **Brushes** palette to load the texture options. Click the swatch to select a texture from the **Pattern Picker** that opens. You can also set the size, blending mode, depth, and depth variation. Paint in the sample file to fine-tune your results.

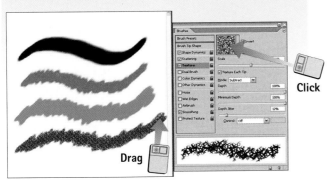

Drag

Click

Continues

7 Set Dual Brush Capabilities

Select the **Dual Brush** option in the **Brushes** palette to create a brush with multiple brush tips in the same stroke. First, set the mode and brush shape for the second brush tip using the **Blend Mode** menu and the **Shapes Preset** palette. Then modify the diameter, spacing, scatter, and count to complete the effect. Remember that these settings affect only the second brush tip shape. Photoshop combines these options with the current settings for the first brush. Paint in the sample file to fine-tune your results.

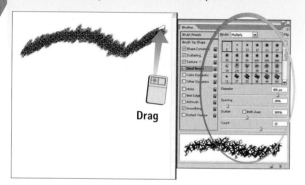

Drag

8 Set Color Dynamics

Select the **Color Dynamics** option in the **Brushes** palette to control color variation within the brush stroke. These settings enable you to blend the foreground and background colors within the stroke and to set variation in hue, saturation, brightness, and color purity. Paint in the sample file to fine-tune your results.

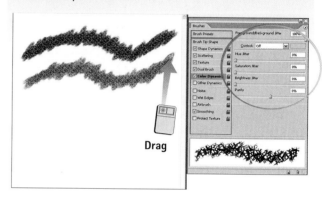

Drag

9 Set Other Dynamics

Select the **Other Dynamics** option in the **Brushes** palette to control the opacity and flow of the brush stroke. Adjust the sliders as needed and paint in the sample file to fine-tune your results.

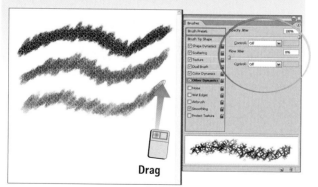

Drag

10 Set Paint Characteristics

The paint characteristics check boxes at the bottom of the list of options on the left side of the **Brushes** palette allow you to enable or disable the **Noise, Wet Edges, Airbrush, Smoothing,** and **Protect Texture** features. These options control the smoothness and texture of the brush stroke; they function predictably based on their descriptions. Experiment with combinations of these options until you get the effect you're looking for.

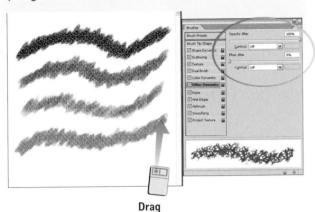

Drag

11 Use the Brush

Close the **Brushes** palette and use the customized brush in your work. If you want to save the custom brush for later use, you can save the custom brush as a tool preset (refer to Part 2, Task 3, "How to Create Custom Tool Presets").

Drag

End

How-To Hints

Setting Up for Pressure-Sensitive Drawing Tablets

Remember to set the associated **Control** menus to **Pen Pressure, Tilt,** or **Thumbwheel** if you're using an input device that supports these features.

Using Custom Brushes with Tool Presets

Remember to save specific settings as a brush preset (refer to Part 2, Task 3, "How to Create Custom Tool Presets"). Also, keep in mind that certain brush settings and options can vary depending on the currently selected paint tool.

How to Use the Pattern Maker

The **Pattern Maker** generates random patterns that can be applied to an image or saved as a preset. This tool goes beyond simply allowing you to save patterns; it assists you in creating custom tiles that can be used to develop amazing abstract patterns and backgrounds.

Begin

1 Open the Image

You can use any image to generate patterns. Select **File, Open** to launch the desired file. To explain how the **Pattern Maker** works, I will use an image with a single text character.

2 Set the Sample Area

Select **Filter, Pattern Maker** to launch the **Pattern Maker** window. Select the **Rectangular Marquee** tool in the upper-left corner of the window and drag to draw a sample area to be used as a starting point for pattern generation.

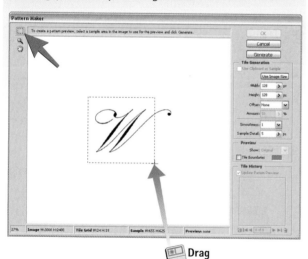

Drag

3 Generate the First Variation

Click the **Generate** button to create the first pattern design. **Pattern Maker** automatically fills the screen with a random design generated from the sampled area. Click **Generate Again** to create additional variations of the pattern.

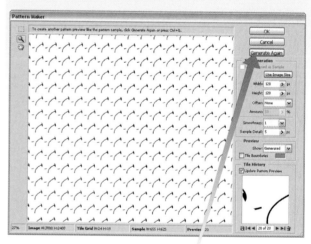

Click

4 Modify Tile Size and Offset

In the **Tile Generation** section of the **Pattern Maker** window, enter alternative values in the **Width** and **Height** fields to change the tile proportions in the pattern. To offset the tile alignment, use the **Offset** drop-down menu. Select a vertical or horizontal offset and enter an offset percentage in the **Amount** field. Click **Generate Again** to create a new pattern.

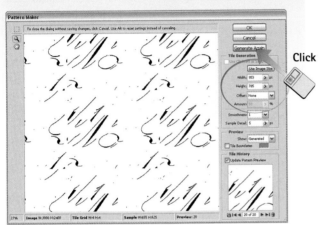

Click

5 Set Smoothness

To modify the smoothness of the rendering, set the **Smoothness** drop-down menu to **1**, **2**, or **3**. To control how much detail is present in the pattern, set a pixel value in the **Sample Detail** field. Click **Generate Again** to create another pattern that reflects these changes.

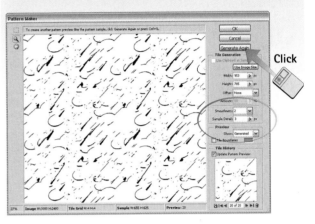

Click

6 Apply or Save Pattern

Click **OK** to apply the pattern to the current image. You can also click the **Save Preset Pattern** icon at the bottom of the **Tile History** section to save the tile as a pattern preset.

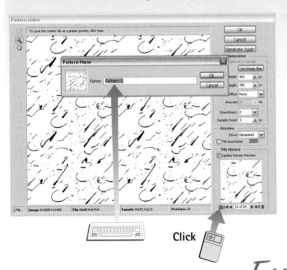

Click

End

How-To Hints

Using the Clipboard As a Sample

You can use any image data saved to the Clipboard as a source for a pattern. To do this, copy any image content and enable the **Use Clipboard As Sample** check box in the **Tile Generation** section of the **Pattern Maker** window. Click **Generate** to view the results.

Previews and Navigation

The last 20 tiles generated in a given session are saved in the **Tile History** section for review and evaluation. Use the forward and back arrows to browse the various iterations of the pattern, which you can save or apply to the image.

How to Apply Gradients

A *gradient* is a fill that gradually blends two or more colors together. These color blends can be applied in circular-shaped, diamond-shaped, and cone-shaped gradients, as well as standard linear and bar shapes. When you apply a gradient, it expands to fill the entire selected area. Gradients are useful as background fills behind an object and in layer masks to fade out an image (see Part 10, Task 8, "How to Add a Layer Mask," for details).

Begin

1 Select the Fill Area

Open the image file with which you want to work. If necessary, select the area to be filled with the gradient. If no area is selected, Photoshop fills the entire image with the gradient effect.

2 Select Gradient Type

Select the **Gradient** tool from the toolbox. If it is not visible, click and hold the **Paint Bucket** tool and select the **Gradient** tool from the pop-out menu. In the **Options** bar, select the **Linear, Radial, Angle, Reflected,** or **Diamond Gradient** tool.

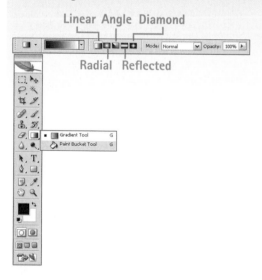

3 Set Foreground/Background Colors

The colors in the gradient are applied using the foreground and background colors specified in this step. In the toolbox, click the **Foreground** and **Background** color swatches and select the desired gradient colors from the **Color Picker** that appears.

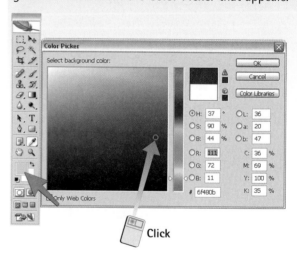

Click

4 Set the Gradient Colors

In the **Options** bar, click the gradient swatch (the first icon) to open the **Gradient Editor** dialog box. Click to select the first swatch in the palette. The gradient sample displayed changes to reflect the colors you selected in step 3. Click **OK** to close the dialog box.

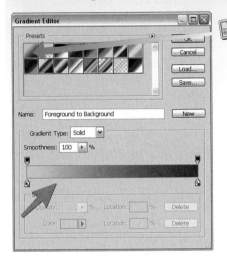

Click

5 Set Options

In the **Options** bar for the **Gradient** tool, set the **Opacity** slider as desired, choosing a setting of less than **100** to create a transparent gradient. If you want, you can also select a different gradient type by clicking one of the icons in the bar. Leave the **Transparency** check box disabled and enable the **Dither** check box if you want to reduce banding in the gradient. Finally, enable the **Reverse** check box if you want to switch the colors in the gradient.

Click

6 Apply the Effect

Position the mouse pointer in the image where you want the gradient to start. Click and drag, releasing the mouse to apply the effect. Remember that the gradient will cover the entire image; the point at which you release the mouse determines the end of the gradient transition from the foreground color to the background color you selected.

Drag

End

How-To Hints

Applying Gradients in Their Own Layers

For full flexibility, apply gradients in their own layers. Doing so allows you to go back and adjust transparency, blending modes, and positioning as needed. You can also use layer masks to control the visibility of the gradient.

Tweaking a Gradient

If you are not satisfied with the angle or tone break, drag again to reapply the gradient, overwriting the previous attempt. This works only if the **Mode** option in the **Options** bar is set to **Normal** *and* if the **Opacity** slider is set to **100**.

How to Create Custom Gradients

Building a custom gradient in Photoshop involves defining the number of colors in the gradient and specifying how those colors fade and transition. You can also build transparency into the gradient, which allows the layers below the current layer to show through. Gradients are similar to custom brushes in that you can customize them for each image. Photoshop lets you create and save custom gradients and add them to the preset list for easy access. After you create a gradient, you can use it with any of the gradient shapes selected from the **Options** bar.

Begin

1 Select a Gradient Tool

Select the **Gradient** tool from the toolbox. In the **Options** bar, click the gradient swatch to launch the **Gradient Editor** dialog box.

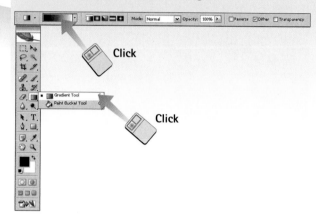

Click

Click

2 Select a Preset

From the palette at the top of the dialog box, select one of the existing gradient presets if you want to use it as a starting point. Starting with a preset is a good idea if you want to predefine many of the parameters (such as color choices and color stops).

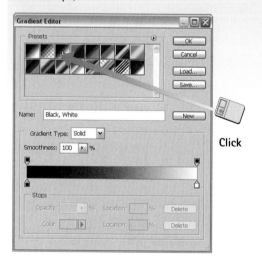

Click

3 Select the Starting Color

Double-click the left color stop in the gradient bar in the **Gradient Editor** dialog box to open the **Color Picker**. Select a color you want to use in the gradient you are creating and click **OK** to close the **Color Picker**. The new color appears on the left end of the gradient bar, and the gradient is updated.

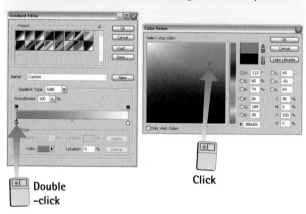

Double
-click

Click

4 Select the Ending Color

Double-click the right color stop in the gradient bar in the **Gradient Editor** dialog box to open the **Color Picker**. Select another color you want to use in the gradient you are creating and click **OK** to close the **Color Picker**. The new color appears at the right end of the gradient bar, and the gradient is updated.

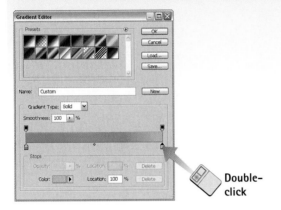

Double-click

5 Set the Break

The *break* in a gradient determines where a 50% mix of the two colors occurs. By default, the break is in the middle of the gradient, but you can adjust the placement by dragging the diamond that appears below the gradient bar. By adjusting the break point, you can designate a dominant color for the gradient.

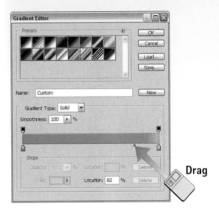

Drag

6 Add Additional Colors

Double-click in the color stop section below the gradient bar to add a third color stop. This action also opens the **Color Picker**. Select the third color you want to add to the gradient, click **OK** to close the **Color Picker**, and add the color to the gradient. Drag the new color stop as necessary to control the color placement in the gradient. Notice that a new diamond is placed between each color to control the breaks between colors.

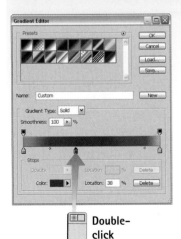

Double-click

7 Save the Gradient

Click **New** to save the gradient and add its swatch to the gradient palette. Click **OK** to close the **Gradient Editor**. If you want, you can click the **Save** button to save the gradient as a separate file to be loaded later. When you do this, a **Save As** dialog box opens for you to name the gradient file and specify where it goes.

End

How-To Hints

Using Transparency

You can build transparency into a gradient to allow lower layers to show through. Photoshop includes opacity stops along the top of the gradient bar. Select a stop and enter a value in the **Opacity** field. Move the stop to control how the transparency transitions through the effect.

Task

PART 8

Using Type

*T*here was a time when using text in Photoshop was a pretty bad idea. In the pre-version 2.5 days, there were no layers, History brushes, or multiple undos, so when you placed text on an image, it was there permanently. Kerning or leading was out of the question—and heaven forbid if you had a typo! Unless you were very brave or very stupid, text was the domain of illustration and layout programs.

This began to change when Adobe added layers with version 3. Then an enhanced text tool, vertical type, and kerning controls hit the scene. One of the biggest enhancements has been Photoshop's capability to keep text as an editable item at all times. When text was placed as a bitmap, if you misspelled the word, you were out of luck. With editable text, however, you just reopen the dialog box and make the correction.

The tasks in this part profile the primary features for working with type in Photoshop. As a general rule, you still should not set large amounts of type in Photoshop. Keep your use of text to headlines and a few paragraphs, and you'll find that Photoshop's text capabilities are a full-featured option that was well worth the wait. ●

How to Add Type to an Image

When you add text to an image in Photoshop, it is placed on a separate layer. It remains editable at all times—unless you intentionally convert the image to pixels for further editing (as you must if you want to apply filters that work only on raster layers) or integration. When text is added, a new layer is created. The text is the only element in the layer; all other areas are transparent. Photoshop can access all fonts in your system and makes them available through the **Type Tool** dialog box.

Begin

1 Select the Type Tool and Orientation

With the image you want to work with open, click the **Horizontal Type** or **Vertical Type** tool in the Photoshop toolbox.

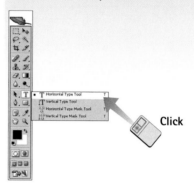

Click

2 Select the Font

From the **Font** menu in the **Options** bar, select a typeface. From the **Font Style** menu, select a typestyle (bold, oblique/italic, and so on). You can also select the font size, alignment, and antialiasing method.

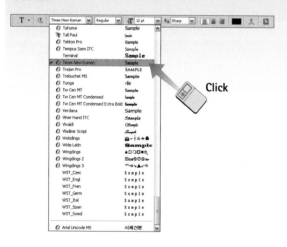

Click

3 Set Parameters

Click the **Palettes** button in the **Options** bar (next to the **Warp Text** icon) to launch the **Paragraph** and **Character** palettes. In the **Character** palette, set the *kerning* (the spacing between individual pairs of letters), *tracking* (the horizontal spacing between the text letters), *baseline shift* (whether the letters sit on an invisible baseline or "float" above or below it), *leading* (the vertical spacing between multiple lines of text), horizontal or vertical scale, and type color. You can also change the font from this palette. In the **Paragraph** palette, you can align the text to the left, center, or right (in relation to the entry point), and you can set justification parameters, paragraph indentation, and hyphenation.

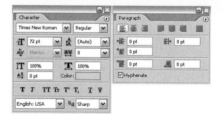

4 Set Antialiasing Method

Antialiasing determines how sharp or smooth text appears. In the **Options** bar, select the antialiasing method for the type. The sharpness of the image, the kind of background on which the text sits, and your overall intentions will determine this setting. Use your eye to judge type for the Web. For print, use the **Strong** or **Crisp** option, unless you want a softer effect.

Click

5 Place the Text Starting Point

Move the mouse pointer into the image area and click to set the text entry point and create a new type layer for the image.

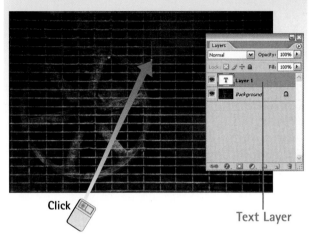

Click

Text Layer

6 Type Text

With the image as the active window, type the text you want to add. Highlight the text and use the **Options** bar and palettes to change any of the characteristics of the text. Select any other tool or click the check mark in the upper-right corner of the **Options** bar to commit the text.

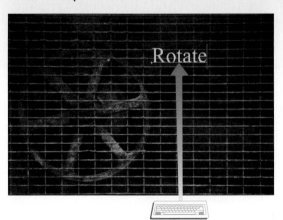

7 Edit the Type

The type is represented as a separate layer on the image, denoted as a type layer by the **T** icon in the **Layers** palette. Select **Window**, **Layers** (if the **Layers** palette is not already showing), and then click the type layer to make it active. Select the **Type** tool and highlight the text to make further changes. The layer name changes to reflect any changes.

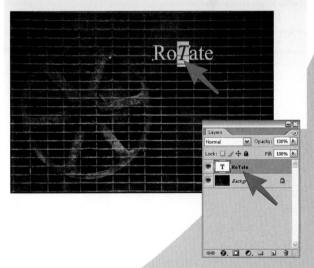

End

How to Create 3D Text

3D text refers to type that includes shading or modeling to create a three-dimensional effect on the page or image. These effects can include drop shadows, embossing, and other impressive options. This current task is specific to creating great-looking type.

1 Create the Text

Follow the instructions in Task 1 to create a text layer. When you have created the text layer, verify its existence by selecting **Window**, **Layers** to open the **Layers** palette.

2 Select Bevel and Emboss Effects

Select **Layer**, **Layer Style**, **Bevel and Emboss** to launch the **Layer Style** dialog box. Make sure that the **Preview** check box is enabled.

Click

3 Select the Bevel Style

From the **Style** menu in the **Structure** section of the dialog box, select the desired bevel style. Options are **Outer Bevel**, **Inner Bevel**, **Emboss**, **Pillow Emboss**, and **Stroke Emboss**. Because the **Preview** check box is enabled, you can select each option and see the results in the main image window.

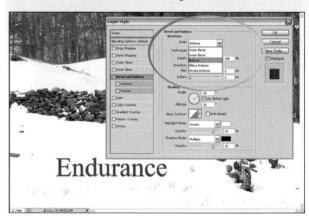

4 Set the Depth

The **Depth** slider determines the thickness of the bevel. The "proper" thickness depends on the font size selected and the overall resolution of the image. The **Size** and **Soften** sliders control the spread of the effect and its sharpness. Click and drag the sliders to increase or decrease these effects.

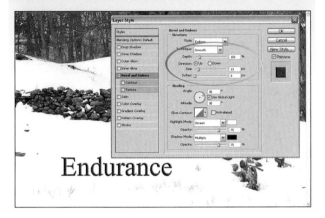

5 Set the Angle

The **Angle** option determines the angle at which the "light" falls on the text. The angle setting determines the shadows and highlights on the text. In the **Shading** section, click inside the **Angle** circle and drag to change the angle direction. You can also type a numeric angle value in the **Angle** text box.

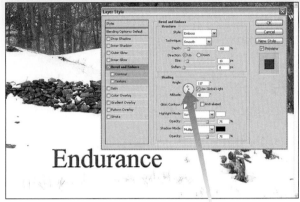

 Drag

6 Change Color for Highlights and Shadows

If necessary, you can change the color for the highlight and shadow. In the **Shading** section of the **Layer Style** dialog box, click the color swatch at the end of the **Highlight Mode** or **Shadow Mode** line to open the **Color Picker**, from which you can select a new color for the shadow or the highlight. Click **OK** to close the dialog box and apply the effects.

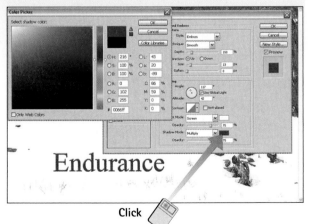

Click

End

How-To Hints

Setting the Modes for Text Shadow and Highlight

When you tweak the shadow and highlight colors in the **Layer Style** dialog box, you can also set the modes for these two elements. Select the **Highlight Mode** and **Shadow Mode** from the pop-up menus and set the relative opacity for each mode with the associated slider. Both these options act in much the same way as layer blending modes do—except they are confined to the actual highlight and shadow areas you're creating with the effect.

How to Create Typographic Style Sheets

The standard tool presets described in Part 2, Task 3, "How to Create Custom Tool Presets," are especially effective in creating text-based style sheets that help manage type treatments in image and web design. Style sheets provide full control over all type parameters, including font, font color, alignment, and spacing options. Now you can easily select a specific type tool for headlines and another for captions, body text, or any other format present in the project.

Begin

1 Select the Type Tool

Select either the **Horizontal Type** or **Vertical Type** tool from the toolbox.

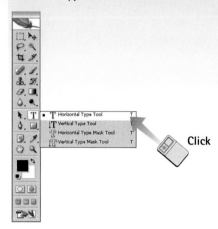

Click

2 Select the Font Parameters

Use the **Options** bar to set the basic font settings including type orientation, font, size, and sharpness.

Click

3 Set Line and Character Spacing

Select **Window**, **Character** to launch the **Character** palette. Set the leading, tracking, baseline shift, and vertical or horizontal shift as desired.

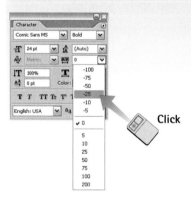

Click

4 Set Alignment

Select **Window, Paragraph** to open the **Paragraph** palette. Set the alignment, justification, and indent settings as desired.

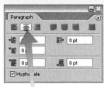

Click

5 Select a Font Color

If you want to include a text color in the preset, click the font color swatch in the **Options** bar or in the **Character** palette. When the **Color Picker** opens, select the desired color for the text and click **OK**.

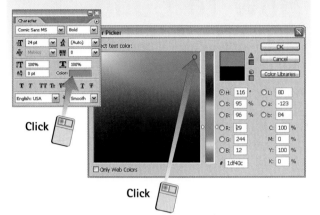

Click

Click

6 Save the Preset

Select **Window, Tool Presets** to open the **Tool Presets** palette. Select **New Tool Preset** from the palette menu, name the preset in the dialog box that appears, and click **OK** to save. Now you can access this text preset to load these precise text parameters whenever you need them.

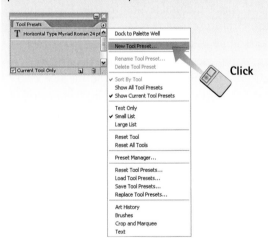

Click

How-To Hints

Don't Forget Warped Text

You can include warped text settings as part of a text preset. Select the **Warp Text** option as explained in Task 5, "How to Warp Text," before saving the text preset.

End

How to Build Filtered Text Effects

Instead of placing text as straightforward characters, you might want the text to appear as lightened or darkened areas of the image itself. You also can apply a textured effect to delineate the text characters. This task uses Photoshop filters to modify a text selection mask, creating an effect that integrates the text with the background image. In addition to filters, you can use color shifts, contrast changes, and texture effects when applying the filtering technique. Part 13, "Special Effects," introduces some of the techniques available.

Begin

1 Duplicate the Target Layer

Open the image file and determine the layer that will serve as the background for the effect. Select that layer in the **Layers** palette and select **Duplicate Layer** from the palette menu. After the **Duplicate Layer** dialog box opens, provide a name for the layer you are creating and click **OK**.

Click

2 Select the Horizontal Type Mask Tool

Select the **Horizontal Type Mask** tool from the Photoshop toolbox. In Photoshop, *masking* refers to a process of identifying a particular area for selecting or making specific modifications. In this case, we are selecting an area in the shape of the text letters.

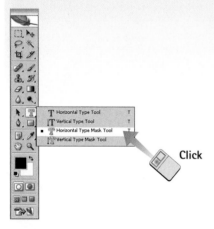

Click

3 Place the Text Starting Point

Move the mouse pointer into the image area and click to set the text entry point. A colored type mask appears as you click or as you type. The color mask represents the text character selection. The background might be masked and the text characters might be reversed out of the masking color, based on the current Photoshop Quick Mask configurations (more on that later).

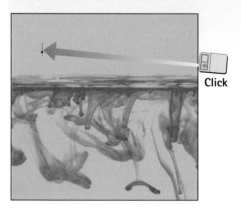

Click

4 Set Text Parameters

In the **Options** bar, set the font and font attributes for the text you want to add to the image. For filtered text effects, "fat" typefaces in fairly large point sizes (20 points or larger) work best.

Click

5 Enter Text

Type the text in the image. As you type, the text and mask appear. Click the check mark on the **Options** bar, or select any other tool to set the type and create the selection (the "text" appears in the image in a kind of marching-ants, marquee fashion). If the size of the text is wrong, click the **Type** tool anywhere in the image to deselect the text selection, change the text parameters, and retype the text. To reposition the text, choose any selection tool in the toolbox and drag the selection.

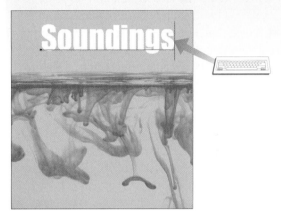

6 Apply a Filter

Click the **Move** tool to create the selection. From the **Filter** menu in the menu bar, select any of Photoshop's filters. This example uses the **Halftone Pattern** filter (**Filter, Sketch, Halftone Pattern**) with the **Size** set to **4**, **Contrast** set to **40**, and **Pattern Type** set to **Line**. Click **OK** to apply the effect.

How-To Hints

A Mask Is a Mask (Sort Of)

Although they share some of the same preference characteristics, **Quick Mask** and **Type Mask** are two different functions. For details on using **Quick Mask**, refer to Part 3, Task 4, "How to Use Quick Mask."

End

How to Warp Text

Warping text takes the idea of text on a path to a new level. This Photoshop feature enables you to distort the contents of an entire text layer, twisting, bloating, or stretching it into a wide range of effects. You have 15 warping effects from which to select, and all allow bending as well as horizontal and vertical distortion.

Begin

1 Create the Text

Follow the instructions in Task 1 to create a text layer. You can warp any type of text, including vertical and horizontal type and type masks.

Oceans of Fun

2 Select Warp Text

In the **Options** bar for the **Text** tool, click the **Warp Text** button. The **Warp Text** dialog box opens.

Click

3 Select Warp Text Style

From the **Style** menu in the **Warp Text** dialog box, select the desired warp variation. In addition, enable the **Horizontal** or **Vertical** radio button to determine the axis for the distortion.

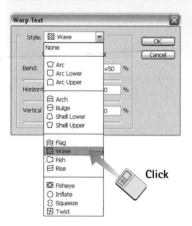

Click

Oceans of Fun

4 Warp the Text

Adjust the **Bend** slider as desired to create the initial warp shape, as determined by the selection you made in step 3. You can also experiment with the **Horizontal Distortion** and **Vertical Distortion** sliders to further pinch or stretch the effect. Click **OK** to apply the distortion.

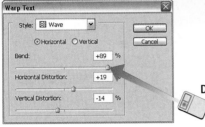

Drag

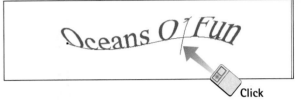

5 Edit the Text

Most warped text remains editable at all times. To edit the text effect you just created, select the **Text** tool from the toolbox. Move the pointer over the warped text and click to create a blinking text insertion point. Type as you normally would to edit the text. You can also drag to select a section of text for resizing or adding color. The one exception to this rule is the type mask, which cannot be edited after it has been deselected and the mask has been turned off.

Click

End

How-To Hints

Combining with Text on a Path

Combine the warped text effect with the text-on-a-path feature in the following task to create some truly unique text distortions.

Cool Animation

Text warping provides a great starting point for doing GIF animations for the Web. Check out Part 12, Task 9, "How to Build Filter-based GIF Animations," for step-by-step details.

How to Set Text on a Path

Photoshop CS2 can create text with a baseline that follows a curving, directional path (or any other path you can imagine). Yet no matter how convoluted the path, the text still remains fully editable.

Begin

1 Open the Image

Select **File**, **Open** and select the image to which you want to add text on a path.

2 Create the Path

Select the **Pen** tool from the toolbox. Make sure the **Paths** icon option is chosen from the **Options** bar, and draw a path in the image window along which you want the text to align. See Part 9, "Using Paths," for details on creating paths.

Drag

3 Select the Type Tool

Select the **Horizontal Type** tool from the toolbox. Note that you can also select the **Vertical Type** tool or either of the **Type Mask** tools by selecting that tool from the **Type** tool pop-out menu.

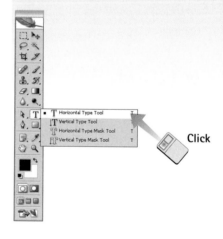

Click

4 Set Type on Path

Move the pointer over the path you drew in step 3 and click to create a text insertion point (where you click determines where the text will start). Select type parameters such as the font, font size, font color, and so on from the **Character** and **Paragraph** palettes; then type the text.

5 Edit the Text

Text on a path remains editable at all times. To edit the text effect you just created, move the pointer over the text and click to create a blinking text insertion point. Type as you normally would to edit the text. You can also drag to select a section of text for resizing or adding color.

Click

End

How-To Hints

Repositioning Text

To change the text's starting point, hold down the **Ctrl** key (Windows users) or the ⌘ key (Mac users) and move the pointer over the text insertion point (a black arrow is added to the pointer as you do this). Click and drag along the path to change where the text starts. If you drag the cursor below the path, the text inverts so that the text baseline follows the bottom of the path line.

Transforming the Path

If you hold down the **Ctrl** key (Windows users) or the ⌘ key (Mac users), a bounding box appears around the path. Click and drag to scale, rotate, or apply other transformation changes to the path in the same way you would transform a layer. See Part 10, Task 6, "How to Transform Layers," for details on the transform options.

Task

Using Paths

Paths offer the capability to outline shapes or areas within Photoshop files. You then can convert the paths into selections, fill the paths with color, or outline the paths as borders.

Paths offer many advantages. They add very little to the overall file size, and they use standard vector controls such as Bézier curves, points, and direction handles. If you know how to create curved segments in Adobe Illustrator or Macromedia FreeHand, you will quickly catch on to the Photoshop path controls.

Other advantages to paths include the flexibility of being able to export them to other files and programs. If you use the **Paths** palette, you can drag paths from the palette for one image window into another open window (an easy way to move paths between Photoshop files). In addition, you can export individual paths as .ai files that you can open in Illustrator, FreeHand, and many other programs that support vector graphics. Doing so gives you more flexibility in illustration and layout programs when mixing vector graphics with the bitmapped images created or modified in Photoshop. ●

How to Create a Straight-Edge Path

You can use paths to define an image area that you then can select, fill, or outline. Paths are especially valuable for graphic shapes you might want to select repeatedly. You create a path using the **Pen** tool, clicking points that are connected automatically with line segments. This task begins by creating a simple path with straight-line segments; later tasks show you how to create more complex path shapes.

Begin

1 Open the File

Select **File, Open** to launch the desired file.

2 Select the Pen Tool

Select the **Pen** tool from the toolbox (you might have to select it from the pop-out menu of tools that appears after you click this button in the toolbox). Click the **Paths** icon located on the left end of the **Options** bar.

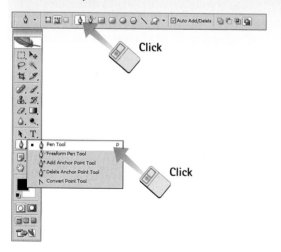

Click

Click

3 Place the First Point

Position the pen over the image area at the spot where you want to start the path. Click once to place an anchor point.

 Click

4 Place Additional Points

Click additional points as necessary to complete the path. Notice that a straight line is drawn between the points you click with the **Pen** tool.

5 Close the Path

Place the last point over the starting point to close the path. A circle appears next to the **Pen** tool when the tool is positioned properly.

 Double-click

6 Edit the Path

To edit the path, select the **Direct Selection** tool from the toolbox (click and hold the tool in the toolbox to activate the pop-out menu and select the desired tool). Click and drag the anchor points on the image to modify the path. The **Direct Selection** tool (which looks like a hollow arrow) allows you to edit and reposition individual anchor points or specific path segments between anchor points. The **Path Selection** tool (the solid arrow) enables you to select the entire path.

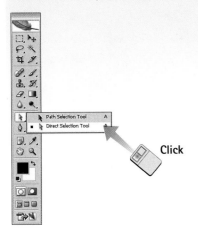 Click

7 Save the Path

Select **Window**, **Paths** to launch the **Paths** palette. Double-click the tile for the path you just created (the tile has the name **Work Path**). The **Save Path** dialog box opens. Type a name for the path and click **OK** to save the path.

How-To Hints

Deleting and Duplicating Paths

Press the **Delete** key twice to delete the path you are currently drawing. Alternatively, select **Delete Path** from the **Paths** palette menu to delete a selected path or segment.

After you have saved a path, you can duplicate it: From the **Paths** palette, select the desired path and select **Duplicate Paths** from the **Paths** palette menu.

End

How to Create a Curved Path

Although the straight-line path you learned to create in Task 1 is good for basic shapes, you might want to create paths with curved lines as well. This task shows you how to draw paths with curved segments, enabling you to create more complex and detailed paths.

Begin

1 Open the File

Select **File**, **Open** to launch the desired file. Select the **Pen** tool from the toolbox (you might have to select it from the pop-out menu that appears after you click the tool in the toolbox).

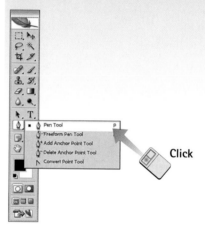

Click

2 Place the First Point

Positionthe pen over the image area at the spot where you want to start the path. Click once to place an anchor point.

Click

3 Create the First Curved Segment

Click and drag while placing the second point to create a curved path segment. Two handles appear out of the second point as you drag, showing the direction of the curve.

Drag

4 Modify the Curve

Press and hold the **Ctrl** key (Windows users) or the ⌘ key (Mac users) to change the **Pen** cursor into the **Direct Selection** tool. Click and drag either of the handles to change the shape of the curve.

Control + **Drag**

⌘ +

5 Complete the Path

Continue adding points to create additional straight or curved segments as necessary. Click the first point again to close the path, if desired.

Click

6 Save and Name the Path

Open the **Paths** palette by selecting **Window, Paths**. In the palette, double-click the tile for the path you just created (the tile has the name **Work Path**). In the **Save Path** dialog box that appears, type a name for the path and click **OK** to save the path.

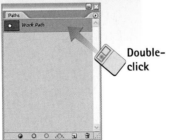

Double-click

How-To Hints

Editing Curved Segments

Instead of editing each curved segment as you make it, it might be easier to approximate all the curve points and fine-tune the segments all at once. When you work this way, you can select the **Direct Selection** tool directly from the toolbox instead of pressing the **Ctrl** key (Windows users) or the ⌘ key (Mac users) as you did in step 4.

End

How to Edit a Path

Photoshop offers a number of ways to edit a path; you can add, subtract, or move points with ease. You can edit a path at any time—as you're creating it or later in the process. This task shows all the ways to edit a path, enabling you to pick and select the options applicable to your project.

Begin

1 Open the File with the Path

Select **Window, Paths** to launch the **Paths** palette. Click the tile of the desired path to select it. The path becomes visible in the image window.

Click

2 Move a Point

Select the **Direct Selection** tool in the toolbox. Click in the middle of a line segment to show the points on the path. Click and drag a point to move it. If the point is related to a curved segment, handles appear when you select the point, enabling you to modify the curve.

Click   Drag

3 Move Multiple Points

To move multiple points as a group, select the **Direct Selection** tool and show the points in the path, as described in step 2. After clicking the first point, press and hold the **Shift** key and click additional points (the points darken to show that they are selected). When multiple points are selected, click and drag to move them as a group.

⬆Shift + Drag

4 Add a Point

To add a point to a path, begin by selecting the **Add Anchor Point** tool from the **Pen** tool pop-out menu in the toolbox. Select the path you want to edit from the **Paths** palette, position the cursor over the path segment, and click to add a new point. Click and drag to create a point with a curved path segment.

Click

5 Delete a Point

To delete a point from a path, begin by selecting the **Delete Anchor Point** tool from the **Pen** tool pop-out menu in the toolbox. Select the path you want to edit from the **Paths** palette, position the cursor over the point to be removed, and click to delete.

Click

Click

6 Convert an Anchor Point

A *complex path* consists of both curved and straight-line segments, which are determined by smooth and corner anchor points, respectively. To convert between smooth and corner points, select the **Convert Point** tool and position it over the point to be converted. Click to convert a smooth point to a corner point; click and drag to convert a corner point to a smooth point.

Click

Click

End

How-To Hints

Delete Alternative

You can also use the **Pen** tool to delete points if the **Auto Add/Delete** option is enabled in the **Options** bar. When you move the mouse pointer over an anchor point, a minus sign appears next to the pointer, indicating that the anchor point will be removed when you click that anchor point.

How to Convert a Path to a Selection

One of the primary reasons for creating a path is to convert it to a selection. You can convert a path to a selection as long as the path is available. Because paths take less disk space to save than selections do, you probably shouldn't save a selection when you can save the path.

Begin

1 Open the File

Select **File, Open** to launch the desired file.

Click

2 Create the Path

Use any of the methods described in the preceding tasks to create a path.

3 Select Make Selection

Select **Window, Paths** to launch the **Paths** palette. With the path tile selected, choose **Make Selection** from the palette menu. The **Make Selection** dialog box opens.

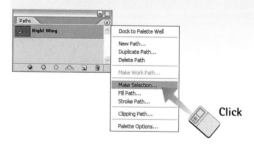

Click

4 Enter the Feather Radius

Enable the **Anti-aliased** check box and enter a feather amount if you want a selection with soft edges (or if you are making a selection around fine details, such as hair). Click **OK** to make the selection. Photoshop automatically hides the path so you can see only the selection.

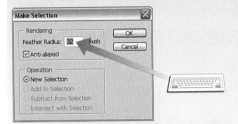

End

How-To Hints

Combining Selections

You can use paths to create selections that interact with existing selections, as determined by the **Operation** section of the **Make Selection** dialog box. If no selection is active in the image area when you choose **Make Selection**, only the **New Selection** radio button is available. If another selection is active when you open this dialog box, you can select to add to, subtract from, or intersect the path selection with the current one.

Converting a Selection to a Path

If an area is already selected, you can easily convert the selection line to a path. With a selection active, select **Make Work Path** from the **Paths** palette menu, select a tolerance level, and click **OK**. If the result is a path with too many points, undo the conversion and set a higher tolerance level. The result is a work path you can save and name as you want.

How to Stroke Paths

Stroking a path draws an outline around a selected path. This capability is useful for outlining a rectangle for a text box, building buttons for the Web, or outlining letter forms you have saved as paths. You can create the outline by using any of Photoshop's painting or drawing tools for a wide range of effects. You can even specify the brush size, opacity, and blending mode for full control over the final result.

Begin

1 Open the File

Select **File**, **Open** to launch the desired file.

2 Create or Select a Path

Use any of the methods described in the preceding tasks to create a path.

3 Configure the Stroke Tool

In the toolbox, select the paint tool (such as a pencil or brush) you want to use to stroke the path. In the **Options** bar for that tool, configure the tool as desired. Select a brush and brush size from the **Brush** menu.

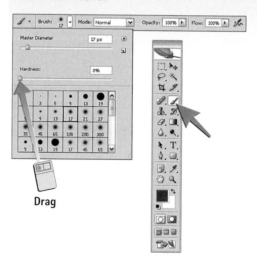

Drag

4 Select the Stroke Path

If it's not already open, select **Window**, **Paths** to launch the **Paths** palette. With the desired path active, select **Stroke Path** from the palette menu. (If the path is not named, the menu option is labeled **Stroke Subpath**.) The **Stroke Path** dialog box opens.

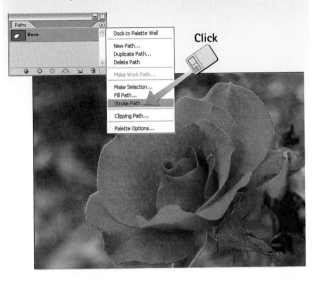

Click

5 Stroke the Path

The tool you configured in step 3 should be selected in the **Stroke Path** dialog box when it opens. If you want to use a different tool, select it from the **Tool** drop-down list and click **OK**. A line is drawn, in the current foreground color, along the selected path using the tool you selected and applying the current settings for that particular tool.

Click

6 Deselect the Path

In the **Paths** palette, click a blank area below the path title to deselect it. This action hides the displayed path and shows only the final result.

Click

How-To Hints

Making an Object Glow

To create an easy glow effect using the stroking method, select the **Brush** tool as the stroke tool, click the **Airbrush** icon on the **Options** bar, and stroke the path with a large brush at a low **Flow** setting. Stroke the path several more times, reducing the brush size and increasing the opacity with each stroke, to build up a glowing effect.

Filling a Path

You can also fill a path with a color or pattern. Select **Fill Path** from the **Paths** palette menu and select the fill contents, blending mode, and feather details from the dialog box.

End

How to Create Clipping Paths

Clipping paths refer to a method of exporting a file for use in a vector or layout application in a format that masks out part of the image. The most common use is to drop out the background in a product shot so that only the product object is visible. Although the file looks normal in Photoshop, when it is placed in the new application, everything not contained in the path is masked out.

Begin

1 Open the File

Select **File**, **Open** to launch the desired file.

Click

2 Create and Name the Path

Use any of the methods described in the preceding tasks to create a path. In the **Paths** palette, double-click the **Work Path** tile and name the path you just created.

3 Select the Clipping Path

Select **Clipping Path** from the **Paths** palette menu to launch the **Clipping Path** dialog box. From the **Path** drop-down list, select the path you want to use for the clipping path. In this example, I have only two options: **None** and the path I selected and named in step 2.

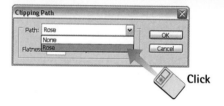

Click

4 Set the Flatness

Set the **Flatness** level to **0.2** and click **OK** to set the clipping path. The **Flatness** setting affects how smooth the path will be.

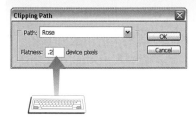

5 Save the File

The Photoshop PSD file format has become an industry standard; however, to preserve the clipping path along with the file so that the clipping path can be imported into a layout or illustration program, you might have to save the file in the TIFF format. Select **File**, **Save As** to save a copy of the file. From the **Format** drop-down list in the **Save As** dialog box, select **TIFF**, type a new name for the file, and click **Save**.

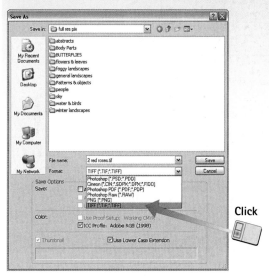

Click

6 Set TIFF Options

The TIFF file format has a number of options. For ease of transportability, you should leave most of them disabled. Set **Image Compression** to **None** and **Pixel Order** to **Interleaved**. Both of these options can save file space, but not all applications can read compressed TIFF files. **Byte Order** doesn't matter for most modern applications, but just in case, leave it set to your computer type. **Save Image Pyramid** can speed up display times with some layout programs, but support is spotty and the option increases file size, so leave this option disabled. Click **OK** to save the file.

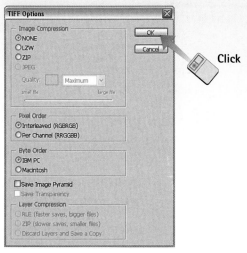

Click

How-To Hints

Watching the Flatness

If the resulting path creates printing or PostScript errors, reset the clipping path using a higher **Flatness** setting (as described in step 4). A higher **Flatness** setting creates fewer points when the path is interpreted by the printer, which eliminates most printing errors.

End

Task

PART 10

Working with Layers

*L*ayers deliver flexibility, color control, and silhouetting options that factor into most intermediate to advanced image-editing tasks. It's hard to imagine doing any sort of image montage or text integration without taking advantage of layers—in some cases, it's just impossible.

Layers isolate parts of an image in a separate, *um...layer* that you can edit and modify without altering the other layers around it. Think of layered sheets of acetate stacked on top of each other. Viewed from the top, they flatten out and show an entire scene, yet they keep the elements separate from each other.

You can reposition layers in the stack to control how different components overlap with each other. You also can hide layers from view or display them with varying levels of transparency.

A feature first introduced in Photoshop CS is the **Layer Comps** command, which allows you to create and save specific layer configurations—recording layer order, transparency, and other parameters. When you have a file with 50 layers and you start lowering the transparency on 1 layer and adding a layer effect on another, it can get pretty hard to remember how to go back to where you started. **Layer Comps** enable flexible experimentation by preserving specific states of layer configurations (including where you started) for easy recall at any time.

The tasks in this part explore the essentials involved in creating and combining layers, building the foundation for professional image compositing. ●

How to Create and Move Layers

You should create a layer any time you want to isolate an element from the rest of the image. The element can be text, a second image, or an area of flat color. You can create a layer by using the **New Layer** command, pasting an element, or duplicating an existing layer. After you create the layer, it appears in the **Layers** palette, named in numerical sequence. To rename a layer, double-click its existing name and type a new name there.

Begin

1 Open the File

Click the **Go to Bridge** icon from the **Options** palette and select the image file you want to modify.

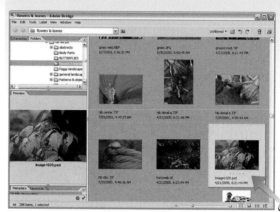

Double-click

2 Open the Layers Palette

Select **Window, Layers** to open the **Layers** palette. In the **Layers** palette, notice that the original image is called **Background**. Any layers you create appear by default above the **Background** layer in the stack.

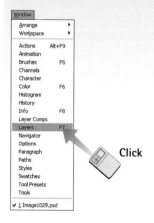

Click

3 Create a Text Layer

To create a new layer, select **Layer, New, Layer**. In the dialog box that appears, name the layer and click **OK**. By default, the layers are given sequential numbers (**Layer 1, Layer 2,** and so on). For this example, create at least two layers and make **Layer 2** a type layer by selecting the **Type** tool and clicking the cursor on the image (if no layer is active, a new type layer is automatically created). Add some text and format it in a large, bold typeface (refer to Part 8, "Using Type").

4 Control Layer Visibility

To turn a layer's visibility on and off, look at the **Layers** palette. The far left column contains boxes with eye icons. Click the box next to the layer for which you want to control the visibility to display or hide the eye icon—also called the *visibility icon*. In this example, I've added a horizontal green line to **Layer 1**; I can see how the image looks with and without the line simply by clicking the visibility icon for the line layer.

5 Change the Order of the Layers

You can change the order of the layers that form the image. In the **Layers** palette, click the layer you want to move in the stack and drag it to its new position. By changing the order of various layers, you can change the apparent order of the objects that reside on these different layers—a powerful feature.

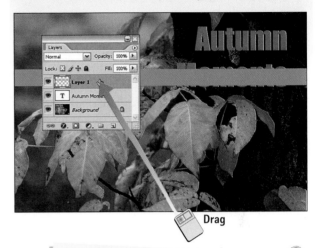

Drag

6 Change Layer Opacity

To make a layer more transparent, select the layer in the **Layers** palette to make it the active layer. Adjust the **Opacity** slider at the top of the **Layers** palette until the active layer has the desired degree of opacity. If a layer style has been applied to a layer, you can fade the layer contents without fading the layer style. To do this, adjust the **Fill** slider. See Part 8, Task 3, "How to Create Typographic Style Sheets," for more on layer styles.

Drag

End

How-To Hints

Repositioning the Background Layer

The **Background** "layer" has special properties. It cannot be repositioned in the layer stack, cannot have any transparent areas, and is locked at 100% opacity. To move the background, you first must rename it (thus "converting" it from the background/base image to a layer). Double-click the layer's name in the **Layers** palette and enter a new name in the dialog box that appears. (You can also accept the default new name of **Layer 0**.) After you rename the ex-background layer, it behaves like any other layer.

Preserving Transparency

You can preserve the transparent areas of a layer—that is, prevent them from being edited—by selecting the layer in the **Layers** palette and clicking the **Lock Transparent Pixels** icon. This option ensures that you color within the lines, so to speak, and prevents any painting or editing from registering in the transparent areas.

How to Link Layers

As you accumulate multiple layers in a file, you can link certain layers together to preserve alignment or visibility. After you link layers, they all move together as you reposition the multiple layers on the screen—even as they maintain their identities as separate layers. You also can merge linked layers together with a single command, as explained in Task 9, "How to Merge and Flatten Layers," of this part.

Begin

1 Open the File

Locate and open the file you want to edit by either selecting **File, Open** or clicking the **Go to Bridge** icon in the **Options** bar.

Double-click

2 Open the Layers Palette

Select **Window, Layers** to open the **Layers** palette. This example starts with an image that contains several layers in addition to the basic **Background** layer.

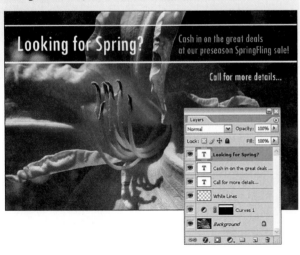

3 Select the Primary Layer

In the **Layers** palette, click the layer to which you want to link other layers. The layer you select here becomes the *primary* layer, or the *active* layer. In this example, the **Background** layer was chosen.

Click

4 Link Secondary Layers

Hold down the **Ctrl** key (Window users)) or the ⌘ key (Mac users) and click any additional layers you want to link. Click the **Link Layers** icon in the bottom-left corner of the **Layers** palette. A chain icon appears to the right of the layer's title, indicating that the layers are linked.

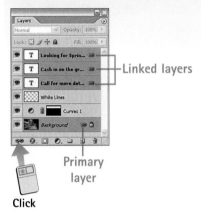

Linked layers

Primary layer

Click

5 Unlink Layers

To unlink layers, click any linked layer to select it and then click the **Link Layers** icon in the bottom-left corner of the **Layers** palette to remove the links. When the link icons are gone, the layers are no longer linked. Alternately, you can **Shift**+click a layer's link icon to temporarily unlink that layer. When you want to relink the layer, **Shift**+click again on its link icon (which now appears with a red × across it, signifying its temporary unlinked status).

Click

End

How-To Hints

Transforming Linked Layers

Linked layers do more than just move and align together. You also can apply the **Transform** command, as outlined in Task 6, "How to Transform Layers," to modify all the linked layers at once.

How to Create Clipping Masks

Clipping masks in Photoshop use the transparency of the bottom layer of a sequential stack of layers as a mask for the other layers. This means that the upper layers are visible only through the "window" created by the transparency of the bottom layer (anything that appears on top of a transparent area is hidden). You also can use a layer mask for the bottom layer in the group instead of actually erasing part of that layer to create transparency (see Task 8, "How to Add a Layer Mask"). When layers are clipped, the thumbnails in the upper layers in the **Layers** palette are indented and shown with arrows, and the layer name of the clipping mask layer is underlined.

Begin

1 Open the File

Select **File, Open** or click the **Go to Bridge** icon on the options bar and select the image file you want to modify.

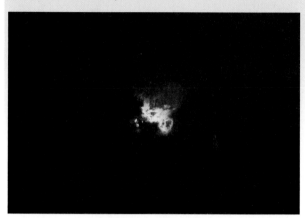

2 Arrange Layers

Select **Window, Layers** to display the **Layers** palette. Move the layers you want to clip so they are adjacent; make sure the layer to serve as the clipping mask is positioned immediately below them. In this example, the **Background** layer is at the bottom of the stack, followed by a copy of the **Background** layer with the rooftop erased (this will be our clipping mask) and an image layer that has been pasted in from another file (this will be the clipped layer).

3 Clip Layers

Click the first layer to be clipped to make this the active layer. Select **Layer, Create Clipping Mask.** Alternatively, hold down the **Alt** key (Windows) or the **Option** key (Mac) and click the line separating two layers (the pointer changes to two interlinked circles). Repeat this process for any additional layers to be clipped. You can identify clipped layers by the arrow icons to the left of the layer thumbnail and the way the layer names are indented above the clipping mask layer. The clipping mask layer be identified by its underlined layer name.

4 Examine the Results

Notice how the topmost image layer is visible only in the areas that are transparent in the clipping mask layer under it. Neither of the two image layers has been altered in any way, yet we now have an entirely new image made from the combination of the two.

5 Unclip Layers

If you want to unclip a layers, first select the clipped layer in the **Layers** palette; then select **Layer, Release Clipping Mask**. Alternatively, you can hold down the **Alt** key (Windows) or the **Option** key (Mac) and click the boundary line between the clipped layer and the layer below it. If you unclip the layer immediately above the clipping mask layer, that action unclips any remaining clipped layers.

Click

End

How-To Hints

Setting Opacity and Mode

Set the opacity and mode by highlighting the base layer that is used as the clipping mask and modifying the **Mode** drop-down list and the **Opacity** slider at the top of the **Layers** palette.

The Power of Clipping Masks

Clipping masks can mask any number or type of layers, including type and adjustment layers. Clipping masks provide a great deal of control in complex layer situations. Try duplicating a **Background** layer, adding an adjustment layer that changes its hue, and then adding another adjustment layer that adjusts its contrast. Finally, add a type layer with some text below the new layers. Select the layer immediately above the type layer and select **Layer, Create Clipping Mask**. Watch for the changes in the image that occur. One by one, add the remaining layers to the clipping mask and examine the changes. The final result is difficult to replicate with other methods—and you can still edit the text and make other nondestructive changes.

How to Create Layer Groups

So far, you've seen that you can link layers to move them as one and can clip layers to create a masking effect. This task explains how to create groups of layers that can be activated, hidden, or copied as a single unit. The *layer groups* feature, introduced in Photoshop 6 (and known as *layer sets* in past versions), has been a godsend, especially for interface designers who can finally organize the dozens of layers necessary to build a website.

Begin

1 Open the File

Select **File**, **Open** or click the **Go to Bridge** button on the **Options** bar and select the image file you want to modify.

2 Display the Layers Palette

Select **Window**, **Layers** to display the **Layers** palette. Using what you've learned in the preceding tasks, create the desired layers for the group.

3 Select the Layers for the Group

Hold down the **Ctrl** key (Windows) or the ⌘ key (Mac) and click each of the layers you want to include in a group (or set). As you select each new layer, it is highlighted. Here I've selected just the type layers.

Control +
⌘ + Click

4 Group the Selected Layers

Select **Layer**, **Group Layers** to create a new layer group from the selected layers. A **Group 1** layer appears in the **Layers** palette with a folder icon and an arrow that allows you to collapse or expand the list of layers that appear within the new group "folder." Double-click the **Group 1** title to rename the group folder (to help organize the groups).

Click

5 Add Layers to the Layer Group

To add more layers to the group, first click the arrow next to the folder icon to expand the group. Drag the layer into place in the group folder. The line separating the layers darkens to show where the layer will be placed. Here I'm dragging the **White Lines** layer to the top of the **Text Layers** group. To insert an entirely new layer, you can highlight the group folder (or any layer within a group) and select **Layer**, **New**, **Layer** from the menu bar or select **New Layer** from the **Layers** palette menu.

6 Create Nested Layer Groups

Photoshop CS2 provides the ability to nest layer groups within other layer groups. Any layer group can be dragged into any other layer group folder to nest it. Drag and drop other layers into the group folders to organize information as desired. Here I made a new group for the remaining design elements for this image and then dragged the **Text Layers** group into the **Design Elements** group to nest them.

Layer group nested within another layer group

How-To Hints

Adding the Background Layer to a Group

The **Background** layer must be converted to a standard layer before it can be added to a layer group. To convert the **Background** layer, double-click it in the **Layers** palette, name it in the dialog box that appears—or accept the default **Layer 0** name—and click **OK**.

Links, Clipping Masks, and Groups

The differences between layer links, clipping masks, and layer groups can be classified as repositioning, masking, and unification. Linking layers enables you to reposition a series of layers as one unit, and clipping masks enable you to use the transparent areas of the lower layer as a mask for the upper layers. Layer groups unify multiple layers as a single unit that can be activated, hidden, or duplicated as one.

End

How to Create Smart Objects

New for Photoshop CS2, **Smart Objects** are essentially containers for one or more layers. The Smart Object container can be transformed, and you can change layer styles, opacity, and blend modes for the Smart Object. The important part (the "smart" part) about Smart Objects is that no matter what you do to them, the original layers remain untouched and editable. If you edit any of the original layers that make up a Smart Object, the Smart Object is updated to reflect the edits to the individual layers.

Begin

1 Open the File

Select **File, Open** or click the **Go to Bridge** icon on the **Options** bar to select the file you want to modify.

2 Display the Layers Palette

Select **Window, Layers** to open the **Layers** palette and show all existing layers. In this example, a **Hue/Saturation** adjustment layer, a white background layer, and a layer mask have been added to the image.

3 Select the Layers

Click the first layer you want to include in the Smart Object, hold down the **Ctrl** key (Windows) or the ⌘ key (Mac) and click the other layers you want to include in the Smart Object. As you click each new layer, it is highlighted.

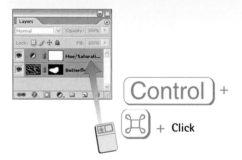

4 Create the Smart Object

Select **Layer, Smart Objects, Group into New Smart Object.** The selected layers are replaced with a single Smart Object layer. The layer thumbnail shows overlapping squares in the lower-right corner to indicate that it is a Smart Object. You can rename the Smart Object just as you can any other layer by double-clicking its name and typing the new name.

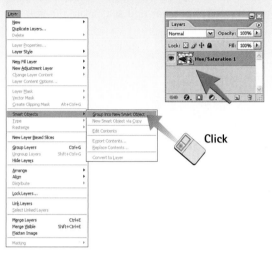

Click

5 Transform the Smart Object

From now on, the Smart Object is similar to any other layer. You can transform it, copy it, and even change its blending mode. Here I made several copies of the Smart Object's butterfly layer and transformed each layer by resizing, flipping, and rotating it. Finally, I added a tree leaf image as a backdrop.

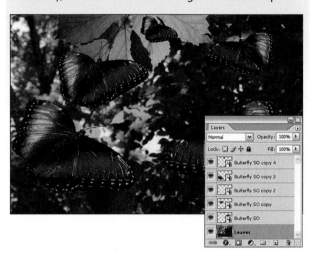

6 Reedit the Original Layers

Double-click any one the Smart Object layers and the original layers open for editing in a new window. Notice that the original layers remain untouched. Here I decided to hide the visibility of the **Hue/Saturation** layer, changing the butterflies

back to their original colors. Select **File, Close** to stop editing the Smart Object. In the dialog box that asks whether you want to save the changes, Click **OK**, and watch whatever changes you made cascade through every instance of the Smart Object.

End

How to Transform Layers

When you *transform* a layer, you modify the position, scale, or proportions of the layer. Transforming a layer is useful for changing the size or placement of a layer, as well as for adding perspective or distortion. You cannot apply the transformation process to the **Background** layer; you must convert that layer to a standard layer before you can transform it. (Double-click the **Background** layer in the **Layers** palette and rename it in the dialog box that appears. Alternatively, duplicate the layer and transform the copy, leaving the original **Background** layer untouched.)

Begin

1 Open the File

Select **File**, **Open** or click the **Go to Bridge** button on the **Options** bar and select the file you want to modify.

2 Open the Layers Palette

Select **Window**, **Layers** to open the **Layers** palette.

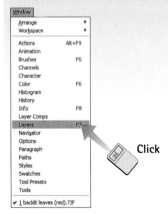

Click

3 Select the Layer to Transform

In the **Layers** palette, click the name of the layer you want to transform. In this example, I select the layer that contains a photo of a leaf.

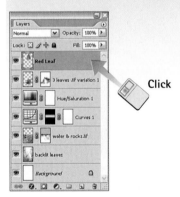

Click

4 Select Free Transform

Select **Edit**, **Free Transform** to begin the transformation process. A bounding box with handles at the sides and corners surrounds the layer or the objects on the layer. To transform just a portion of a layer, select the area before selecting **Free Transform** so that the bounding box covers only the selected area. Background areas left by the transformation will be transparent, allowing lower layers to show through.

Click

5 Modify the Layer

Apply any of the following transformations to the area in the bounding box. **To move:** Place the mouse pointer inside the bounding box and drag. **To scale:** Click and drag a handle (use the **Shift** key to keep the original proportions). **To rotate:** Position the mouse pointer outside the bounding box until it turns into a curved, two-headed arrow; then drag. **To distort freely:** Press and hold **Ctrl** (Windows) or ⌘ (Mac) and drag a handle. **To skew:** Press and hold **Ctrl+Shift** (Windows) or ⌘+**Shift** (Mac) and drag a side handle. Press **Esc** to cancel transformations, or press **Enter** or **Return** to apply the effect.

Drag

End

How-To Hints

Using the Individual Transform Commands

You also can apply individual transformation options by selecting **Edit**, **Transform** and then choosing the transformation option you want from the submenu that appears. This approach limits the transformation to only the selected task, such as rotating or scaling.

Transforming Numerically

You can transform a layer with numeric precision by selecting **Edit**, **Transform**, **Free Transform**. In the **Options** bar, adjust the **Position**, **Scale**, **Rotation**, and **Skew** options. This approach is especially valuable when you have to repeat the same transformation across multiple unlinked layers.

Warp Transform

New in Photoshop CS2 is the **Warp** command (select **Edit**, **Transform**, **Warp**). This transformation is explored fully in Part 6, Task 5, "How to Warp an Image."

How to Create Adjustment Layers

Adjustment layers apply tone or color to all the layers that appear below them in the **Layers** palette, without altering specific layer content. With an adjustment layer, you can also apply a gradient, color, or pattern fill. An adjustment layer acts like a filter, altering the appearance of all the layers underneath it—effectively modifying multiple layers simultaneously. If the result is unsatisfactory, delete or turn off the layer to return to the previous state. Adjustment layers are like other layers in that you can reposition, hide, or duplicate them in the **Layers** palette.

Begin

1 Open the File

Launch **Bridge** by clicking the **Go to Bridge** icon in the **Options** bar, and then double-click the file you want to modify.

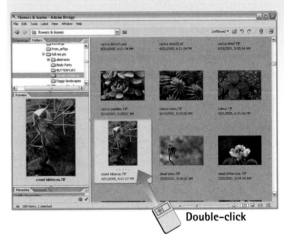

Double-click

2 Open the Layers Palette

Select **Window, Layers** to open the **Layers** palette.

3 Create an Adjustment Layer

Select **Layer, New Adjustment Layer** and select the desired adjustment type. The options are **Levels, Curves, Color Balance, Brightness/Contrast, Hue/Saturation, Selective Color, Channel Mixer, Gradient Map, Photo Filter, Invert, Threshold,** and **Posterize**. Alternatively, you can click the **Create New Fill or Adjustment Layer** button (the half-black circle icon) at the bottom of the **Layers** palette.

Click

4 Create the Adjustment Layer

In the **Name** box of the **New Layer** dialog box that opens, type a name for the layer you are creating. Click **OK** to create the layer. This dialog box is skipped if you use the **Create New Fill or Adjustment Layer** button at the bottom of the **Layers** palette.

Click

5 Apply the Adjustment

An adjustment dialog box appears based on the specific selection you made in step 3. Adjust the controls to your satisfaction (select colors, gradients, saturation, and so on) and click **OK** to set the adjustment.

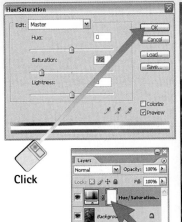

Click

6 Edit the Adjustment

To edit the adjustment settings, double-click the icon on the left side of the adjustment layer in the **Layers** palette. The adjustment dialog box you saw in step 5 opens so you can make further changes.

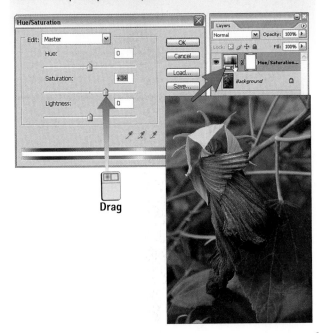

Drag

How-To Hints

Adjustment Layers As Layer Masks

You can paint into an adjustment layer, masking how its effect is applied to the layers underneath. As with other layer masks (described in the following task), painting with black conceals the adjustment effect and painting with white reveals it. With the adjustment layer active in the **Layers** palette, select any paint tool and paint into the image. The color choices convert to grayscale while the adjustment layer is active. The line or area you paint becomes the mask through which the adjustment effect is applied to the remaining layers.

End

How to Add a Layer Mask

A *layer mask* conceals a portion of a layer without actually deleting it, allowing the lower layers to show through. Erasing the layer mask restores the layer's original appearance so that nothing is lost. The general approach to applying a layer mask is to brush it on using any of the paint tools, controlling the visibility and transparency with grayscale values. As you saw in Part 3, Task 4, "How to Use Quick Mask," a black value conceals the layer image, white reveals it, and grayscale dictates the transparency.

Begin

1 Open the File

Select **File**, **Open** or click the **Go to Bridge** button on the **Options** bar and select the image file you want to modify. For this task, I've opened an image with two layers. The lower layer is of a misty landscape with grass in the foreground and an ancient tree in the background; the top layer is of a pull chain. By "painting" in a mask, I'll make it appear as if the pull chain was suspended in front of the camera lens when the landscape was shot.

2 Open the Layers Palette

Select **Window**, **Layers** to open the **Layers** palette.

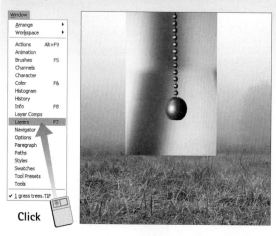

Click

3 Select the Mask Layer

Select the layer to be masked by clicking its name in the **Layers** palette. In this example, select the layer containing the pull chain.

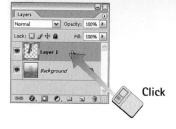

Click

4 Add the Layer Mask

Click the **Add Layer Mask** button at the bottom of the **Layers** palette to add a layer mask to the current layer. The layer mask is indicated in the image tile by a white thumbnail next to the image thumbnail. The border of the new thumbnail is doubled, indicating that the mask is selected.

Add Layer
Mask button

5 Paint the Mask

Select the **Brush** tool from the toolbox. Press **D** for the default black and white colors (if necessary, press **X** to switch black to the foreground). Move the mouse pointer into the image area and paint the areas you want to mask (or remove). As you do so, you'll see the current layer disappearing and the lower layer showing through; the thumbnail mask icon is updated to show the current mask. In this example, notice that the blurred background behind the pull chain is being "erased" and the misty **Background** layer is showing through.

Drag

6 Erase the Mask

To erase or correct painting errors when masking, change the foreground color to white and repaint the mask. The image layer reappears as you work. To paint in transparency, select a gray foreground color or reduce the **Opacity** setting in the **Options** bar for the paint tool you are using. Note that pressing the **X** key enables you to quickly toggle between the foreground and background colors. This is helpful while adjusting the edges of the mask.

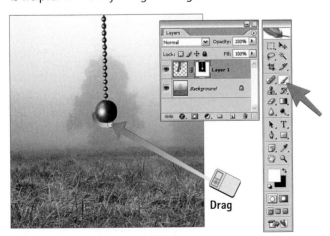

Drag

How-To Hints

Be Sure You Paint the Mask

When applying a layer mask, be sure the mask thumbnail is highlighted in the **Layers** palette before you make any changes. As you're working, you can easily forget that the mask thumbnail should be selected; if it's not selected, you'll be painting directly into the image.

Using Selections with Layer Masks

You can speed the production of layer masks by using selections. Use any selection tool to rough in the area to be left visible before you add the layer mask. Then when you make the layer mask, everything outside the selected area will be black (masked). You can also use selection tools on existing layer masks to fill large areas with black or white (depending on whether you want the area to be masked or revealed).

End

How to Merge and Flatten Layers

In a complex design, it's not hard to accumulate dozens of layers, which can bloat file size and make it hard to find what you're looking for. Whenever possible, you should look for opportunities to merge and flatten layers to keep the design clean and well ordered. *Merging* layers refers to combining some of the layers in a design while keeping other layers separate. *Flattening* the image involves compressing all the layers into one flat background layer.

Begin

1 Open the File

Select **File, Open** or click the **Go to Bridge** button on the **Options** bar and select the file you want to modify.

2 Launch the Layers Palette

Select **Window, Layers** to open the **Layers** palette and show all existing layers.

3 Merge Multiple Layers into One

To merge two layers into one, drag them one above the other in the **Layers** palette and select the layer at the top of the two. Select **Layer, Merge Down** to combine the selected layer with the layer below it in the list. The name of the lower layer is used when you combine layers with the **Merge Down** command.

These two layers will be merged

4 Merge Multiple Layers

To merge more than one layer at a time, click to select the first layer to be merged, hold down the **Ctrl** key (Windows) or the ⌘ key (Mac), and click the remaining layers to be merged. Then select **Layer, Merge Layers** to combine all the selected layers.

These three layers will be merged

5 Merge All Visible Layers

An alternative to merging selected layers is to first turn off the visibility of all layers you do *not* want to merge. Select **Layer, Merge Visible** to combine all visible layers. Then go back to the **Layers** palette and turn the hidden layers back on. The current, or active, layer name is used when you combine layers using the **Merge Visible** command.

These visible layers will be merged

6 Flatten the Image

To reduce all the layers in a document to one, select **Layer, Flatten Image**. If any layers are hidden as you do this, a dialog box appears, asking whether you want to discard the hidden layers or cancel the operation. Click **OK** to flatten the image and delete the hidden layers.

All layers are combined

How-To Hints

Watching the Layer Order When Merging

If selected layers are not adjacent to each other, the image could be altered when you merge the layers. This is especially true when opacity or blending modes have been used.

End

How to Create Layer Comps

Layer comps capture the precise configuration of the **Layers** palette—including layer order, layer styles, transparency, and blending modes. Layer comps enable you to experiment with variations and multiple layer combinations, marking the ones that work best and recalling them with a mouse click.

Begin

1 Open the File

Select **File, Open** or click the **Go to Bridge** button on the **Options** bar and select the file you want to modify.

2 Create a Base Configuration

Create a layer configuration as desired, combining layer order, styles, masks, or any other attributes. In this example there are seven layers using six layer masks and three adjustment layers. In addition, most of the layers use a blending mode and some incorporate various levels of transparency.

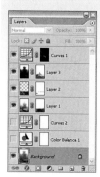

3 Create a Layer Comp

Open the **Layer Comps** palette by selecting **Window, Layer Comps**. Click the **Create New Layer Comp** button at the bottom of the palette; in the dialog box that opens, specify the layer attributes you want to record, name the comp, and add comments. Click **OK** to create the comp, which now appears in the **Layer Comps** palette. This example records the layer configuration at the start of the session to create a safety net you can access if the experimentation goes too far.

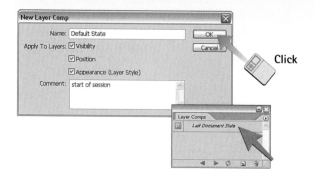

Click

4 Revise Layer Info

Modify the layer attributes as desired, exploring new variations or options in the design. In this example, layer visibility has been enabled in two layers, a blending mode was changed in another layer, and another layer was hidden.

5 Create Additional Layer Comps

Access the **Layer Comps** palette and click the **Create New Layer Comp** button again to create a new comp that records the changes you just made to the **Layers** palette. Repeat this step as necessary to capture additional comp states.

Create New Layer Comp button

6 Using Saved Layer Comps

In the **Layer Comps** palette, click the icon to the left of the desired state to reconfigure the layer attributes. You can also click the forward and back arrows at the bottom of the palette to cycle through the list of layer comps and view the changes to the image with each separate configuration.

End

How-To Hints

Layer Comps Are Not History States

Layer comps preserve only layer attributes such as position, transparency, visibility, and so on. They do not preserve the actual contents of the layer as you edit it. For example, if you capture a layer comp and then apply the **Curves** command to the layer, the initial layer comp reflects the new edited layer contents.

Updating Layer Comps

As you work, you can update a layer comp to reflect the current state by highlighting the comp in the **Layer Comps** palette and clicking the **Update** button at the bottom of the palette. Don't accidentally click the comp's icon if you want to update because it will reconfigure the layers with that comp's settings.

Task

Digital Photography Features

Photoshop CS2 offers many enhancements that attempt to simulate traditional photographic methods. It's curious that an established software program with a name like Photoshop would take so long to build in features and enhancements that target the digital photographer. Although Photoshop has always worked with photographic images, it always manipulated them using digital terminology and methods. Bit depth, pixels, and color models have always dominated the Photoshop terminology landscape, confusing many traditional photographers who were used to f-stops, shutter speeds, and correction filters.

In this part are tasks that explain how to create a contact sheet and create picture packages for easier photo printing. Additional tasks outline how to eliminate red-eye reflections, build image panoramas, and work with 16-bit camera raw files.

Finally, you'll find a task that outlines how to enter and modify keywords and metadata for individual images, making it easier to track, search, and sort your image collection.

Some of these tasks and features have been in Photoshop for some time, whereas others are new with the release of Photoshop CS2. The net result of these photo features is a powerful imaging application that's intuitive and photographer friendly. ●

How to Build a Contact Sheet

A *contact sheet* is a Photoshop file with thumbnail references for all the images in a given folder. You can use contact sheets for a number of tasks, such as sending clients a list of images for approval, archiving, or just organizing your graphics visually rather than with archaic filenames. When you set up contact sheets, you have full control over the page size, the thumbnail size, and the spacing on the page. You can optimize the format of contact sheets for any printer or format.

Begin

1 Select the Images

Click the **Go to Bridge** button on the **Options** toolbar and navigate to the folder containing the images for your contact sheet. Click the thumbnail of the first image you want to include and then ⌘+click (**Ctrl**+click in Windows) the thumbnails of the remaining images you want in your contact sheet.

Click

2 Open Contact Sheet II

In **Bridge**, select **Tools, Photoshop, Contact Sheet II**. The **Contact Sheet II** dialog box opens.

Click

3 Specify Document Settings

In the **Document** area of the dialog box, specify the size of the contact sheet you're building. Enter the dimensions and resolution in the spaces provided. Set the resolution to 72 pixels/inch if you're just viewing onscreen, or use a setting of 300 pixels/inch for printing. The preview area on the right side of the dialog box changes as you modify these values. Leave the **Mode** drop-down menu set to **RGB Color** and verify that the **Flatten All Layers** check box is enabled.

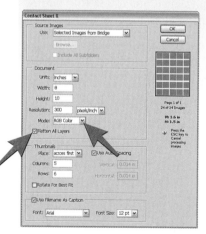

4 Determine Page Grid

Make a selection from the **Place** drop-down list and specify the numbers of **Columns** and **Rows** you want on your contact sheet. Watch the preview area to see how the values you provide affect the size of the thumbnails (based on the overall page dimensions).

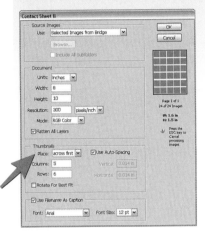

5 Set Captions and Fonts

Enable the **Use Filename As Caption** check box if you want the filenames of the images to appear below the thumbnails on the contact sheet. From the **Font** drop-down menu, select the font you want to use for the captions, and enter the caption font size in the **Font Size** box.

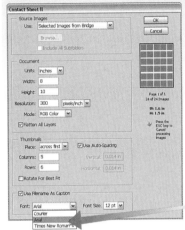

Click

6 Build the Sheet

Click **OK** to start building the contact sheet images. Note that the contact sheet is a Photoshop file; you can modify it any way you want. Consider saving the file as a PDF file because this compact Adobe file format is especially suited for emailing to clients or when disk space is limited. To save an image as a PDF file, select **File, Save As** and select **Photoshop PDF** from the **Format** drop-down menu.

End

How-To Hints

Using More Than One Folder

If you have more than one folder of images to make into contact sheets, consider copying them to a temporary folder and then using the **Folder** option from the **Source Images** drop-down list in the **Contact Sheet II** dialog box. Don't include any images you don't want on your contact sheet because this method cannot skip any images in the folder.

Labeling Contact Sheets

You might want to take the time to label each contact sheet with the folder and path to the images. With the contact sheet still open in Photoshop, use the **Type** tool to add a text layer with your name, the date, and the folder and path to the images on the contact sheet.

How to Make Picture Packages

The **Picture Package** command places multiple copies of a selected image in a page layout, allowing you to make several prints on one sheet of paper. This arrangement saves time and printing materials—and allows you to satisfy the extended family's request for the latest baby pictures. If you print photos on a home inkjet printer, this command makes life a lot easier.

Begin

1 Select Picture Package

Select **File, Automate, Picture Package** to launch the **Picture Package** dialog box.

Click

2 Select Files

From the **Use** drop-down list at the top of the dialog box, select **Folder** or **File**; then click the **Browse** button in Windows (click the **Select** button on the Mac) and navigate to the image or folder you want to use. If the target file is open in Photoshop, or if one or more files are selected in **Bridge**, select **Frontmost Document** or **Select Images from Bridge** from the **Use** menu. If desired, enable the **Include All Subfolders** check box.

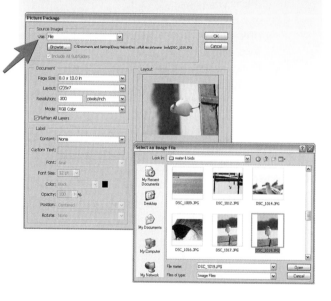

3 Set Page Layout and Size

Select page parameters from the **Document** section of the **Picture Package** dialog box. The **Page Size** setting determines the size of the overall document. Select the size of each print from the **Layout** menu, set the **Resolution** according to your printer specifications (or use the same resolution as the images), leave the **Mode** set at **RGB Color**, and enable the **Flatten All Layers** check box unless you would prefer to save the resulting file as a PSD file (with each image on a separate layer for editing flexibility).

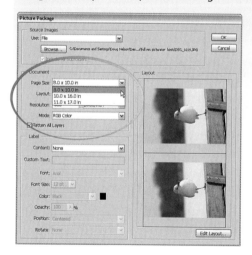

4 Select Additional Images

When you select a **Layout** option, Photoshop automatically populates all image zones within the layout with the images you selected in step 2. You can substitute an additional image by double-clicking its thumbnail in the **Layout** pane of the dialog box and navigating to a different image.

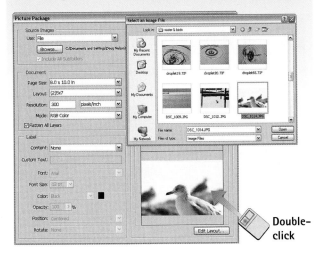

Double-click

5 Set Label Information

To add labels to the images in the layout (the labels appear on top of the images), select a content type for the label from the **Content** pop-up menu. To add a customized text message, select **Custom Text** from the **Content** menu and type the message in the **Custom Text** field. Select any desired text parameters such as **Color**, **Font**, or **Font Size** from the remaining lists in the **Label** section of this dialog box.

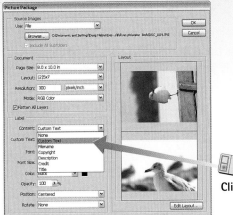

Click

6 Create the File

Click **OK** to build the **Picture Package** file. Photoshop launches the image, resizes it, and populates a file that corresponds to the page parameters specified in step 3. If you selected a folder in step 2, or if you included subfolders, Photoshop creates a separate document for each target image. Save the files or print them to complete the process.

End

How-To Hints

Creating Custom Layouts

Click the **Edit Layout** button under the preview images in the **Layout** section to design your own layout. In the window that appears, specify a name and page size for the document to be created. If image zones already exist for the layout, you can click them and drag their handles to create images of any size. Click the **Add Zone** button to add more image zones to the layout. As you rearrange image zones, selecting the **Snap to** option in the **Grid** section can make alignment easier.

It's important to remember that the **Layout** window preview does not change to reflect the proportions of a new page size. For example, a 4" × 20" page is still represented in the 8" × 10 " proportion. As a result, image zones are scaled independently for horizontal and vertical dimensions and might not look anything like the dimensions they represent.

TASK 3

How to Use the Red-Eye Tool

"Red eye" happens when the light from the camera flash reflects off the subject's retina. It can make for a disturbingly demonic image, particularly when photographs of angelic children are affected.

1 Open the Image

Select **File, Open** or click the **Go to Bridge** icon in the **Options** bar to launch **Bridge**; then open the file you want to modify.

2 Zoom in Close

Click the **Zoom** tool in the toolbox or repeatedly press **Ctrl++** in Windows or ⌘**++** on the Mac (the Ctrl/⌘ key and the plus key) to zoom in tight on the subject's eyes.

3 Select the Red Eye Tool

Select the **Red Eye** tool from the toolbar. You'll find it nested with the **Spot Healing, Healing,** and **Patch** tools.

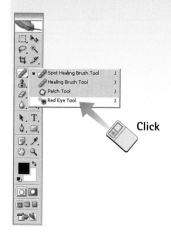

Click

4 Click in the Red

With the **Red Eye** tool active, click in the red area of one eye. If the correction doesn't match the size of the pupils or seems too light or too dark, undo the effect and change the **Pupil Size** or the **Darken Amount** setting on the **Options** bar and then reapply. When you're satisfied with the result, click in the red area of the other eye.

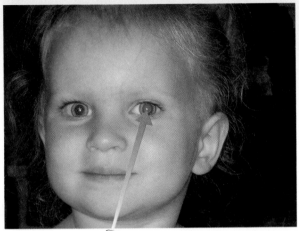

Click

5 Evaluate the Results

The final result should look natural, not drawing attention to itself in any way.

End

How-To Hints

Fixing Non-Red Eyes

Many animals have a special reflective layer at the back of their eyes to help with their night vision. This can cause green or white eye instead of red eye. The **Red Eye** tool looks for red, so it isn't of any help if you want to correct green or white eye. Instead, use the **Sponge** tool set to **Desaturate** to remove all the color from the affected area and then repeatedly apply the **Burn** tool to the area, set to **Midtones**.

Avoiding Red Eyes

The best solution for the red-eye problem is to avoid red eye to begin with. The effect is usually caused by the flash being too close to the lens. Try increasing the distance between the two, if possible. The problem is made worse when the photograph is taken in a dark room (the dim light makes the subject's pupils even larger), so try turning on more room lights. In addition, some cameras have a red-eye setting that flashes twice—once to contract the subject's pupils and once to actually expose the photo.

TASK 4

How to Reduce Noise

A noisy image has tiny nondetail artifacts that are evenly distributed throughout the image. Noise typically falls into two categories: grain and digital noise. Film scanners often record the actual grains that make up the image, usually in areas of little detail and smooth tone. Digital noise is introduced either by the digital camera during the image-capture process or from post-capture processing and compressing. Photoshop CS2 is now well-equipped to handle all these problems.

1 Select the Reduce Noise Filter

With your image open, select **Filter**, **Noise**, **Reduce Noise**. The **Reduce Noise** dialog box opens.

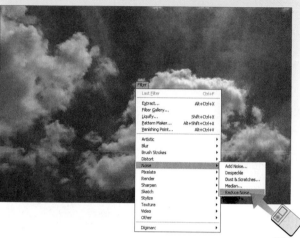

Click

2 Analyze the Noise

Zero all the controls by dragging their sliders to the left. Click the + button under the image preview to zoom in on an area that contains both details and even tones. Click and drag within the image to move it. You're looking for overall noise, not individual specks. Disabling the **Preview** check box at the upper-right of the dialog box speeds up the response.

Drag

3 Set the Strength Slider

Slowly move the **Strength** slider toward the right until the tiny dark and light speckles (known as *luminance noise*) begin to disappear. Keep the **Strength** setting as low as possible to protect important details. You can optionally limit the filtration to specific channels by selecting the **Advanced** option.

Drag

4 Set the Preserve Details Slider

Removing noise also softens image detail, but you can restore much of that detail with the **Preserve Details** slider. Set it as high as possible, although you'll notice a tradeoff between the amount of detail restored and the amount of noise reduced. Check several areas of the image before deciding on a setting.

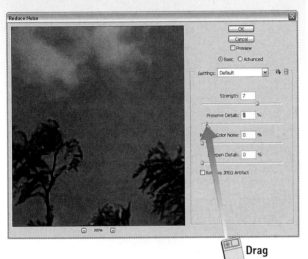

Drag

5 Set the Reduce Color Noise Slider

Even after eliminating all the luminance noise, some colored speckles (known as *chromatic noise*) might remain. Get rid of those by dragging the **Reduce Color Noise** slider toward the right. Just as with the **Strength** slider, keep this slider set at the lowest value you can get away with.

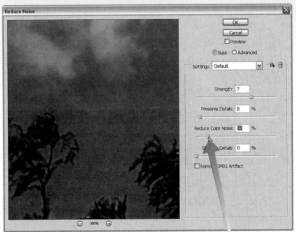

Drag

6 Set the Sharpen Details Slider

You can sharpen the image with the **Sharpen Details** slider. If you're going to make further edits to the image, leave this slider set to 0 and sharpen later (refer to Part 4, Task 6, "How to Sharpen Images," for details). When you've checked several areas of the image and are satisfied with your settings, click **OK**.

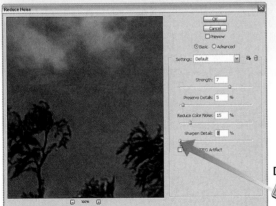

Drag

End

How-To Hints

Removing JPG Artifacts

The JPG file format compresses an image's file size by throwing out image details. If an image is overcompressed, a distinctive square pattern is introduced. JPG compression artifacts are most noticeable in areas with a lot of detail. If your image has JPG artifacts, open the **Reduce Noise** filter, zero all the slider controls, and enable the **Remove JPG Artifact** check box. Click **OK** and do any final touch-up work with the **Clone Stamp** and **Healing Brush** tools.

TASK

How to Build Panoramas

The **Photomerge** command has automated the process of stitching together panoramic images, allowing you to create wide-angle landscapes that are seamless and highly detailed. To complete this task, start with a group of images taken in a linear sequence—across a horizon, for example. Although the **Photomerge** command makes the process of creating a panorama very easy, a common misconception is that the process is fully automated. This task explains how to use **Photomerge** as one tool in the process, with the understanding that you must still tweak the image layers manually to complete the effect.

1 Launch Photomerge Interface

Select **File, Automate, Photomerge** to launch the **Photomerge** dialog box.

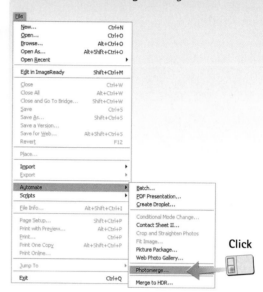

Click

2 Select Source Files

The first **Photomerge** screen that appears asks you to select the files to be stitched together for the panorama. Click the **Browse** button, navigate to the desired files in the window that appears, and click **Open**. Repeat this selection step for as many files as you want to use to create the panorama. If the images are located in the same folder, **Ctrl**+click (Windows) or ⌘+**click** (Mac) to select more than one file. Alternatively, group all the images in a single folder and select **Folder** instead of **Files** from the **Use** pop-up menu. When all the images are selected, click **OK** to launch the Photomerge script.

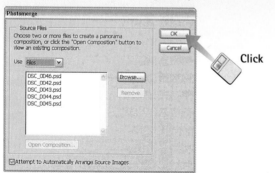

Click

3 Zoom to Inspect

Photomerge automatically opens each target file and attempts to combine all the pieces into a cohesive panorama within the **Photomerge** window. The preview will be quite small by default, so drag the **Zoom** slider in the **Navigator** section of the window to the right to enlarge the preview.

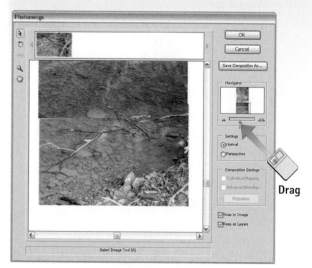

Drag

4 Edit in Photomerge

The **Snap to Image** setting is active by default, which should cause the images to snap into alignment. If the alignment doesn't look right, drag each image to correct the alignment. Files Photomerge can't match up automatically are displayed along the top of the dialog box. Drag these files into the main window and manually align them. Enable the **Keep As Layers** check box to preserve each image as a separate layer in the final file. When you're satisfied with the results, click **OK**.

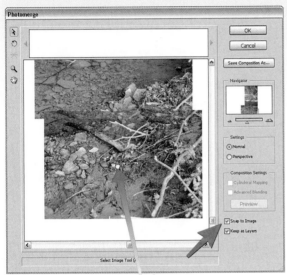

 Drag

5 Edit the Image

Because you're combining multiple images taken from different angles, the chance of having each exposure match perfectly is pretty slim. But each is on a separate layer, so adjusting color and hiding seams is greatly simplified. Finally, to square things off, use the **Crop** tool from the toolbox, drag a marquee to define the rectangle for the image, and double-click to crop the image. Close the file as you normally would to save the changes.

End

How-To Hints

Using Match Color

Occasionally, the images you're combining will have color shifts as the exposure gets lighter or darker. A good way to fix this problem is to use the **Match Color** command, using a single layer as the source for the corrections. For more on **Match Color**, see Part 5, Task 2, "How to Use the Match Color Command."

Leaving Plenty of Overlap

When shooting images for a panorama, make sure that the shots overlap somewhat so Photomerge has enough data to work with as it combines images. The visual overlap of the images can also help if you use layer masks to combine layers manually (see next hint).

Using Layer Masks to Merge Images

When the panorama opens in Photoshop, each of the original images is listed on a separate layer. If the layers do not line up exactly right, and you have enough image overlap between the layers, try to blend the layers with a layer mask. Click the **Layer Mask** icon at the bottom of the **Layers** palette, select the **Brush** tool with black as the foreground color, and paint to blend the two layers.

How to Organize Images with Custom Metadata

The photo industry is developing some consistent standards for how images should be organized, categorized, and labeled. There's EXIF data that profiles camera information and IPTC data for journalistic information such as writers, sources, and deadlines. (File Data, EXIF, Camera Raw, GPS, and IPTC information is also referred to as *metadata*.) Then there are basic keywords and comments for keeping things straight. Photoshop has organized all this information with the **Metadata** and **Keywords** tabs in **Bridge**.

Begin

1 Create Keywords and Sets

With **Bridge** open, click the **Keywords** tab and click the **New Keyword** icon. A new keyword appears in the list, ready to be labeled. Type the desired keyword, and repeat this step to create a list of keywords you expect to use often. To help organize a lengthy list of keywords, click **New Keyword Set** to create a new folder, which you can use to organize keywords into thematic groups.

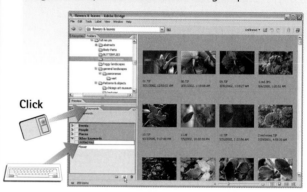

Click

2 Assign Keywords to Images

Select one or more files in **Bridge** and click the box to the left of any keyword to assign it to the selected images. A dialog box appears to confirm that you want the keyword to apply to all selected images; click **Yes**. The *keyword* is a searchable descriptor word that helps categorize the contents of the image. Images can have multiple keywords such as *outdoors*, *family*, and *purple*, allowing you to search for each keyword individually or to combine keywords for more specific search results.

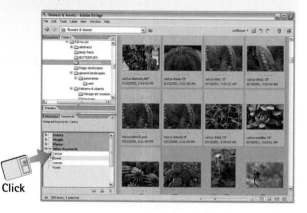

Click

3 Open File Info

Metadata is attached to a file with the **File Info** command. Select a file in **Bridge** and select **File**, **File Info** from the **Bridge** menu. *Metadata* information is supplemental information about a file that can help with identification, copyright protection, searching, or workflow management. Photoshop allows for six metadata subcategories: File Properties; EXIF Camera Data; Camera Raw; GPS; Edit History; and project-based IPTC information that shows authorship, assignment information, and other workflow data points.

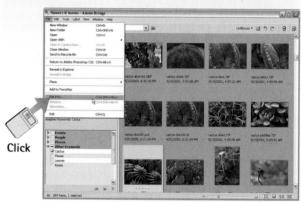

Click

4 Add Metadata

The **File Info** window features 12 categories of information, listed in a column on the left. Click a category in the column to access that information. Enter relevant information for each category as it relates to your work (notice our assigned keyword has been stored). If your camera captures shooting information in EXIF format, some of the fields in the **Camera Data** categories might already be filled in.

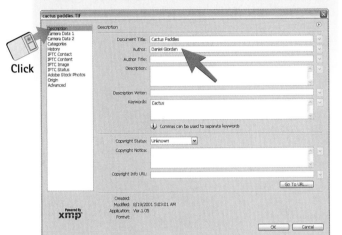

Click

5 Select Find

After keywords and metadata are assigned to your images, you can use this information to search and sort your images just like records in any other database. To search for images with keywords or metadata using **Bridge**, select **Edit**, **Find** from the **Bridge** menu.

 Click

6 Enter Find Data

In the **Find** dialog box that appears, select the target folder or folders you want to search using the **Look in** menu or the **Browse** button. Enable the **Include All Subfolders** check box if necessary. In the **Criteria** section, select the search variable from the first menu and construct a search string using the second menu and typing a search term such as a keyword or author name. Search variables include filenames and types, dates created/modified, labels, ratings, keywords, and metadata. Click the plus sign to expand the fields and allow additional search variables in the same search. Enable the check box for **Show Find Results in a New Browser Window** if you want a new **Bridge** window to open and display the results.

Click

7 View Search Results

In the **Find** dialog box, click **Find**. **Bridge** returns all the results. If you selected the new browser window option, **Bridge** opens a separate window called **Find Results**. Every time you perform a search, the search results are placed in a new window, so you can compare the results of two searches.

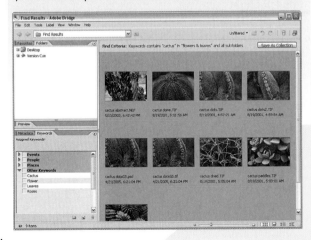

End

How to Work with Camera Raw Images

Camera raw images are 16-bit image files saved from professional and semiprofessional digital cameras. When you open one of these raw images, Photoshop launches a separate window that applies tone and sharpness corrections to the raw data as the file is opened, allowing you to save the result as a separate file. This capability enables you to explore and push the limits of the extended 16-bit file depth while preserving the original data values. Note that the controls for raw images are extensive. I won't attempt to explain all of them, but the steps that follow cover the majority of standard imaging corrections.

Begin

1 Open File

Click the **Go to Bridge** icon in the **Options** bar to launch **Bridge**. Navigate to the desired file and double-click its thumbnail to open it. If the file is a camera raw file, Photoshop automatically launches the **Camera Raw** window.

Double-click

2 Adjust Exposure

Adjust the **Exposure** slider to lighten or darken the primary tonal range. At the top of the **Raw Plug-in** dialog box are check box options for **Shadows** and **Highlights** that you can toggle on or off to highlight clipping in these areas. Avoid clipping tonal areas in most cases because doing so results in a loss of detail.

Drag

3 Adjust the Shadows

Increase the **Shadows** slider to deepen the shadows in the image (note that too much darkening can cause a loss of shadow detail). Enable the **Shadows** clipping option at the top of the dialog box to highlight tonal areas within each channel that would be lost.

Drag

4 Adjust the Remaining Exposure Controls

Modify the **Brightness**, **Contrast**, and **Saturation** sliders to complete the tonal modifications. If enabled, the **Shadow** and **Highlights** check box options highlight any clipped areas.

Drag

5 Adjust Sharpness

Click the **Detail** tab and adjust the **Sharpness** slider as needed. Be sure to select **100%** from the **Zoom Level** menu at the bottom of the window to see the actual sharpening results.

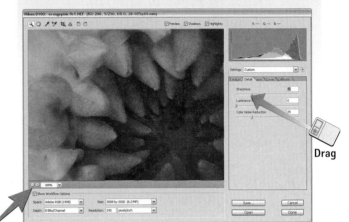

Drag

6 Adjust for Chromatic Aberration

Chromatic aberration is a misalignment of color channels that is sometimes visible at the edges of digital images. It appears as colored fringing that corresponds to either a red/cyan or blue/yellow polarity (that is, the fringe will be red on one side of the image and cyan on the other). Click the **Lens** tab and adjust the **Chromatic Aberration R/C** or **Chromatic Aberration B/Y** slider as needed.

Drag

How-To Hints

Save, Done, or Open?

Instead of a simple **OK** button, the **Camera Raw** dialog box has three options to save your adjustments: **Save** saves a copy of the adjusted file; **Open** moves the adjusted image into Photoshop for further editing; and **Done** saves the adjustment settings in either a database file or in a *sidecar file* (a small file in the same folder the original image file), depending on the **Preferences** setting. **Camera Raw** never changes the actual raw image file.

Color Correction with Temperature

The **Temperature** slider in combination with the **Tint** slider (on the **Adjust** tab) is good for compensating for color casts from light sources. Use these sliders to neutralize green fluorescent lights or the harsh yellow of interior incandescent lighting. Together, the two sliders can help to adjust for a better white balance.

End

Task

PART 12

Building Web Files

*A*dobe has done an excellent job transforming Photoshop from an advanced image-editing tool into an advanced web-production tool, without losing the image-editing features along the way. Using the ImageReady feature set, users now can build tables, create JavaScript rollovers, and slice an image into multiple images with custom optimization for each piece.

In addition, file optimization has never been easier; both Photoshop and ImageReady save and optimize files in a range of Web-ready formats such as JPEG and GIF. These controls allow real-time previews, transparency adjustments, and more.

Note: Some of the work in the tasks in this part will be done in ImageReady and not in Photoshop itself. Moving back and forth between the two programs is easy, calling on the strengths of each as necessary. In fact, the two programs are closely linked and you can open one from the other and move files back and forth between the applications.

Photoshop and ImageReady automatically optimize, rename, and generate solid HTML code on-the-fly, supporting a wide variety of web tasks. The code is saved as a separate HTML file that can dovetail with an existing page or, in the case of tables, be used on its own.

Be sure to set the HTML settings in both Photoshop and ImageReady to ensure that the code being created is optimized for the platforms and browsers for which you're developing. In addition, you should check out the filenaming conventions in the ImageReady and Photoshop **Preferences** dialog boxes to ensure that the autonaming schemes are compatible with your overall process. Refer to Part 1, "Getting Started with Photoshop," for details on setting these preferences. ●

How to Preview Files in Browsers and Platforms

Image files can look different on Macs than they do on PCs and from browser to browser. Uncalibrated PC monitors have a higher gamma setting than uncalibrated Mac monitors, so image midtones can appear darker when displayed on PCs. (see the Hint following this section). Differences in browser types tend to show themselves when you're building tables or working with other layout issues. When preparing files for the Web, it is imperative that you check each file on all platforms and in as many browsers as possible.

Begin

1 Open the File in ImageReady

Open the image file in ImageReady. Although you can do this in Photoshop, ImageReady offers a few general advantages for web optimization, such as GIF animation and Java rollovers.

2 Preview for Windows

If you're on a Mac and want to see what the file might look like on a Windows machine, select **View, Preview, Standard Windows Color.** This command adjusts the image's appearance to approximate the 2.2 gamma setting typical for uncalibrated PCs. In Photoshop, select **View, Proof Setup, Windows RGB.**

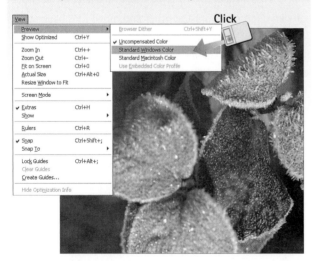

3 Preview for Mac

If you're on a PC and want to see what the file might look like on a Macintosh, select **View, Preview, Standard Macintosh Color.** This command adjusts the image's appearance to approximate the 1.8 gamma setting typical for uncalibrated Macs. In Photoshop, select **View, Proof Setup, Macintosh RGB.**

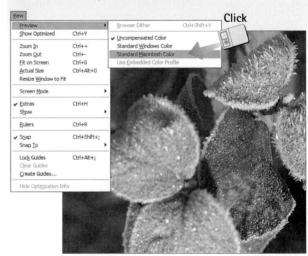

4 Preview As JPEG

After you set the preview to Mac or PC, you should determine the best compression format for your image. To test the results of JPEG compression, select **Window, Optimize** to open the **Optimize** palette. Select **JPEG** from the **Format** drop-down list and click the **Optimized** preview tab.

Click

Click

5 Preview As GIF

To test the results of GIF compression, select **Window, Optimize** to open the **Optimize** palette. Select **GIF** from the **Format** drop-down list. Look at the status line at the bottom of the image area: With the **Optimize** tab selected, the file's original size appears, followed by the size the file will be if saved as a GIF. For details on GIF optimization, see Task 2, "How to Build GIF Files for the Web."

Click

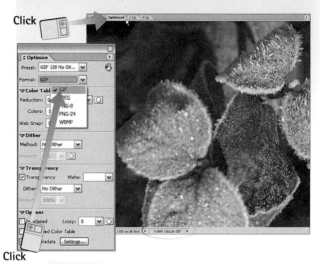

Click

6 Preview in Browsers

To preview a file or table in a browser, click the **Browser Preview** button in the toolbox. The specified browser launches and loads the current file. Here the image is shown in the Internet Explorer browser. To select an alternative browser, click and hold the tool button and select from other browser options. You can also select **File, Preview In,** *<Browser Name>* to select a browser.

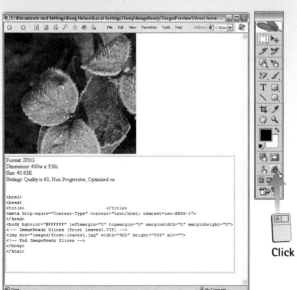

Click

End

How to Build GIF Files for the Web

GIF files are efficient, compact files perfect for use on the Web. GIF files enable you to build in transparency and animation while keeping the file size small. GIF files do not handle photographic images well, however. If you want your photographic images to maintain detail, consider the JPEG file format.

Begin

1 Open and Save File in Photoshop

Open the file you want to convert to GIF format. Select **File, Save for Web**. The **Save For Web** dialog box opens, and Photoshop creates a duplicate image, leaving the original image untouched. Click the **Optimized** tab to preview the file compression results based on your settings.

Click

2 Select Optimized File Format

From the first drop-down menu in the dialog box, select **GIF**. Leave the next two options set at **Selective** and **Diffusion** (these options refer to the color conversion and dither patterns).

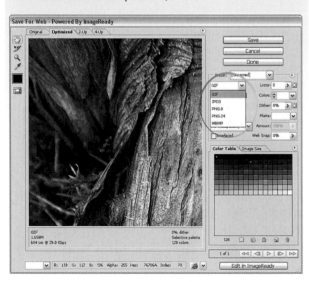

3 Set Lossy and Dither Sliders

Set the **Lossy** and **Dither** sliders. Start by setting **Lossy** to **100** and **Dither** to **0**. To reduce the file size (displayed under the preview), keep the **Dither** value as low as possible and the **Lossy** value as high as possible. The image is updated to reflect the changes you make. Watch the image changes to help make a final decision when it comes to applying the various settings. If the image is too grainy, lower the **Lossy** slider. If it appears solarized and graphic, raise the **Dither** value.

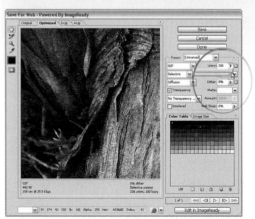

4 Set the Number of Colors

Your next goal is to create a GIF file with as few colors as possible. Shoot for 32 or 64 (some graphics files can use as few as 8 or even 4 colors without compromising the image much). Click and hold the **Colors** drop-down list and select the number of colors. (Alternatively, highlight the number in this field and type the desired value.)

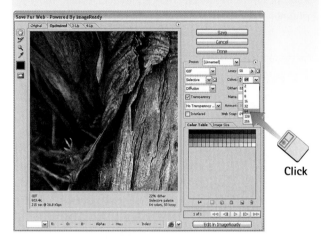

Click

5 Set the Image Size

You can further reduce file size by reducing the image size. You also should ensure that your image is small enough to be seen fully without any zooming (usually less than 800 pixels wide and 600 pixels in height). Click the **Image Size** tab and enable the **Constrain Proportions** check box. Enter an appropriate height and width and then click the **Apply** button to preview the new size.

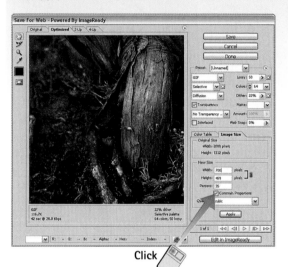

Click

6 Save the File

Click **Save** to close the **Save for Web** dialog box. The **Save Optimized As** dialog box opens. Verify the name and location of the file and click **Save** to save the file.

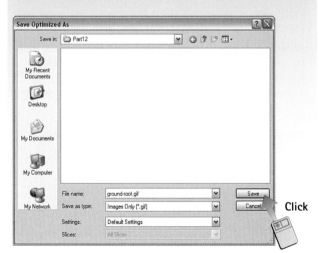

Click

End

How-To Hints

Using 2-Up or 4-Up Comparison Tables

If you're unclear about multiple compression settings, click the **2-Up** and **4-Up** tabs in the **Save for Web** dialog box. These tabs enable you to compare options side by side.

Previewing in Browsers

If you're unsure about how an image will look in a given browser, use the **Browser Preview** feature: While still in the **Save for Web** dialog box, either click the **Browser Preview** button or use the **Select Browser** menu to select the desired target browser. Both the button and the menu are at the bottom of the dialog box (in these examples, the button shows the Internet Explorer icon; access the menu by clicking the arrow next to this button).

How to Optimize GIF Color Sets

The more you work with GIF conversion, the more you realize that the most critical step is in mapping the original colors to a minimal yet representative table set. To most people, it sounds inconceivable that 32 colors can replace the thousands of colors in an image. Although you *can* do it, you must be careful about which colors you keep and which you throw away.

1 Open and Save File in Photoshop

With your image open in Photoshop, select **File, Save for Web**. The **Save For Web** dialog box opens and Photoshop creates a duplicate image, leaving the original image untouched. Click the **Optimized** tab to select it.

Click

2 Set Basic GIF Settings

Refer to Task 2 and set the compression type (**GIF**) and the **Dither** and **Lossy** settings. From the **Colors** list, select the lowest number of colors while keeping the file's integrity intact.

3 Lock Important Colors

Click the **Color Table** tab. Click the **Eyedropper** tool located at the upper-left side in the **Save for Web** dialog box, and click a prominent color in the image. The corresponding color in the **Color Table** is highlighted. Lock the selected color by clicking the **Lock** button at the bottom of the **Color Table**; locking a color prevents it from being removed or dithered. Repeat this step for other critical colors in the image.

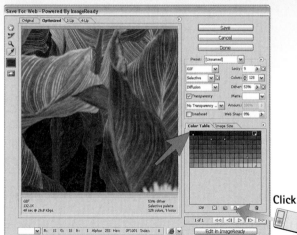

Click

4 Eliminate Close Colors

With the image showing on the **Optimized** tab, select **Sort by Luminance** from the **Color Table** palette menu. In the **Color Table**, select a color close to a locked color and click the **Trash Can** icon in the **Color Table** section. The screen redraws to delete the selected color from the image. Continue deleting colors until you get a core set that represents the image well.

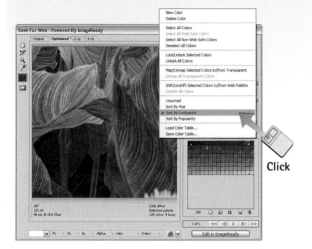

Click

5 Changing Individual Table Colors

With the important colors locked down, determine whether you need to change other colors. To change color swatches, double-click the color in the **Color Table**; the **Color Picker** dialog box opens. Change the current color, paying close attention to the web-safe icon in the picker (the three-sided box icon), which shows you the nearest web-safe color.

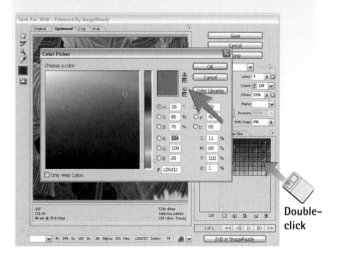

Double-click

6 Save the Color Table

If you're working with the same kind of image or want a series of images to use the same color set, save the color table you just fine-tuned. Select **Save Color Table** from the **Color Table** palette menu. In the **Save As** dialog box that appears, type a name for the color table and click **OK**.

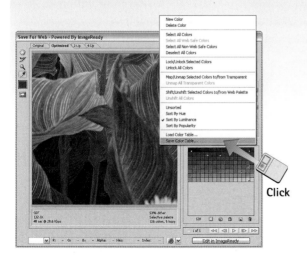

Click

How-To Hints

Using a Saved Color Table

To load a saved Color Table profile, open the **Save for Web** dialog box and select **Load Color Table** from the **Color Table** palette menu.

Using Web-Safe Colors

Use the **Web Snap** slider in the upper-right corner of the **Save for Web** dialog box to convert existing colors to web-safe colors. Change the slider and monitor the results in the preview. The higher the value in the **Web Snap** slider, the more exactly colors are transformed to the web-safe palette. The *web-safe palette* refers to a subset of colors that can be reproduced exactly the same on all platforms and with all browsers. Use these colors to ensure that people who view your web graphics see exactly the colors you intended them to see.

End

How to Create a GIF Transparency

GIF files have an advantage over JPEG files in that they enable you to set certain areas as transparent. This means you can create silhouette effects to place over web page backgrounds. The transparent areas in a GIF file are completely invisible. This task uses ImageReady to create the transparency.

Begin

1 Open File in ImageReady

In ImageReady, select **File, Open**. In the **Open** dialog box, select the file you want to work with and click **Open**.

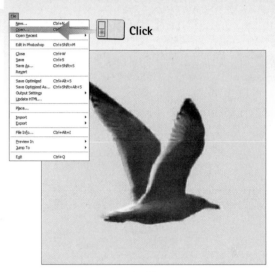
Click

2 Select the Area to Be Transparent

Using any of ImageReady's selection tools (such as the **Magic Wand** tool to select areas of similar color), make a selection representing the area you want to make transparent. Here, I selected the sky.

3 Apply a Layer Mask

Open the **Layers** palette by selecting **Window, Layers**. With the selection from step 2 still active, press and hold the **Option/Alt** key and click the **Add A Mask** button at the bottom of the **Layers** palette. This action "masks out" the selected area, giving you an idea of what the final result will be. If the button is grayed out, rename the **Background** layer.

Option + Alt +
Click

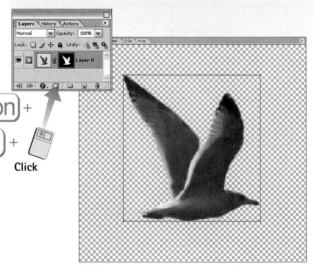

4 Build Optimize Settings

When the transparency is the way you want it, select **Window**, **Optimize** to open the **Optimize** palette. Then specify the appropriate settings. (Refer to Task 2, "How to Build GIF Files for the Web," for instructions on setting up a GIF file.) Make sure that the **Transparency** option is checked. Inspect the results in the **Optimized** window.

5 Preview in a Browser

Select **File**, **Preview In**, *<Browser Name>* or click the **Browser Preview** button in the toolbar to look at the file as it will appear in a browser.

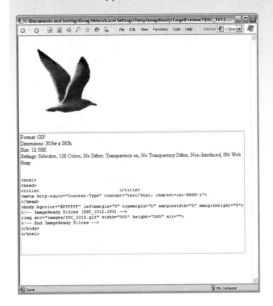

6 Save Optimized File

If the file looks good, close the browser and return to ImageReady. Select **File**, **Save Optimized** to save the file using the settings in the **Optimize** palette.

Click

How-To Hints

Fixing the Transparency

If the transparency in the layer mask in step 3 is not right, click the **Add a Mask** button in the **Layers** palette and paint the transparent selection as you would with any layer mask. (See Part 10, Task 7, "How to Add a Layer Mask," for details on layer masks.)

Transparency in Photoshop

You can also set GIF transparencies using Photoshop's **Save for Web** dialog box. Select the color in the **Color Table** and click the **Transparency** icon at the bottom of the **Color Table**.

End

How to Build JPEG Files for the Web

The JPEG format works well for continuous-tone images, such as photographs. Even though the compression format creates artifacts that pixelate the image, these snags are hardly visible in photographic-quality images (although they can degrade the quality of hard-edged graphics). Photoshop has a blur function built in to the JPEG dialog box that is helpful for many images. You can smooth over many of the artifacts that surface when the quality level gets too low.

Begin

1 Open File in Photoshop

In Photoshop, select **File, Open**. In the **Open** dialog box, select the file you want to compress with the JPEG format.

2 Set JPEG Options

Select **File, Save for Web** to open the **Save for Web** dialog box. From the **Optimized File Format** drop-down list, select **JPEG**. The main control in this section is the **Quality** slider. This setting determines the level of compression in the file, as well as the corresponding quality. Adjust the setting to high, medium, or low, remembering that the higher the quality, the bigger the file size and the lower the quality, the smaller the file size.

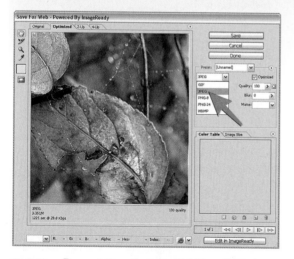

3 Select 4-Up to Compare Settings

Click the **4-Up** tab to look at the original image and three variations. This comparison can help you select the setting that creates the highest-quality image combined with the lowest file size.

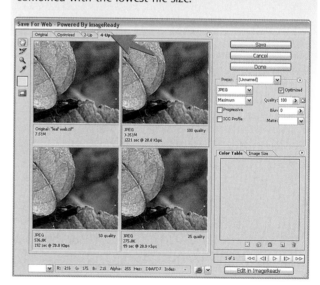

4 Tweak Blur Slider

Click the **Optimized** tab to return to that page, and then slightly raise the **Blur** slider to see whether this adjustment helps smooth the image. Click **OK** and rename the file to optimize it and save it as a separate file.

Drag

5 Reopen File

To check the quality of the image you just created, select **File, Open**. From the **Open** dialog box, select the optimized file you just created. Check it against the original file to ensure that the detail is solid and the color is good.

Original TIFF file

JPEG file

6 Test Unsharp Mask Filter

Because JPEG files tend to soften the original image, you might find that a slight **Unsharp Mask** filter helps bring back some detail (the filter also adds to the file size). Select **Filter, Sharpen, Unsharp Mask**. Start by setting the **Amount** field to **50%** or **100%**; set the **Radius** field to a value between **.7** and **1.0**. Gradually increase the settings until you like the results. Click **OK** to apply the sharpening or click **Cancel**.

Drag

End

How-To Hints

Moving the Image Around

While working in the **Save for Web** dialog box, you can place the mouse pointer over the preview image; when the pointer changes to the hand icon, move the image around so you can look at specific details in the image. You can also select the magnifying glass tool and zoom in and out of the image to check details.

Keeping Consistent Color

Enable the **ICC Profile** check box in the **Save for Web** dialog box to embed the profile in the compressed image. Only a few browsers support ICC profiles, but the feature can offer color consistency when you share your files with others.

How to Optimize Files with Variable Compression

Variable compression enables you to alter image compression and quality in different areas of the same image. You can focus more detail around a central character or image while allowing details to erode in unimportant areas, such as the background or flat areas of color. The result is an optimized image that delivers higher quality and lower bandwidth. This task describes the compression process in Photoshop; although you can optimize a file with additional channels in ImageReady following the same process, ImageReady does not add or modify channels.

1 Open File in Photoshop

The first part of this task involves creating a mask in Photoshop. To do this, open Photoshop and select **File, Open**. From the **Open** dialog box, select the file you want to optimize.

2 Create a New Channel

Select **Window, Channels** to launch the Channels palette. Next, select **New Channel** from the Channels palette menu. Modify any parameters as desired in the **New Channel** dialog box (including mask color and area definition options) and click **OK** to create the new channel.

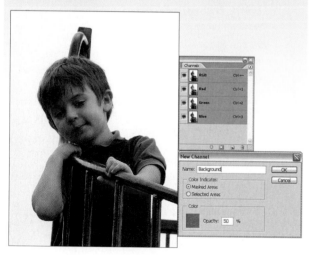

3 Create the Mask

Initially, the new channel turns the image black. To view the channel and the image as a composite, go to the **Channels** palette and turn on visibility for all channels, including the new channel you just created. In the final compressed image, white areas of the alpha channel will carry the most detail; black areas will have the least detail. With this in mind, paint the channel to emphasize image detail using any of Photoshop's paint tools. When finished, turn off visibility for the alpha channel in the **Channels** palette.

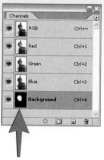

4 Save for the Web

Select File, Save for Web to launch the Save for Web dialog box. With the mask in place, you now have the option of opening the file and optimizing it in ImageReady as well.

Click

5 For JPEG Files

In the Save for Web dialog box, select JPEG from the Optimize File Format menu. Click the icon next to the Quality control to launch the Modify Quality Setting dialog box. From the pop-up menu, select the channel created in step 2. With the Preview box checked, adjust the slider to specify the minimum or maximum quality setting to be applied, based on the selected channel. Remember that the pure white channel areas correspond to the maximum settings and the black areas correspond to the minimum settings. Click OK.

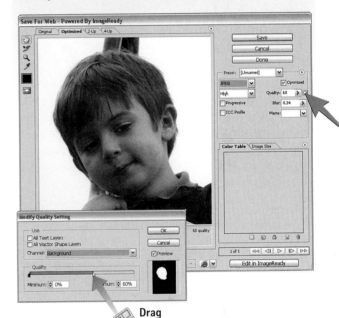

Drag

6 For GIF Files

In the Save for Web dialog box, select GIF from the Optimize File Format menu and set the GIF settings as desired. You can use channels to modify the Dither, Lossy, and Color Reduction settings by clicking the icon next to the associated control to open a dialog box and following the process in the preceding step.

How-To Hints

Feathering Masks for Gradual Effects

When building the mask in Photoshop, use the Blur filter or the Brush tool set to Airbrush to create soft, graduated areas between light and dark sections of the mask. Doing so reduces the crisp transitions between areas of different quality.

Don't Forget PNG Files

You can also use channels to modify the quality in a PNG-8 file. Use the process outlined in step 6 to alter the Dither and Colors settings.

End

How to Slice Images for the Web

Slicing an image for the Web involves dividing a larger image into smaller tiles that are assembled in a table as the page is loaded. These smaller tiles often load faster than one large image and are necessary if you want a portion of a large image to act as a *rollover* or an *animation*. ImageReady lets you divide a graphic with a grid of horizontal and vertical lines and then creates individual files on-the-fly, including the necessary HTML code to build the table.

Begin

1 Open the File in ImageReady

In ImageReady, select **File, Open** and select the image file you want to modify.

2 Show Rulers

If the rulers are not already visible, select **View, Rulers** to display rulers along the top and left sides of the image window.

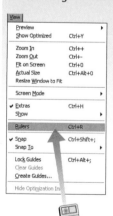

Click

3 Drag Guides

Position the mouse pointer over one of the rulers and hold down the mouse button until the pointer changes to a double-headed arrow. Drag into the image to create a horizontal or vertical guide. Position guides to correspond to the slices you want to create.

Drag

4 Slice Along Guides

Select **Slices, Create Slices from Guides** to slice the image along the current guidelines. The slices show up on the image area as rectangular sections outlined in a highlight color. The currently selected slice appears in gold.

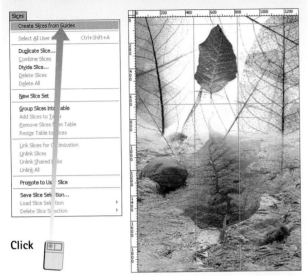

Click

5 Optimize Slices

Click the **Slice Select** tool from the toolbox and click the first slice in the image area to select it. Then open the **Optimize** palette (select **Window, Optimize**) and set the optimization for that section, just as you would for an entire file. Repeat this step for each slice in the image area. Preview your optimizations by clicking the **Optimized** tab.

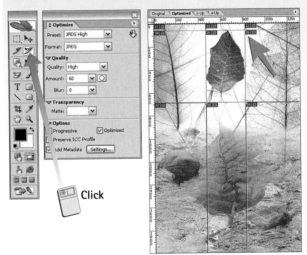

Click

6 Save Files

Select **File, Save Optimized** to open the **Save Optimized** dialog box. Select **HTML and Images** from the **Save As Type** menu (the **Format** menu on the Mac) if you want ImageReady to create the HTML file for the associated table. If you are saving a large number of slices, you might want to click the **New Folder** button and name the new folder to keep all the associated files in one place. Click **Save** to save and optimize each slice. Multiple files will be created, each file containing a single slice. The files have the original filename and a sequentially assigned number appended to the filename.

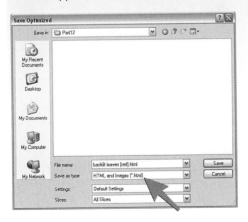

End

How to Build Imagemaps

Imagemaps enable you to create *hot spots* in web images that link to other pages, actions, or information. You could create a graphic with buttons, elaborate text treatments, or image-based information, designating the exact areas within the image for the links. ImageReady lets you easily designate areas for imagemaps, allowing you to specify the link information and even save the necessary HTML code to finish the effect.

Begin

1 Open the File in ImageReady

In ImageReady, select **File**, **Open** and select the desired image file. In this image, I will draw imagemap areas around each line of text, which will link to the respective pages in a website.

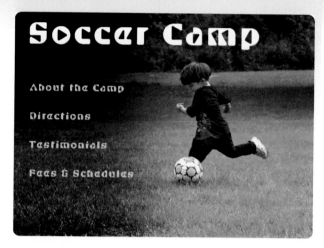

2 Select the Image Map Tool

Click and hold the **Image Map** tool in the toolbox to display all the ImageMap tools in a pop-out menu. The tool options enable you to draw rectangles, circles, and polygonal shapes. There is also a tool for selecting the imagemap shapes after they're drawn. Select the desired shape tool from the menu.

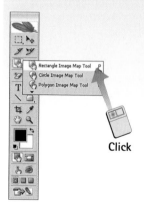

Click

3 Draw the Imagemap Shapes

Move the mouse pointer over the image and click and drag to draw the shape—it appears outlined with handles on each side. To edit the shape after it is drawn, select the **Image Map Select** tool, select the imagemap shape, and move the handles as desired to resize.

Drag

4 Open the Image Map Palette

If it's not open already, select **Window, Image Map** to open the **Image Map** palette. Adjust the **X** and **Y** settings in the **Dimensions** section to control the exact placement of the shape. Adjust the **Width, Height,** or **Radius** control (depending on the shape type you selected in step 2) to resize the shape.

5 Set HTML Information

Enter a unique name for the imagemap shape you just drew, as well as the target URL for the link. After entering a URL, you can select a target value to control the kind of window in which the link will open. Select **Blank** for a new window or **Self** for the current window (the **Parent** and **Top** options are used primarily for frameset targeting). If desired, enter an **Alt** value, which appears if someone views the page with the graphics off.

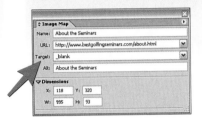

6 Save the Files

To save the image and the HTML parameters, you must save a graphic file *and* an HTML file. To do this, optimize the file as explained in Task 2, "How to Build GIF Files for the Web," and then select **File, Save Optimized**. In the **Save As Type** menu (the **Format** on the Mac), make sure that **HTML and Images** is selected and that the files are in the desired directory. Click **Save** to save the image and HTML files.

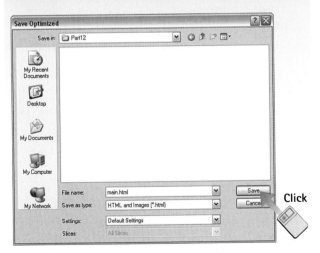

Click

End

How-To Hints

Aligning Shapes

When working with multiple imagemap shapes, use ImageReady's precision alignment tools to center the shapes or align them along an edge. Select the **ImageMap Select** tool and hold down the **Shift** key to select multiple shapes. You can then select from any of the align or distribute tools that appear in the **Options** bar.

Imagemaps from Layers

If you have a shape isolated on its own layer (such as a graphic button), select **Layer, New Layer Based Image Map Area**. This option creates a new imagemap shape based on the currently active layer.

How to Build Filter-Based GIF Animations

Photoshop and ImageReady enable you to create impressive animation sequences using progressive applications of various texture filters or distortion filters. By creating duplicate layers of the same file and then applying a filter with increasing intensity, you can easily animate the filter application. In this task, we take a close-up image of a flower and apply the **Motion Blur** filter in successive layers to create a nifty animation. Although you can start with any type of file, animations must be saved in the GIF format.

Begin

1 Open the File

In Photoshop, select **File**, **Open** and select the file you want to animate with a filter.

2 Duplicate Layers

Select **Window**, **Layers** to open the **Layers** palette. Select **Duplicate Layer** from the palette menu multiple times to create several individual states for the animation. In this example, I created three more layers.

Create multiple duplicate layers

3 Filter the Layers

Select the first layer in the **Layers** palette and open the desired filter (for this example, I selected **Filter, Blur, Motion Blur**). Apply a modest filter amount and click **OK**. Select the other layers in sequence, applying the filter to each layer with increasing intensity.

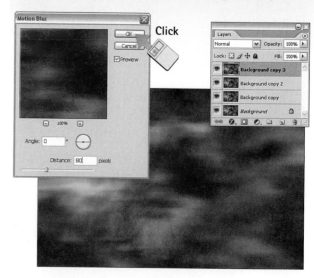

Click

4 Open the Animation Palette

Select **Window, Animation** to open the Animation palette.

5 Create Frames

Select **New Frame** from the **Animation** palette menu to create a new animation frame. Repeat this step to create a corresponding frame for each filtered layer you created in step 3. For example, if you have the original layer and created three filtered copies in step 3, create four animation frames now.

Make as many frames as you have filtered layers

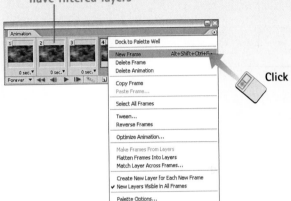

Click

6 Assign Layers to Frames

With both the **Layers** and **Animation** palettes visible, click the first animation frame and select the corresponding first layer of the filter progression. Click the visibility icons (the eye icons) for all the other layers so that only the selected layer is visible. Then click the next animation frame and select the next filtered layer in the **Layers** palette, making sure that only the selected layer is visible. Continue until each frame is assigned to a layer.

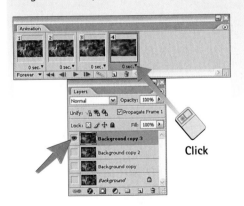

Click

How-To Hints

Using ImageReady if Necessary

If you have a pre-CS2 version of Photoshop, the **Animation** palette is available only from within ImageReady. However, Photoshop offers many more filter options than does ImageReady, so you still might want to perform steps 1–3 of this task in Photoshop. After you have filtered all the layers, click the **Jump to** button at the bottom of the toolbox to open the file in ImageReady and continue with step 4.

Continues

7 Play Back

Click the **Play** button at the bottom of the **Animation** palette to play the animation. Check for smoothness, alignment, and timing between frames. The animation will replay continuously; click the **Stop** button to stop the playback.

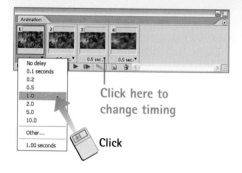

Click

8 Set the Loop Count

The **Loop Count** option controls whether an animation plays once, forever, or a specific number of times. Select **Once** or **Forever** from the pop-up menu; alternatively, select **Other** and enter the number of repetitions in the dialog box that appears.

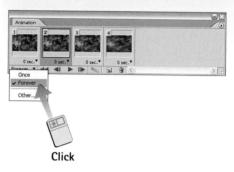

Click

9 Set the Frame Timing

To add a timing delay for a single frame, click the timing pop-up menu underneath the frame you want to modify and select the desired time delay. For example, you might want to add a longer delay to the first frame to emphasize the original state of the image.

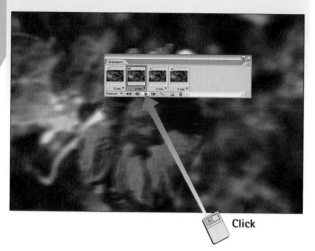

Click here to
change timing

Click

10 Launch Save for Web

Select **File**, **Save for Web** to open the **Save for Web** dialog box. Optimize the animation as a GIF file as explained in Task 2, "How to Build GIF Files for the Web."

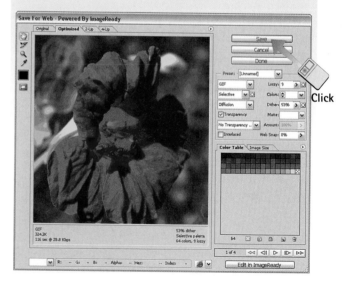

Click

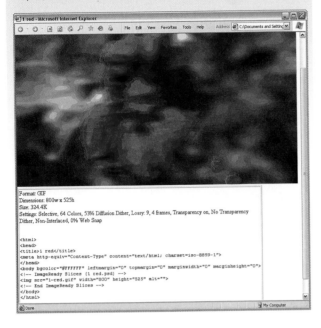

11 Preview in a Browser

Click the **Preview in Browser** button. The animation file opens in the specified browser with information about the file size, file type, and compression type displayed at the bottom of the window.

12 Save As GIF

Configure the GIF format settings in the **Optimize** palette and select **Save** to save the GIF file. For details on how to save GIF files, refer to Task 2, "How to Build GIF Files for the Web."

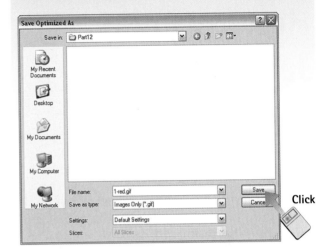

Click

End

How-To Hints

Optimizing and Saving Animation Files

If you are using ImageReady for your animation, remember to save the file as a GIF in step 12. Optimizing the file as a GIF in step 10 sets the number of colors and so on; it does not save the file. You must save the file using the **GIF89a** format; otherwise, the file will not animate.

Keeping the Number of Animation Frames to As Few As Possible

Animation frames dramatically increase file size and, consequently, download times. Keep the number of frames to a minimum to ensure fast download times and to guarantee fast-loading pages.

Animating Text with Warp Text

Consider using the **Warp Text** tool for sophisticated text animation. Create the text with the **Type** tool, build animation frames, and apply **Warp Text** effects gradually to each frame. **Warp Text** is an icon in the upper-right corner of the **Options** bar for the **Text** tool.

How to Build JavaScript Rollovers

Rollover animations are graphics that change as you pass the mouse over a specific spot onscreen. These animations are useful for emphasizing links, especially in graphics that might not be clearly marked. Rollovers consist of a normal state, mouse-over state, and click state, so this task creates a separate image variation for each state. To explain the rollover effect, this task creates a basic button and then changes the state of the button. After you create the button and its three states, you must save the HTML code as well as the graphics and then paste the code into the target web page.

Begin

1 Create a New ImageReady File

In ImageReady, select **File, New** to open the **New Document** dialog box so you can create a new file. For this task, specify a width of **340** pixels and a height of **240** pixels for the image size; then select the **White** radio button. Click **OK**.

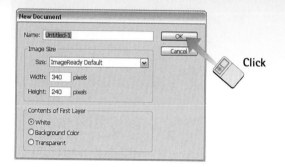

Click

2 Create the Button

Make a new layer, select the **Elliptical Marquee** tool, and **Shift**+drag within the image to draw a circle the size of the final button. Select **Edit, Fill** and fill the button shape with black.

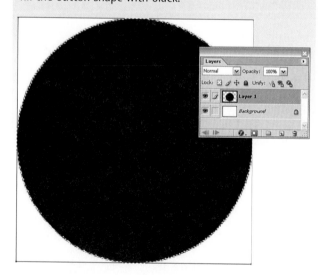

3 Add the Layer Effect

To give the button a 3D effect, select **Window, Styles** to open the **Styles** palette. Then click the **Green Gel** style. This action automatically assigns pre-designed layer styles to the active layer.

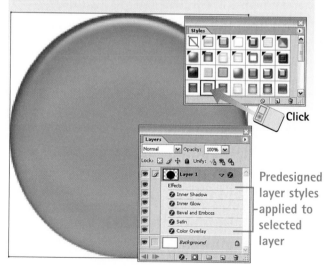

Click

Predesigned layer styles applied to selected layer

4 Make Layer Duplicates

From the **Layers** palette menu, select **Duplicate Layer** to copy the button and its effects. Select **Duplicate Layer** again to create a total of three layers, each of which shows the same button and styles.

5 Color the Layers

In the **Layers** palette, select the **Layer 1 Copy** layer and double-click the **Color Overlay** style to open the **Layer Style** dialog box. Click the color swatch to open the color picker, select a new color, and click **OK** to accept the color. Click **OK** again to accept the style change. Go back to the **Layers** palette and select the **Layer 1 Copy 2** layer and repeat this step, selecting a different color.

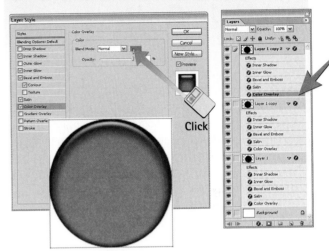

Click

6 Create Rollover States

Select **Window, Web Content** to open the **Web Content** palette. Select **New Rollover State** from the palette menu to create a new rollover state called **Over**. Select **New State** again to create another new rollover state called **Down**. You now should have a total of three states: the Normal state and two rollover states labeled **Over** and **Down**. (And, unbeknownst to you, ImageReady is creating the JavaScript code to make all this work!)

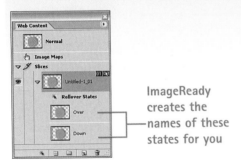

ImageReady creates the names of these states for you

7 Assign Layers to States

In the **Web Content** palette, select the **Normal** state; in the **Layers** palette, select the layer that shows the color you want the button to be in its normal state. Repeat this for the **Over** and **Down** rollover states. Select **File, Save Optimized** to save the file, making sure that **Format, HTML and Images** is selected.

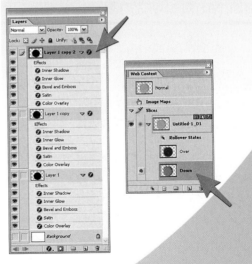

End

How to Build a Web Gallery

The **Web Photo Gallery** feature in Photoshop is a great way to quickly post to the Web a thumbnail directory of images that includes links to full-sized images, filenames, and the photographer's name. Anyone who wants to post a directory of images should take advantage of this feature, which is built around Photoshop's **Actions** technology. You place images into a single folder, set the parameters, and step back. The script runs everything right before your eyes, building the code, optimizing the images and thumbnails, and creating all the links.

Begin

1 Select Web Photo Gallery

In Photoshop, select **File**, **Automate**, **Web Photo Gallery** to open the **Web Photo Gallery** dialog box. Select a page layout from the **Styles** pop-up menu, observing the thumbnail on the right side of the dialog box to evaluate the results.

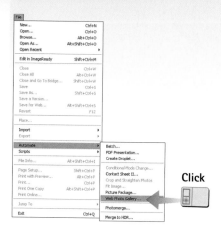

Click

2 Set File Source and Destination

In the **Source Images** section, click the **Browse** button (the **Select** button on the Mac) and navigate to the source folder (the folder that contains all the images). Click **OK** (**Select** on the Mac) to close the **Select Image Directory** dialog box. Now click the **Destination** button and navigate to the destination folder (where the final files and HTML documents will be stored). Click **OK** (**Select** on the Mac) to make your selection.

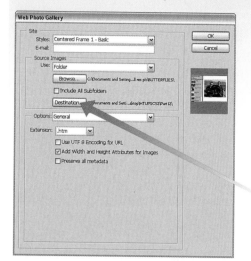

Click

3 Name and Date the Site

From the **Options** menu, select **Banner**. In the bottom section of the dialog box, fill in all appropriate fields, listing the site name, date, and photographer information. You can also select the date. The **Font** and **Font Size** options can be specified only with some site styles.

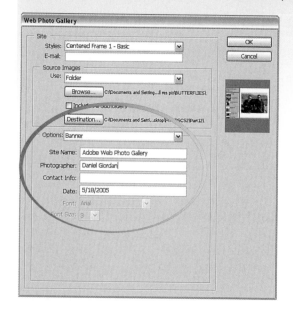

4 Resize Images

From the **Options** menu, select **Large Images** to see more options. Enable the **Resize Images** check box if you want to resize the main images that open from the thumbnails. With this box enabled, select the image size from the adjacent pop-up menu and the JPEG compression rate from the **JPEG Quality** pop-up menu. To enter a specific JPEG compression value, select the quality setting from the **JPEG Quality** menu.

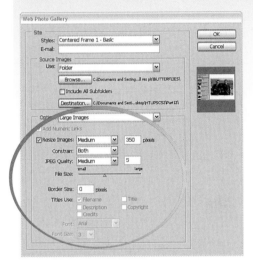

5 Set the Page Layout

Select **Thumbnails** from the **Options** pop-up menu. To use the filename or the text stored in the **File Info** section as a caption, enable the appropriate check box. Some title options are not available for all site styles.

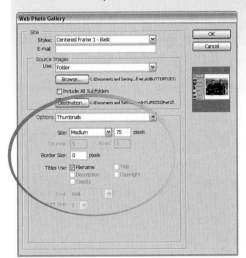

6 Build and Test the Site

Click **OK** to build the Web Photo Gallery site. Photoshop runs the script on its own, opening files, compressing, and saving everything to the source folder you specified in step 2. When the script is complete, Photoshop launches the **Web Photo Gallery** in a browser window for you to test. Click the thumbnails to test the links and ensure that everything is listed properly.

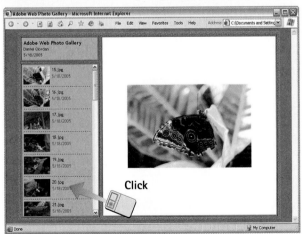

Click

How-To Hints

File Structure

Photoshop creates several files and folders within the destination folder you designated to support the Web Photo Gallery. All the images are stored in an images folder; thumbnails go into a thumbnails folder. A separate HTML page also is created for each image and is stored in a folder called pages. The main gallery page is called index.htm. There can also be other support files, depending on the site style you select. When posting your gallery page online, be sure to upload the entire contents of the destination folder, including its subfolders and their contents, to your server.

Custom Colors

Select **Custom Colors** from the **Options** menu to specify the text, link, background, and banner text colors. Click each color swatch to launch the **Color Picker** and select the desired color. Enable the **Only Web Colors** check box in the **Color Picker** to restrict the choices to web-safe colors.

End

Task

PART 13

Special Effects

*Y*ou can perform two kinds of tasks with Photoshop. One is the basic, utilitarian task of image processing, and the other is the dynamic, eye-catching effects you can create by using filters and special Photoshop commands.

Until this point, you've only looked at the image-processing side of things—exploring how to crop, rotate, and paint images. Although you almost always will need these skills more than you will need creative special effects, the reality is that special effects are just more fun. To that end, the tasks in this part of the book look at a variety of special effects you can apply fairly easily in Photoshop.

A good special effect is often the result of a careful selection so that the effect applies to only a portion of the image. A good special effect might also combine a filter or an effect with surrounding layers or the previous image state. By creating effects in combination or by applying them to specific areas, you can create effects that are professional and distinctive.

Be sure to check out the **Artistic** and **Brush Strokes** filters, which create a staggering variety of strokes, textures, and abstractions. These filters have been combined into an interactive interface called the **Filter Gallery** that allows you to simultaneously combine multiple filter effects.

The tasks in this part spend a fair amount of time looking at various filter options; with more than 100 native Photoshop filters built in to Photoshop CS2, we won't scratch the surface of all that's available. I've selected certain filters you can combine with other effects, such as blur or lighting effects. The filters I've selected also let me explain the general approach to working with filters, emphasizing the use of the **Fade** command and filter color selection. ●

TASK 1

How to Use Blending Modes

Blending modes are one of the fastest ways to experiment with imaging effects in your Photoshop files. Think of them as preset functions that apply a range of imaging effects that standard Photoshop commands can't touch. The basic function of a blending mode is to compare two sets of pixel data and combine them in different ways. Although I could write an entire chapter on exactly how these options work, 99% of Photoshop users simply experiment until they get an effect they like.

1 Blending Modes in Layers Palette

Open or create a file with more than one layer and select **Window, Layers** to open the **Layers** palette. The **Blending Mode** drop-down menu is at the top of the palette. Highlight the topmost layer tile in the list and click and hold the menu to select one of the modes. The contents of the selected layer are compared with all the layers below it to achieve the result. Keep in mind that you cannot apply a blending mode to the **Background** layer.

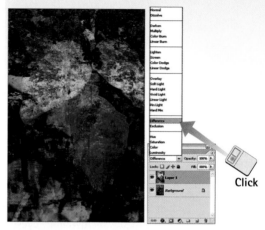

Click

2 Blending Modes in Paint Tools

You can select most of the paint tools and apply them using the blending modes. With the tool selected, select an option from the **Mode** menu in the **Options** bar. This approach to modes compares the values from the paint color or source data (if you're using the **Clone Stamp** or **History Brush** tool) with the underlying image. Blending modes are available with the following tools (including the tools nested with them): **Brush, Healing Brush, Clone Stamp, History Brush, Blur,** and **Gradient**.

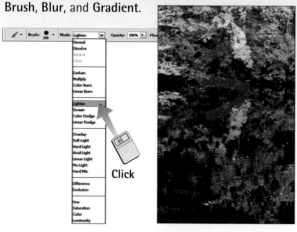

Click

3 Blending Modes with Filters

After applying a filter, select **Edit, Fade <filter name>**. The Fade dialog box opens with an **Opacity** slider and a **Mode** menu. Select the desired mode from the menu and click **OK** to apply the effect. This approach to modes compares the original image data with the results of the filter effect.

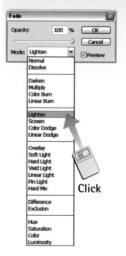

Click

4 Blending Modes with Fills

Select **Edit**, **Fill** to launch the **Fill** dialog box. Select **Foreground Color**, **Background Color**, or **Color** from the **Use** menu and then select the desired blending mode from the **Mode** menu. If you want, you can enter a percentage value in the **Opacity** text box to apply the mode with a degree of transparency. This approach to modes compares the current foreground or background color with the image.

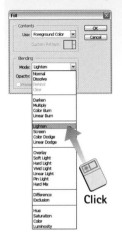

Click

5 Blending Modes with Pattern Fills

Select **Edit**, **Fill** to launch the **Fill** dialog box. Select **Pattern** from the **Use** menu and select a pattern preset from the **Custom Pattern** list. Select the desired blending mode from the **Mode** menu. If you want, enter a percentage value in the **Opacity** text box to apply the mode with a degree of transparency. This approach to modes compares the pattern values with the image.

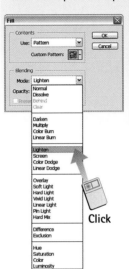

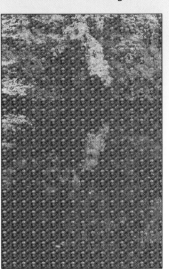

Click

6 Blending Modes with History

Follow the steps in Part 7, Task 4, "How to Use the History Brush," to set the History source in the **History** palette. Then select **Edit**, **Fill** to launch the **Fill** dialog box. Select **History** from the **Use** menu and select the blending mode from the **Mode** menu. If you want, enter a percentage value in the **Opacity** text box to apply the mode with a degree of transparency. This approach to modes compares the selected history state with the image.

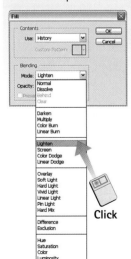

Click

How-To Hints

Previewing Blended Fills

When using **Color**, **Pattern**, or **History** fills, note that there is no **Preview** option. However, after you have accepted the fill, you can select **Edit**, **Fade Fill** to change the fill's blending mode with a full preview.

Blending Modes with Tone and Color Adjustments

Because a blending mode requires the comparison of two sets of data, you can't apply modes when using the color and tone adjustments found in the **Image**, **Adjustments** menu. However, you can create an adjustment layer and apply a blending mode to *that* layer as described in step 1. This achieves the same result and also provides the flexibility of being able to hide or move the layer.

End

TASK 2

How to Build a Glow Effect with Stroke Path

You can add an effect around a featured object that looks like a glowing halo that softly fades into the background. In addition to having aesthetic appeal, the effect described in this task works well when you're silhouetting an object against a white or dark background. It also works to separate the object from its background.

1 Open the File and Draw a Path

Select **File**, **Open** and select the file you want to modify. Select the **Pen** tool from the toolbox and select the **Paths** option in the **Options** bar. Use the techniques described in Part 9, "Using Paths," to draw a path around the desired object.

2 Select the Glow Color

Double-click the **Foreground** color swatch in the toolbox; after the **Color Picker** opens, select a color for the glow. Click **OK** to close the **Color Picker**.

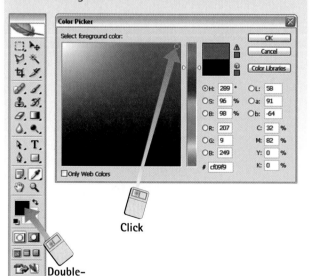

Click

Double-click

3 Configure Settings

Select the **Brush** tool from the toolbox. On the **Options** bar, click the **Brush Preset** icon and set the **Master Diameter** and **Hardness** sliders for the brush. You'll want a large, very soft brush. Select the **Airbrush** icon in the **Options** bar and set the **Flow** to about 8% or 10%.

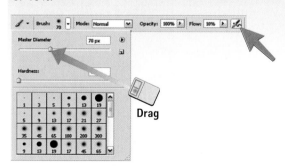

Drag

4 Stroke the Path

With the new path selected in the **Paths** palette, select **Stroke Path** from the palette menu. In the **Stroke Path** dialog box that appears, click **OK** to apply the stroke using the brush settings specified in step 3.

Click

5 Modify Brush Settings

Restroke the path several times by repeating steps 3 and 4. Each time you reapply the stroke, select a smaller brush size. This intensifies the stroke as it gets closer to the object, simulating the glow effect. Deselect the path in the **Paths** palette by clicking anywhere below the path title to view the effect without the path in the way.

End

How-To Hints

Hiding the Path

Evaluating the effect of the stroke while the path is selected can be hard because the outline of the path obscures the image edge. After you apply each stroke, you might want to deselect the path in the **Paths** palette. After evaluating the stroke results, reselect the path (by clicking the **Path** title in the **Paths** palette) and continue building the effect.

Other Path-Creation Methods

You can also use any other method described in this book to create a selection. For example, you can use **Quick Mask** to paint a selection or use the **Magnetic Lasso** tool. After you create the selection, you can easily transform it into a path by clicking the **Make Work Path** icon at the bottom of the **Paths** palette. You can then edit the path using any of the **Pen** tools from the toolbox.

How to Create Lighting Effects

The **Lighting Effects** filter casts multiple spotlights of different colors falling across the image as though it were a flat surface. The filter gives you full control over the focus and direction of the light, as well as the color, exposure, surface texture, and ambient light characteristics. Use this filter to add depth and drama to an image, as well as to build interest into a composition by highlighting a focal point.

Begin

1 Open the File

Select **File, Open** (or select **Window, File Browser**) and select the file you want to modify.

Double-click

2 Select Lighting Effects

Select **Filter, Render, Lighting Effects** to open the **Lighting Effects** dialog box. You will see a thumbnail of the image on the left side of the dialog box, with one spotlight already placed over the image.

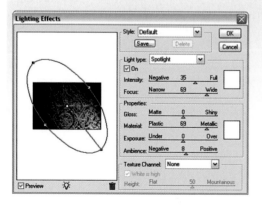

3 Reposition the Light

Click and drag the center of the light to reposition the light circle in relation to the thumbnail image. Then click the point where the light-source line meets the light circle and drag to move the light source. Finally, drag the handles on the light circle to widen or narrow the light beam as it is cast on the image.

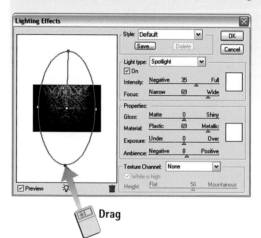

Drag

4 Configure the Light Type

Modify the **Intensity** and **Focus** sliders as desired to brighten the image and focus the light beam. Click the color swatch to display the **Color Picker** so you can select a color for the light itself.

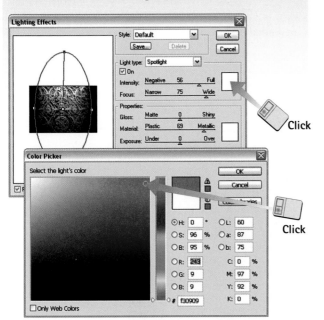

Click

Click

5 Configure Properties

The four **Properties** sliders control the appearance of the surface of the image as well as the overall brightness of the exposure. Adjust the **Gloss** and **Material** sliders to modify the surface brightness. The **Exposure** slider controls image brightness, and the **Ambience** slider controls the amount of secondary ambient light. You can click the color swatch in this area of the dialog box to modify the color of the ambient light.

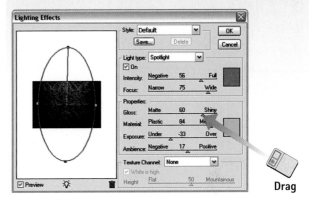

Drag

6 Add Other Lights As Needed

To add other light sources, drag the light bulb icon into the thumbnail image. Reposition and reset the parameters as described in steps 3–5. The **Style** drop-down list at the top of the **Lighting Effects** dialog box contains many more fun options with which you can experiment. If you want to remove a light, drag it to the trash can icon at the bottom of the dialog box. Remember that you need at least one light source.

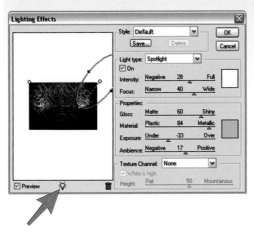

7 View the Results

Click **OK** to apply the filter and view the results.

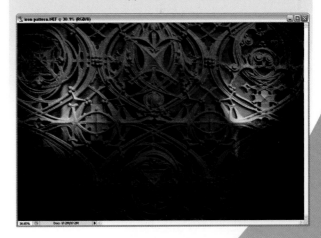

End

How to Apply a Radial Blur

A *radial blur* is an interesting effect that blurs an image in toward a center point or rotates it around a center point. The effect is similar to the photography technique of making a zoom lens time exposure that creates a tunnel effect in toward the subject. This is a good way to create emphasis on a central subject or image area and to control the composition as a whole.

Begin

1 Open the File and Select the Filter

Select **File, Open** and select the file you want to modify. Select **Filter, Blur, Radial Blur** to open the **Radial Blur** dialog box.

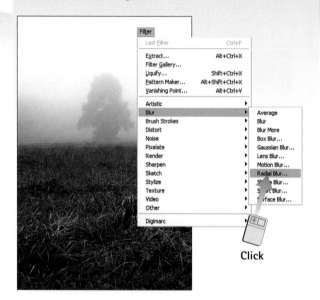

Click

2 Set the Amount Slider

Drag the **Amount** slider to control the degree of blur being applied to the image.

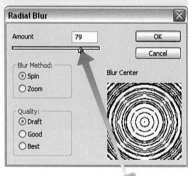

Drag

3 Set the Blur Method

Select either **Spin** or **Zoom** to determine whether the blur rotates around a center point in the image or zooms straight into the image.

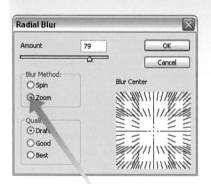

Click

4 Set the Quality Setting

Select **Draft**, **Good**, or **Best** as the **Quality** mode, keeping in mind that the higher the quality, the longer it takes to apply the effect. Note that higher quality does not affect the file size—just the amount of time it takes to display the image.

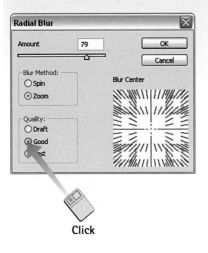

Click

5 Apply the Filter

Click **OK** to apply the **Radial Blur** filter.

End

How-To Hints

Moving the Center Point

While working in the **Radial Blur** dialog box, click and drag in the grid preview section to move the center point of the effect. Try to position the center point of the grid over the corresponding focal point of the image.

Fading the Effect

Because the blur effect often obscures much of the image, consider restoring some of the image by selecting **Edit**, **Fade Radial Blur** immediately after you apply the **Radial Blur** filter and reducing the opacity or using a blending mode.

TASK 5

How to Apply a Ripple Effect

Photoshop is full of filter effects that can create wavy, distorted lines within an image. In fact, an entire filter submenu, called **Distort**, is full of these effects. The ripple effect described in this task uses the **ZigZag** filter to create the look of rippling concentric circles across the image surface.

Begin

1 Open the File

Select **File**, **Open** and select the file you want to modify.

2 Open the ZigZag Filter

Select **Filter**, **Distort**, **ZigZag** to open the ZigZag dialog box.

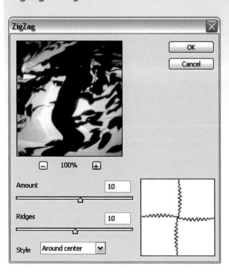

3 Set the Style

From the **Style** drop-down list, select a distortion pattern. This example uses the **Around Center** pattern, which spins the image as it creates concentric distortion. Other options include **Out from Center** (which eliminates the spin) and **Pond Ripples** (which adds highlights and shadows to the distortion). The pattern you select is reflected in the wire frame preview window at the bottom of the dialog box and in the preview window at the top of the dialog box.

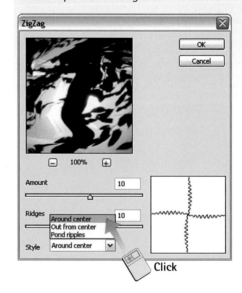

Click

4 Set the Amount

Adjust the **Amount** slider to control the percentage of distortion. Watch the effect of your changes in the preview windows.

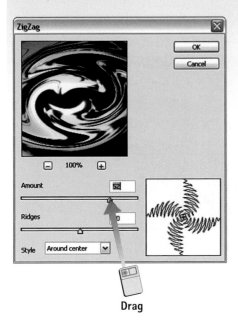

Drag

5 Set the Ridges

Adjust the **Ridges** slider to control how many circular ridges are applied in the pattern.

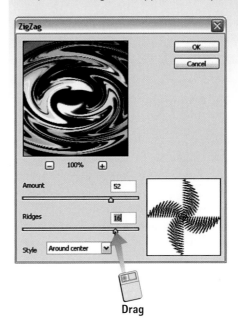

Drag

6 Apply the Filter

Click **OK** to close the **ZigZag** dialog box and apply the filter.

End

How-To Hints

Negative Amounts Implode

Use negative percentages with the **Amount** slider in step 4 to create an imploding effect that draws into the center rather than emanates out from the center.

How to Add a Lens Flare

Adding a *lens flare* to an image creates a bright spot of light that simulates the lens flare created when a photographer points a camera lens into the sun. Although this is a bad thing for photographers, the lens flare effect often works as a design element, adding a specular accent (a white highlight) to a digital composite.

Begin

1 Open the File

Select **File, Open** and select the file you want to modify.

2 Select the Lens Flare Filter

Select **Filter, Render, Lens Flare** to open the **Lens Flare** dialog box.

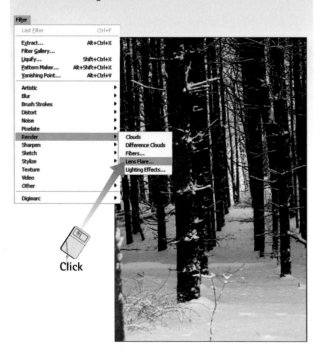

Click

3 Move the Flare Center

A small lens flare preview appears in the **Flare Center** thumbnail of the dialog box. Click and drag the cross at the center of the flare to reposition it in relation to the image.

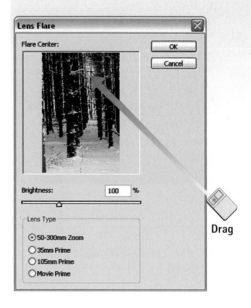

Drag

4 Set the Brightness

Adjust the **Brightness** slider to control the intensity of the flare. Observe the effect in the preview window.

Drag

5 Select the Lens Type

Select one of the four **Lens Type** options at the bottom of the dialog box to specify the type of lens simulated in the effect. Each lens effect mimics the effect of a different focal-length camera lens.

Click

6 Apply the Effect

Click **OK** to close the **Lens Flare** dialog box and apply the filter.

How-To Hints

Building Lens Flare Animations

The **Lens Flare** is a perfect filter to use when building a progressive GIF animation, as described in Part 12, Task 9, "How to Build Filter-Based GIF Animations." Increase the brightness progressively in the animation to create the effect of a starburst.

End

How to Add Noise Texture

In digital imaging, *noise* refers to a coarse, pointillist pattern that is applied to create a graphic feel in an image. Noise is often used when an image is blurry to start with and resists sharpening with Photoshop's standard filters. In this case, you might like the effect created when you add noise and create a graphic look for the image, masking the lack of sharpness.

Begin

1 Open the File

Select **File**, **Open** and select the file you want to modify.

2 Select the Noise Filter

Select **Filter**, **Noise**, **Add Noise** to open the **Add Noise** dialog box.

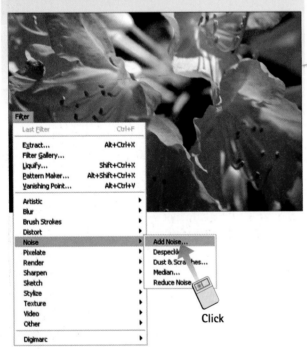

Click

3 Set the Amount

Move the **Amount** slider to control the amount of noise in the image. Observe the effect in both the preview window in the dialog box and the original image area.

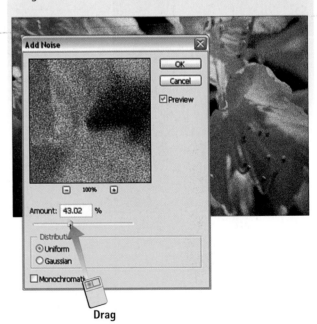

Drag

4 Set the Distribution

Select either the **Uniform** or **Gaussian** option to control how the effect is applied. The **Gaussian** option tends to mimic more closely the noise that appears on the emulsion of photographic film.

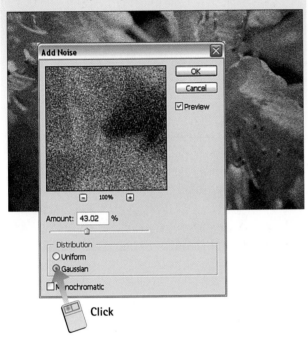

Click

5 Select the Monochromatic Effect

Enable or disable the **Monochromatic** check box and observe the effect this option has on the image. By default, noise is added to an image using randomly colored pixels. These colors can be distracting in some images; the **Monochromatic** option adds noise using grayscale pixels.

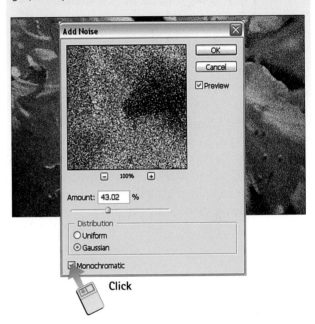

Click

6 Apply the Effect

Click **OK** to close the **Add Noise** dialog box and apply the effect.

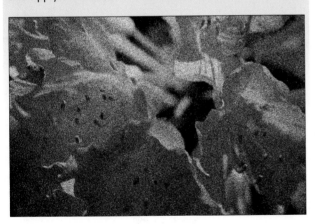

How-To Hints

Noise on a Layer

Instead of applying the **Noise** filter directly to the image, create a new layer filled with a color. Apply the **Noise** filter to the new layer and then adjust the opacity or blending mode to combine the color layer with the image layer. This approach lets you turn the effect on and off and apply it selectively using layer masks (refer to Part 10, Task 8, "How to Add a Layer Mask").

End

How to Use the Fibers Filter

The **Fibers** filter transforms the contents of a layer or selection to a monochromatic fiber texture that resembles handmade paper or textiles. At first look, this filter seems limited in its application because there's not much demand for monochromatic fiber images. The filter does have its applications, however, as this task demonstrates by combining the fiber texture with layers and blending modes to create the look of a print on handmade paper.

Begin

1 Open the File

Select **File**, **Open** and select the file you want to modify.

2 Create Duplicates of the Background Layer

Open the **Layers** palette and drag and drop the **Background** layer onto the **New Layer** icon to duplicate the layer. Repeat this step so you have two copies plus the original **Background** layer. Because the **Fibers** filter is based on the current background color, press **D** to get the default colors (white should be the background color); this way, you can achieve the grayscale effect shown in this task.

—Make two copies of the Background layer

3 Rotate Image

Because the **Fibers** filter is applied vertically and we want a combined vertical-and-horizontal fiber effect, we must rotate the canvas for one of the filter applications. Select **Image**, **Rotate Canvas**, **90° CW** to rotate the canvas 90° clockwise.

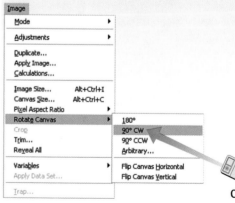

Click

4 Apply Fibers Filter

Highlight the **Background Copy 2** layer and select **Filter, Render, Fibers** to launch the **Fibers** dialog box. For this effect, I set the **Variance** to 5 and the **Strength** to 11 to create a soft contrasted, streaked result. Click **OK** to apply the effect to the selected layer.

Drag

5 Rotate Image and Reapply Fibers Filter

Select **Image, Rotate Canvas, 90° CCW** to rotate the canvas 90° counterclockwise, back to its original state. Highlight the **Background Copy** layer and select **Filter, Render, Fibers** to launch the **Fibers** dialog box. Use the same settings you used in step 4 to create a second layer of fibers at right angles to the first. Click **OK** to apply the filter.

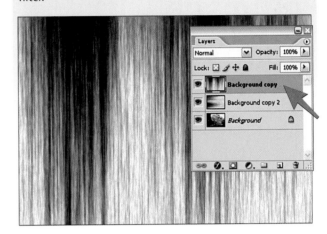

6 Adjust Blending Modes and Transparency

Set the blending modes for both duplicate layers to **Overlay**, and modify the layer **Opacity** setting until the layers blend together. In this example, the layer opacities were set to **50%**. The result is an image with a horizontal and vertical fiber texture and high saturation.

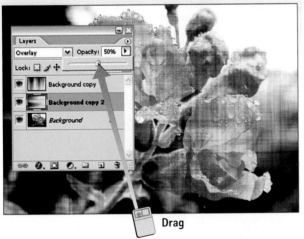

Drag

How-To Hints

Strength Controls the Edges

Although the **Variance** slider controls the overall smoothness of the pattern application, it's the **Strength** slider that dictates the main texture characteristics of the filter. A high **Strength** setting creates sharp, crisp lines, whereas a low setting softens the texture for a more organic feel.

End

How to Distort an Image with Liquify

Liquify is a fun, interactive set of controls that enables you to push and smudge the pixels in an image, creating a brushed-in, fluid distortion. The entire process feels something like finger painting because you can vary the brush size and pressure as you work, create masks to preserve certain areas, and revert to any set along the way.

Begin

1 Open the File

Select **File**, **Open** and select the file you want to modify.

2 Select Liquify

Select **Filter**, **Liquify** to launch the **Liquify** interface window.

3 Protect Image Areas

Select the **Freeze Mask** tool from the toolbar on the left of the window, specify the brush size and pressure in the **Tool Options** section, and brush a mask over the areas you want to protect. The distortion effect will *not* be applied to the areas you freeze. (Make sure that the **Show Mask** check box is enabled in the **View Options** section so you can see the mask as you paint.)

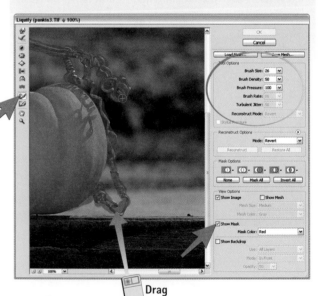

Drag

4 Distort the Image

Select any of the distortion brushes from the toolbar. From the **Tool Options** section, select a brush size and pressure and then paint the effect into the image. Drag the brush with a circular motion and let the effect build to the desired intensity. The distortion tool options include **Warp**, **Turbulence**, **Twirl**, **Pucker**, **Bloat**, **Push**, and **Mirror**. Hold the **Alt/Option** key when painting to reverse the direction of the distortion.

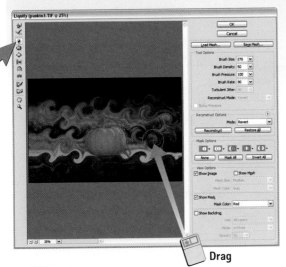

Drag

5 Reconstruct the Original Image

To diminish or erase the effect from step 4, select the **Reconstruct** tool and select the desired mode from the **Reconstruction Options** section. Brush over the distorted area until the effect is reduced or eliminated. Use the **Mode** menu in the **Reconstruction Options** section to control the linear and expressive aspects of the reconstruction. You can also click the **Reconstruct** button to gradually restore the entire image all at once based on the option in the **Mode** menu.

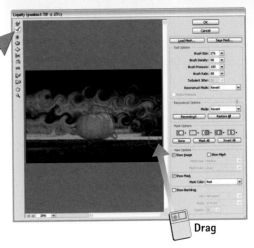

Drag

6 Modify the Protected Area

To modify the mask created in step 3 so you can make further modifications, select the **Thaw Mask** tool from the toolbar and brush over the mask to erase or lighten it. You can continue to apply distortions, erase them, and adjust the mask until you achieve the desired effect. Click **OK** to close the **Liquify** window.

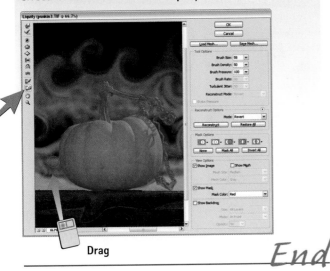

Drag

End

How-To Hints

When All Else Fails, Restore All!

If the distortion gets out of hand and you want to go back to where you started, click the **Restore All** button in the **Reconstruction Options** section of the **Liquify** window. Similarly, you can click the **None** button in the **Mask Options** section to completely erase an existing mask.

Viewing Options

To control how effects and masks are presented in the **Liquify** window, make modifications in the **View Options** section. You can control the presentation of the image, the mesh grid that controls the actual distortion, and the mask visibility and color. You can even save the mesh grid and reapply it to another image. In addition, because the **Liquify** command is applied to a single layer, you can also turn on the visibility of other layers in the image so you can view the effect against the backdrop of the overall image.

How to Use the Filter Gallery

The **Filter Gallery** enables you to explore multiple combinations of the Photoshop **Artistic** filters in a fluid, interactive interface. It allows you to combine 47 filter effects, with full control over all filter settings and variables, complete with real-time preview updates that reflect the cumulative filter results.

Most filters that result in a color image have color thumbnails. On the other hand, most filters with black-and-white thumbnails use the foreground and background colors from the toolbox. However, some filters use combinations of both methods, and some have their own color logic.

Begin

1 Open the Gallery Interface

With the target image open on the desktop, select **Filter, Filter Gallery**. The **Filter Gallery** interface window consists of four main areas: the preview window, **Filters** palette, **Filter Controls** section, and **Effect Layer** palette.

Filters palette   Filter Controls section

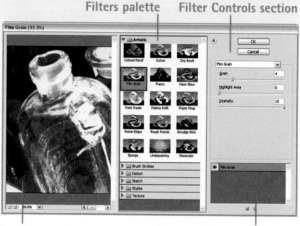

Preview window   Effect Layer palette

2 Select a Filter

In the **Filters** palette, click the arrows next to the folders to display the categories of individual filter thumbnails. Click a thumbnail to select a filter. When you do, the filter name appears in the **Effect Layer** palette and its controls appear in the **Filter Controls** section.

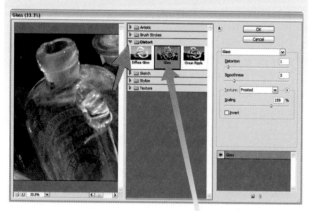

 Click

3 Modify Filter Controls

Depending on the size of your image, it might take a moment for Photoshop to apply the filter settings to the preview image. Modify the filter controls until you're satisfied with the results. Here I adjust the controls for the **Glass** filter (found in the **Distort** category).

 Drag

4 Zoom to Preview

The **Filters Gallery** automatically scales the image preview to fit the size of the preview window. You should zoom in to 100% and check your results after you select the first filter. To do this, click the + or – button in the lower-left of the preview window until 100% is showing next to the buttons. You can also select a magnification rate from the magnification pop-up menu (the black triangle next to the % box). Click and drag inside the preview window to move the preview area.

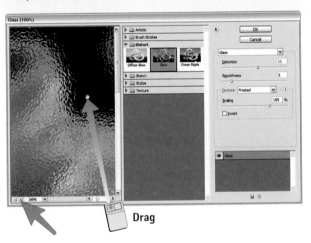

Drag

5 Add Another Effect Layer

Photoshop allows only one filter per effect layer, so you must create a new effect layer before you can add another filter. To do this, click the **New Effect Layer** icon at the bottom of the **Effect Layer** palette.

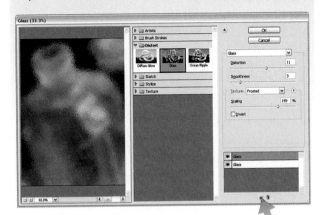

 Click

6 Add Another Filter

Click another filter thumbnail to apply a new filter layer over the effect layer created in step 5. Adjust the filter controls and zoom in to check the results as you work. Apply additional filters as desired by repeating steps 5 and 6.

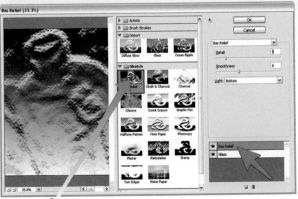

Click

7 Explore Filter Combinations

Modify the filter controls and effect layer combinations to fine-tune the cumulative effect of the filters. Hide or reveal effect layers (click the eye icon next to the effect layer name), or change the order of the layers in the **Effect Layer** palette. Select an effect layer and change the filter controls to fine-tune the results. After the effect is complete, click **OK** to apply the results.

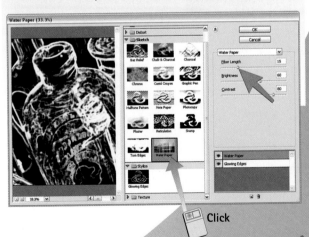

Click

End

How to Add Texture

Texture emphasizes the surface of an image, even as it creates a global graphic effect. Photoshop offers built-in texture maps that simulate sandstone, burlap, canvas, and other surfaces. To apply the **Texture** filter, you select a surface and then control the light direction and the size of the texture as it is mapped onto the surface of the image. The **Texture** controls are located in the **Filter Gallery** interface. For details on how the **Filter Gallery** works, refer to Task 10, "How to Use the Filter Gallery."

Begin

1 Open the File and Select Filter Gallery

With the target file open, select **Filter, Filter Gallery**. Expand the **Texture** folder in the **Filters** palette and select the **Texturizer** filter.

 Click

2 Set the Texture Type

In the **Filter Controls** section, access the **Texture** drop-down list box and select **Brick, Burlap, Canvas,** or **Sandstone**. Notice the results as they appear in the preview window.

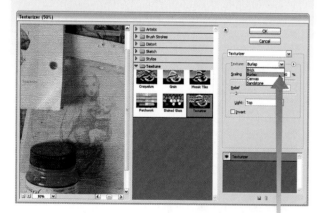

Click

3 Set the Scaling

Scaling refers to the size of the texture effect in relation to the image. In this example, the **Scaling** setting affects how coarse the weave of the canvas looks. Adjust the **Scaling** slider to the desired setting, watching the results in the preview window.

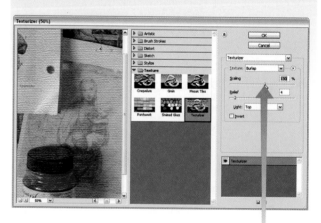

Drag

4 Set the Relief

Relief determines the strength of the texture as it is applied to the image. In this example, the **Relief** setting affects just how "thick" the canvas pattern looks. Adjust the **Relief** slider to achieve the desired effect.

Drag

5 Set the Light Direction

Select a light direction from the **Light** drop-down list. Experiment with selections and observe the effect produced in the preview window.

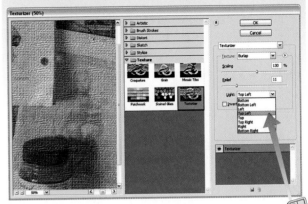

Click

6 Apply the Effect

Click **OK** to close the **Filter Gallery** dialog box and apply the effect.

End

How-To Hints

Using Other Texture Filters

In addition to the **Texturizer** filter, five other texture filters are offered in the **Texture** category: **Craquelure, Grain, Mosaic Tiles, Patchwork,** and **Stained Glass**. Create additional effect layers and experiment with all of these to see how they differ and how you can use them to enhance your image.

More Texture Enhancements

Combine standard **Texture** filters with other filters such as **Rough Pastels, Underpainting,** and **Diffuse Glow**. Create a new effect layer for each, drag the tiles to change the layer order, and explore the wide range of texture combinations.

How to Create a Halftone Pattern

The **Halftone Pattern** filter creates a graphic effect that simulates a halftone screen being applied to an image. This effect reduces the image to two colors and creates a stylized graphic feel that is distinctive and unique. The colors used for the filter are taken from the foreground and background colors, so be sure to select these colors before applying the filter, as explained in step 1. The **Halftone Pattern** controls are located in the **Filter Gallery** interface. For details on the **Filter Gallery**, refer to Task 10, "How to Use the Filter Gallery."

Begin

1 Select Colors

Because the halftone effect uses the foreground and background colors, you must set these colors before applying the filter. Click the **Foreground** color swatch in the toolbox and select the desired color from the **Color Picker**. Click the **Background** color swatch and select the second color.

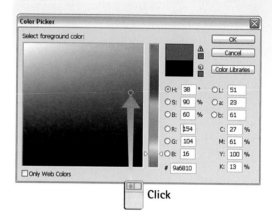

Click

2 Open the File and Select Filter Gallery

With the target file open, select **Filter, Filter Gallery**. Expand the **Sketch** category folder in the **Filters** palette and select the **Halftone Pattern** filter. Notice that the image is reduced to the two colors you selected in step 1.

 Click

3 Select the Pattern Type

From the **Pattern Type** drop-down list box, select **Circle**, **Dot**, or **Line** to determine the actual halftone pattern to be used. Observe the effect your selection has in the preview window.

 Click

4 Select the Size and Contrast

Adjust the **Size** slider to control the size of the halftone pattern relative to the image. Adjust the **Contrast** slider to control how prominently the effect is applied to the image.

Drag

5 Apply the Effect

Click **OK** to close the **Filter Gallery** and apply the effect to the image.

End

How-To Hints

Fading with Blending Modes to Combine Effects

Halftone pattern effects work very well with blending modes because of their graphic feel and flat areas of color. When combined with the original image, interesting hybrid effects can be achieved. Select **Edit, Fade Filter Gallery** directly after applying the filter to use the blending modes and change the opacity of the filter.

Switching the Color Order

The **Halftone Pattern** filter applies the foreground color to the shadows and the background color to the highlights. If you don't like the color distribution as initially applied, undo the filter and click the **Switch Colors** icon in the toolbox to reverse the foreground and background colors. Reapply the filter and compare the results.

How to Use the Vanishing Point Filter

One of the most exciting new tools in Photoshop CS2 is the **Vanishing Point** filter. The term *vanishing point* refers to the most distant point in perspective, and perspective is what the **Vanishing Point** filter is all about. It has several tools that replicate normal tools you'd find in the Photoshop toolbox, only these tools are all perspective-aware.

Begin

1 Open Vanishing Point

With your image open, select **Filter, Vanishing Point** to launch the **Vanishing Point** window.

2 Create the Editing Plane

Select the **Create Plane** tool and click in the image area to place four corners that you know are square in relation to each other in the real world (as opposed to in the image). If there aren't four obvious corners, use your best guess. You can adjust these points in the next step.

Click

3 Adjust the Editing Plane

Select the **Edit Plane** tool and drag the handles on the sides of the editing plane until they cover the area to be edited. Try to reference real-world perspective cues such as corners and edges. If the edges are at a different angle than the lines on the editing plane, drag the corner handles to match the angles.

Drag

4 Edit the Image

Select one of the editing tools and notice how it behaves differently from its regular counterpart. Each tool changes to match the relative size of the editing plane. Here I'm using the **Stamp** tool—in the **Vanishing Point** window, it actually deforms the wood grain to match the perspective of the image.

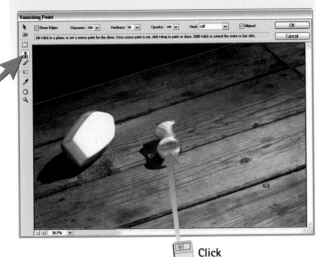

Click

5 Examine the Image

Click **OK** to commit your **Vanishing Point** edits and return to Photoshop's main work area.

6 Reopen Vanishing Point

Launch the **Vanishing Point** window again, and you'll find that the editing plane you established in the last session is still in place. Photoshop saves the editing plane as part of your image file so that any additional edits you make are based on the same perspective points.

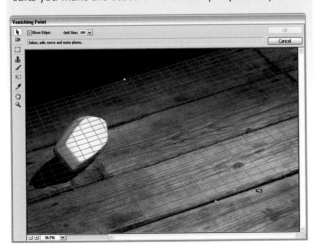

How-To Hints

More on Tools

The toolbox in the **Vanishing Point** window might look a bit sparse (in addition to the two plane tools, the **Marquee, Stamp, Brush, Transform, Eyedropper, Hand,** and **Zoom** tools are the only choices), but that short list is deceptive. The **Marquee, Stamp,** and **Brush** tools each has two healing modes, which effectively adds the **Healing Brush** and **Patch** tools to your editing arsenal, plus one tool with no other Photoshop equivalent (the healing paintbrush). In addition, the **Stamp** and **Brush** tool pointers are much more sophisticated than their Photoshop equivalents, displaying the actual feathering and image data that will be applied instead of just a simple outline or icon.

Perpendicular Planes

If you hold down the **Ctrl/⌘** key before dragging a handle with the **Edit Plane** tool, you can "tear off" a new plane that is perpendicular to the exiting plane. This new plane perspective is great for going around corners or up walls from the floor.

End

Glossary

A

actions   Preset scripts that automate repetitive tasks. With just a single mouse click, you can create special effects without having a clue as to how they are done.

adjustment layer   A nondestructive layer that enables you to adjust the tone or color in an image without altering the content of the layers beneath it.

alias   The name for the jagged edges (*jaggies*) that are seen when an image doesn't contain enough information to make a smooth transition on angled or rounded edges. It's also called *stair-stepping* because the edge can look like a series of steps.

alpha channel   An extra channel in which you can save a selection.

antialiasing   The method of reducing jagged edges in an image or text by slightly blurring the edges of shapes and text to make them appear smooth.

B

baseline shift   The process of raising or lowering text characters to control positioning or alignment in a design. A positive baseline shift value raises the text and a negative value lowers it, as calculated from the initial baseline positioning.

bicubic   An interpolation method that delivers quality results when changing the size or resolution of an image. The Bicubic Sharper method is optimized for image size reduction, and the Bicubic Smoother method is optimized for image enlargement. Other interpolation methods include Bilinear and Nearest Neighbor.

blending modes   Preset functions that compare a source image with new data such as a separate layer or paint tool. Blending modes compare and combine these two sets of pixel data to create unique imaging effects.

border   The outlined edge of a path or selection. Borders can be selected independently and can be filled and stroked.

Bridge   Photoshop's native file browser and organizer that allows you to open files, sort and preview images and camera data, and apply batch commands to one or many files simultaneously. Its interface is common to all the Adobe CS2 applications.

C

caching levels   A Photoshop method for speeding screen redraws by storing commonly used elements for rapid access. You can set the number of levels you want to use on the Image Cache page of the Preferences box.

camera raw   A Photoshop plug-in for processing proprietary file formats created by many professional and prosumer digital camera manufacturers. It enables users to make image modifications while keeping the raw camera data intact and unchanged.

chromatic aberration   A photographic distortion that causes the divergence of the blue/yellow or red/cyan color channels. This distortion is visible mostly at the outside edges of an image captured with a wide-angle lens.

clipping paths   A method of exporting a file for use in a vector or layout application. The clipping path format masks out part of the image (for example, you can use this method to drop out the background in a product shot so that only the product object is visible).

CLUT (color lookup table)   *See* GIF file.

CMYK color model   A color process using cyan, magenta, yellow, and black color variables. Used primarily in offset printing, CMYK color sports a smaller color range than its RGB counterpart. The conversion process between RGB and CMYK must be managed to ensure consistent and high-quality results.

CMYK image   A color image that uses the CMYK color model, featuring cyan, magenta, yellow, and black channels.

color model   A way of quantifying color. There are several color models in which you can identify a particular color; CMYK, RGB, HSB, Web, and Lab colors are all supported in Photoshop. In the RGB color model, for example, a particular color is identified as having a particular quantity of red, a particular amount of blue, and a particular amount of green. The range of available color varies between color models, so it is important to use a model that is suited to the specific image, as well as the overall web or printing process being used.

Color Picker   A dialog box from which you can select the foreground or background color. The Color Picker displays a window with a range of color in a particular hue. Move the Hue slider to see a different range of color, or click in the color window to select a color. The selected color is quantified in terms of Hue/Saturation/ Brightness, Red/Green/Blue, Lab, CMYK, and Hexadecimal (if you need to specify your colors to that degree).

color space   The range of unique colors that can be created for a given color model, such as RGB or CMYK.

contact sheet   A Photoshop file that contains thumbnail references for all the images in a given folder. You can use contact sheets to send your client a list of images for approval, to archive, or just to help organize your graphics visually rather than with archaic filenames.

crop   To cut an image down to a specific square or rectangular section, excluding all other unwanted areas.

D

dithering   The process used to fool the human eye into seeing more colors in an image than are really there. The process works by combining two or more existing colors into patterns. When viewed by the human eye, these patterns appear as solid colors.

dot gain   A measurement that describes and anticipates the way ink spreads and is absorbed on different types of paper. For example, ink spreads more on newsprint than it does on glossy card stock, so you have to compensate to keep the dots from filling in completely.

duotone   A grayscale image that is printed with two colors of ink for a graphic effect. Although duotones were originally designed to extend the tonal range of standard grayscale images, designers have embraced them for their graphic look and feel.

E

EPS format   Stands for Encapsulated PostScript file. The process of converting an image into PostScript data while bundling a lower-resolution preview so the image can be viewed and proofed onscreen.

EXIF Data   Photographic reference information attached to digital files by some digital cameras. Information includes camera name and date, exposure data, flash, and compression rates.

exposure   The degree of effect applied to the image. You can also think of it as *intensity* or *pressure*.

F

feather To dissipate the hard-line edge of an area, creating a vignette effect. You can feather a border, for example, so that it fades off into the surrounding area. You can also feather a selection line. When you choose a brush style, you can choose a brush that has a feathered tip.

File Browser *See* Bridge.

file extension The three (or more) letters after the dot in a filename (for example, in **filename.ext**, **.ext** is the extension). The file extension frequently identifies the format of the file. For example, the extension **.txt** tells you that the file is an unformatted text file; the extension **.jpg** tells you the file is a JPEG graphics file.

flatten In the context of layers, flattening the image involves compressing all the layers into one flat background layer.

flip To change the presentation of an image as if by turning a print of the image over on the desktop—any text is now mirrored (reversed) and left hands look like right hands. When you flip an image, be sure that you are not misrepresenting anything.

frameset targeting The web design process of directing links to load contents into a specific frame within an Internet site's frameset.

G

gamma A term used to measure relative monitor brightness. Standard gamma settings are 1.8 for Macintosh and 2.2 for Windows.

gamut The range of unique colors that can be created for a given color model, such as RGB or CMYK. Also referred to as *color space*.

GIF file An efficient, compact file that is perfect for use on the Web. GIF files create a color lookup table (CLUT) for each image; each color (up to 256 colors) in the image is categorized and stored in the CLUT. Because of this table (as well as algorithms that track repeating pixels), GIF files compress well.

gradient A fill that gradually blends two or more colors together.

grayscale The method for creating a continuous-tone monochrome image using a tonal palette consisting of 256 shades of gray.

grid An underlying matrix of lines that can be used for the general alignment of all items on the page.

guide A user-defined alignment line that is drawn from the rulers. Guides can also be used in ImageReady to slice an image for use on the Web.

H

halftone A filter effect that reduces an image to two colors and creates a stylized graphic feel.

Healing Brush A modified version of the Clone tool that uses color, tone, and texture data to smooth blemishes and unwanted areas within an image.

histogram A profile that charts and quantifies the distribution of image pixels across the entire tonal spectrum.

hot spots Active areas within website imagemaps that include links to other pages or actions. These hot spots change the cursor icon as the mouse passes over them; the change in cursor shape identifies the area's additional functionality.

I

image caching A buffering process that speeds screen redraws and scrolling.

image prep tasks *See* preprocessing tasks.

imagemap A web image that includes hot spots with links to other pages or triggers for other actions.

IPTC Data An information standard developed by the Newspaper Association of America (NAA) and the International Press Telecommunications Council (IPTC) to identify transmitted text and images. This standard includes entries for captions, keywords, categories, credits, and origins.

J–K

jitter Variations in brush strokes that can be controlled by the Shape Dynamics options in the Brushes palette.

JPEG file A file format that works well for photographic images. The compression algorithm tends to create artifacts that pixelate the image. Although these effects can degrade the quality of hard-edged graphics, they are easier to hide in photographs.

kerning The spacing between individual pairs of letters.

L

layer A Photoshop method for separating image components for easy access and editing. Layers follow the metaphor of clear acetate overlays that can be stacked and rearranged.

layer group A complete group of layers that can be moved, deleted, or copied in the Layers palette as a single unit. Layer groups can be viewed in the Layers palette and be expanded or compressed as needed to view details of the group's contents.

layer mask A mask that conceals a portion of a layer without actually deleting it, enabling the lower layers to show through those areas of the mask.

layer set *See* layer group.

layer tile In the Layers palette, each layer is represented as a horizontal tile. These tiles can be hidden or revealed, linked, grouped, or combined into working layer sets.

leading The spacing between lines of text. Leading values are usually expressed in points and are compared to the font's point size.

lens flare A bright spot of light on an image that simulates the lens flare created when a photographer points a camera lens into the sun.

lossy A term normally used to describe the nature of the compression method used by the JPEG format. The compression format is referred to as *lossy* because some information is discarded, or lost. It is because of this technique that JPEG images can be compressed to a much smaller file size than images compressed with other formats. In the Save for Web dialog box, the Lossy option removes data from GIF images to create a smaller file size.

M

mask The process of defining an area of an image or layer for selection, modification, or transparency.

merge In the context of layers, *merging* refers to combining some of the layers in a design while keeping other layers separate.

metadata Ancillary reference information attached to an image file. Photoshop supports six metadata subcategories: File Properties; EXIF Camera Data; Camera Raw; GPS; Edit History; and project-based IPTC information that shows authorship, assignment information, and other workflow data points.

mode   A way to apply editing and painting techniques. Palettes have Mode drop-down lists. *See also* palette.

multiple views   More than one window opened for a single image file. You can open two separate windows of the same file, specify a high rate of magnification for editing in one window, and leave the other at full screen size to check your progress as you work.

N

naming format   A process that controls the automatic naming of files when new files are created, as used in ImageReady image slicing. When selected from the File, Output Settings, Slices menu, names can be automatically generated using a wide range of criteria, such as alphanumeric sequences, date stamping, and file format.

noise   Film grain or digital artifacts visible in an image. Also refers to deliberately introduced random pixel variations, added for either artistic effect or production reasons.

O–P

Options bar   The horizontal bar at the top of the Photoshop and ImageReady interface windows that contains all available options for the currently selected tool.

palette   One of many control elements you can use to fine-tune your use of Photoshop and ImageReady tools. A palette is associated with a single element of the image (for example, the Brushes palette controls the size and shape of the cursor when you are using a painting tool). Each palette has a drop-down menu of options associated with the element it controls.

palette menu   When any palette is open, a menu of options specific to that palette is available. Click the right-facing arrow at the top of the palette to display the palette menu of options.

palette well   The darker gray box at the end of the Options bar that collapses and stores palettes for easy access. To add a palette to the well, drag a palette over the dark gray box; the palette collapses so that only the palette's title tab is visible.

path   A vector outline of an image area or shape.

Pattern Maker   A Photoshop filter module that generates complex, random patterns from user-defined image selections.

Photoshop EPS format   *See* EPS format.

Photoshop PDF format   Stands for Portable Document File. A superset of the EPS file format that has largely replaced the EPS format for printing industry use. Also used for portable delivery of multipage documents.

pixels   The smallest individual building blocks of an image, pixels are usually square in shape.

plug-in   User-installable programs, including third-party filters and utilities, that extend the basic functionality of Photoshop.

posterize   To reduce similar tonal areas of an image to flat color, eliminating shading and fine detail.

preprocessing tasks   Preliminary tasks that typically clean up an image and get it ready for layout placement or more in-depth editing. These tasks include cropping, rotating, and sharpening.

Preset Manager   In Photoshop, a single, multi-tabbed palette that enables you to preset the settings for features such as brushes, swatches, and patterns.

quadtone   A grayscale image printed with four colors of ink, usually black and three other colors for a total of four colors (called *plates* in the printing process).

radial blur   An interesting effect that blurs an image away from a center point or rotates it around a center point. The effect is similar to the photographic technique of making a zoom lens time exposure that creates a tunnel effect in toward the subject.

rasterize   The process of creating pixel data from vector elements. The conversion is often necessary before other Photoshop effects can be applied to a type layer.

red eye   An unwanted reflection from the subject's retina seen through the subject's iris. It's common with flash photography.

relief   The strength of a textured filter effect as it is applied to the image. In a burlap filter, for example, the relief affects the perceived depth of the weave.

render layer   *See* rasterize.

resolution   The detail within a digital image, as determined by the number of pixels per inch.

RGB color model   A color process using red, green, and blue color variables. This is the native format for digital files, as created from scanners and digital cameras. There are multiple RGB color spaces to choose from, including Adobe, sRGB, and Apple RGB. Each offers a specific color range, and care should be taken when deciding which model to use.

rollover   A graphic that changes as you pass your mouse over a specific spot on the screen.

rotate   To change the presentation of an image, as if by placing a print of the image on the desktop and spinning it—nothing about the image changes except the presentation.

sample point   The reference point that provides pixel data to determine how certain Photoshop tools operate. For example, the Clone Stamp tool uses a sample reference point to determine which pixel values it should paint into the image. The Background eraser also uses a sample point to determine which part of the image to erase.

scaling   The act of enlarging or reducing an image, a layer, or an effect. Although an entire image can be resized, scaling can also modify the size of a textured filter effect in relation to the image. In a burlap filter, for example, the scaling affects the coarseness of the weave.

scatter   The way the brush stroke spreads out from the line drawn by the mouse or pen. Scatter can be controlled with the Scattering options in the Brushes palette.

scratch disk   A Photoshop term referring to the system hard drive(s) used as a buffer for storing interim versions of images.

sharpening   Enhancing the perceived sharpness of an image by exaggerating the contrast along the boundary edges between details.

slice   To divide a large image intended for the Web into smaller tiles that are assembled in a table as the page is loaded. These smaller tiles often load faster than one large image and are necessary if you want a portion of a large image to act as a rollover or an animation.

Smart Sharpen   A Photoshop filter for sharpening. *See also* sharpening.

Smart Objects   A composite layer that represents one or multiple other layers. Smart Objects can be scaled and rotated, but the source layers remain unchanged. If you edit one of the source layers, all instances of Smart Objects based on that layer are updated.

snapshot An image state that resides in the History palette that was captured to represent a particular stage of image development. These history states are not affected by the History State value listed in Photoshop's General Preferences box, and they remain available for the current editing session until the image is closed and saved.

stroke To draw an outline around a path or selection. Stroking is useful for outlining a rectangle you want to use as a text box, for building buttons for the Web, or for outlining letterforms you might have saved as paths.

T–U

thumbnail A small graphic that represents a larger image. Thumbnails are often used in palettes to give a visual history of the states in the image.

tonality The grayscale values from 0 to 255 that differentiate an image's pixels. Tonality is black and white and shades of gray, and it is one of the most expressive elements in an image. If you want to create a strong feeling in an image, consider exaggerating the tonality in some way.

tool preset A user-defined set of tool parameters accessible through the Tool Presets palette. Options bar information, foreground color, and external palette information (where applicable) can be saved as part of a tool preset.

tracking The spacing between letters in a block of text.

transform To modify the position, scale, or proportions of a layer. Transforming a layer is useful for changing the size or placement of a layer, as well as for adding perspective or distortion.

transparency checkerboard grid The checkerboard background that appears "through" an image when you have made some part of an image transparent. You can control the size and color of the checkerboard grid using the **Preferences** dialog boxes.

tritone A grayscale image printed with three colors of ink, usually black and two additional colors for a total of three colors (called *plates* in the printing process).

V

variable compression A feature that enables you to alter image compression and quality in different areas of the same image. You can focus more detail around a central character or image while allowing details to erode in unimportant areas such as the background or flat areas of color. The result is an optimized image that delivers higher quality and lower bandwidth.

vertical type Text arranged in a descending vertical column down the image.

video alpha capability A special-effect transparency technique available with certain video boards.

W–X–Y–Z

warp A transformation that distorts an image or text selection by twisting, bloating, or stretching it into a wide range of effects. Custom warping allows mesh-based distortion by dragging with the mouse. You can choose from other warping effects, and all allow bending as well as horizontal and vertical distortion.

work path The "line" created whenever the Path tool begins drawing a path. The work path represents the working path that is in progress or under construction. After the path is saved, the new, named path replaces the work path.

Index

G-H

I